CONSTITUTIONAL DYSFUNCTION ON TRIAL

CONSTITUTIONAL DYSFUNCTION ON TRIAL

Congressional Lawsuits and
the Separation of Powers

Jasmine Farrier

CORNELL UNIVERSITY PRESS   ITHACA AND LONDON

First published 2019 by Cornell University Press

Library of Congress Cataloging-in-Publication Data

Names: Farrier, Jasmine, 1970– author.
Title: Constitutional dysfunction on trial : Congressional lawsuits and the separation of powers / Jasmine Farrier.
Description: Ithaca [New York] : Cornell University Press, 2019. | Includes bibliographical references and index.
Identifiers: LCCN 2019015732 (print) | LCCN 2019018379 (ebook) | ISBN 9781501744464 (pdf) | ISBN 9781501744471 (epub/mobi) | ISBN 9781501702501 | ISBN 9781501702501 (cloth) | ISBN 9781501747106 (pbk.)
Subjects: LCSH: Separation of powers—United States—Cases. | Executive Power—United States—Cases. | Legislative power—United States—Cases. | Judicial power—United States—Cases. | Executive-legislative Relations—United States. | Political questions and judicial power—United States.
Classification: LCC KF4565 (ebook) | LCC KF4565 .F37 2019 (print) | DDC 342.73/044—dc23
LC record available at https://lccn.loc.gov/2019015732

To Bonnie, Tovah, and Talia

Contents

CONSTITUTIONAL DYSFUNCTION ON TRIAL

SYSTEMIC CONSTITUTIONAL DYSFUNCTION

President Richard Nixon's expansion of the Vietnam War into Cambodia in 1970 triggered years of social, political, and legal debate. Students at Kent State University were protesting the Cambodia invasion that year when Ohio National Guardsmen opened fire and killed four of them.[1] Between then and 1973, Congress repealed the 1964 Gulf of Tonkin Resolution that authorized the escalation of the Vietnam War, and engaged in prolonged battles over funding and statutory authority related to Cambodia. Although majorities in the House and Senate pushed to end the bombings in appropriations bills, they did not have the needed two-thirds to override Nixon's vetoes. This impasse ended with a compromise between the branches to end operations in Cambodia effective August 15, 1973.[2] Over this same tumultuous period, federal courts were drawn into the fray by novel types of litigants challenging the constitutionality of the Cambodia campaign, including suits by soldiers, their families, taxpayers, the state of Massachusetts, and members of Congress. Federal judges were divided on these claims, but ultimately decided that they did not have the institutional competence and power to end this chapter of the Vietnam War.

Until now, the complex legacies of those first member cases have not received in-depth attention. House members Parren Mitchell (D-MD) and Elizabeth Holtzman (D-NY) filed the first interbranch lawsuits in U.S. history in 1971 and 1973, respectively. Even though Mitchell and Holtzman both lost, their cases spawned a new and controversial arena for constitutional conflict. Echoes of the institutional patterns seen in those first suits have persisted for decades and deserve a new look: presidents repeatedly expand their domestic and foreign policy powers, majorities of Congress do not protect their institutional prerogatives consistently, and federal courts are wary of getting involved. This book is the first to examine all of these cases together and is driven by a simple question: Are member suits a solution to overweening executive power?

This book says no. Congressional litigation is a powerful symptom of constitutional dysfunction, but will never be the cure. Federal courts cannot rebalance the system alone—regardless of plaintiff. For this and other reasons, member litigation can bring special attention to a broken separation of powers system, but not repair it. Presidents repeatedly expand their domestic and foreign policy powers without direct authorization. It is unrealistic for a federal court to order an end to military action and expect a president (any president) to withdraw troops without protest. Judges might fear a double constitutional crisis—on the policy issue and then on their institutional credibility if they are ignored by an ostensibly co-equal branch. The real problem is that Congress defends its powers tepidly and inconsistently, often due to partisan motivations. Congress also undermines systemic health when it attacks itself through various legislative process "reforms" that reduce member powers and majority rule. In both types of cases, federal courts have opted not to force Congress to embrace the fullness of its powers.

Despite the long odds of success, hundreds of members of the House and Senate have filed or joined these suits out of frustration with the status quo. They have sued individually, in groups up to 196 members at a time, and twice with the blessing of a chamber majority. Members have sued ten times to stop military actions ordered by seven presidents, spanning five decades. They have also sued to stop two presidents from unilaterally withdrawing from treaties. Representatives have also sued to overturn executive orders and other administrative actions on domestic environmental protection and health care. Members have gone to federal court five times to stop their own legislative processes that were designed to take power from simple majorities, including base closure commissions, the line-item veto, and even the Senate filibuster.

One problem with these lawsuits is that they rarely succeed, even on their own terms. Judges may buck precedent to take up and rule something unconstitutional, but then what? The very problems that inspired the cases (aggressive presidents and feckless congressional majorities) may complicate the enforcement of the decision. Furthermore, these lawsuits can backfire in various ways. The justiciability doctrines federal courts have used and developed to dispense with these suits inadvertently normalized many of the very institutional problems the suits tried to stop. Before hearing a case on the merits, judges increase the burden on the members to show disapproval of the situation, which usually requires supermajorities. On the very rare occasion that members win a case, majorities of the House and Senate try to get around the decision rather than build upon the institutional victory. Over time, members' partisanship gets in the way of consistency. Republicans in the House and Senate sue Democratic presidents and vice versa, making serious constitutional claims look like legal gimmicks.

The lesson is that if members are serious about taking back power, they should pursue legitimate constitutional claims in "regular politics" outside the judicial system. Constitutional values of representation, deliberation, and accountability ideally result from open and direct engagement between multiple policy, party, and branch perspectives.

While the book agrees with federal judges who say these lawsuits place far too much pressure on courts to solve complex policy problems, we should still appreciate, and even sympathize with, these member-plaintiffs. Members allege institutional injuries that harm Congress as a coequal branch, which they are best suited to articulate. Background interviews for the book with members, one legislative aide, and members' attorneys (a dozen of interviews all together), spanning both parties and a variety of foreign and domestic policy cases, reveal deep frustration with Congress's disadvantage in the modern policy process. These plaintiffs emphasize the human costs of policies at the local, national, and international levels as motivations to sue. Scholars and political observers likewise rue presidential expansionism, as well as the passivity of congressional leaders and members.[3] But members themselves see the policy and institutional damage of these trends up close; litigation provides another outlet for their frustrations and constitutional arguments. Member-plaintiffs often pursue multiple strategies on policy in tandem and are involved in committee and floor lawmaking as well as the legal front. Members often file the lawsuit because they know the regular legislative process will stall or fail to overcome a presidential veto even if they manage to pass a bill that curtails executive branch power.

Member lawsuits deserve attention individually and together as separation of powers phenomena that are distinct from private litigation on the same topics. Private suits are more likely to succeed for a variety of reasons, while member suits provide an index of constitutional dysfunction. Member lawsuits do not offer a simple solution to past, present, or future institutional imbalances, but they certainly provide opportunity for fresh analysis on how constitutional separation of powers principles can fall apart without deep and wide support.

Fraught Role of Courts

Federal courts do not welcome all types of constitutional conflicts. Like Congress and executive branch, the federal court system developed into an extraordinarily broad branch of government that touches every facet of our lives. Unlike the other branches, however, the courts' only real power is their legitimacy. This structural weakness makes the courts wary of taking on certain areas of constitutional law while being particular about the types of cases that are appropriate for legal resolution. *Federalist* 78 describes the constitutional design of federal courts as the "least dangerous branch" as they lack enforcement powers. "It may truly be said to have neither force nor will, but merely judgment; and must ultimately depend upon the aid of the executive arm for the efficacy of its judgments."[4] In part for these reasons, federal judges have long crafted standards on whether, when, and why to take certain cases.[5] The formal role of federal judges includes congressional laws of jurisdiction (whether the court *can* hear a case) and their own developed norms and precedents of justiciability (whether the courts *should* do so). Judicial legitimacy depends upon courts' adhering to standards about whether, why, and how to take cases.

Some justiciability doctrines focus on the litigants' claims of injury and the timing of the case (called *standing, mootness,* and *ripeness*) and while other doctrines are about the issues themselves and whether courts are appropriate venues (called *political questions* and *equitable discretion*). The first issue that judges must grapple with is who or what has been "injured" by the government power or process at issue, as well as whether courts are able to provide a remedy for the alleged injury. These fundamental threshold questions have been central to judicial politics since *Marbury v. Madison* in 1803.[6] Appointed federal judges serving lifetime terms may be more insulated from public opinion than the elected branches, but they are quite aware of their institutional strengths, weaknesses, and potential effects of their powers on politics.

Standing is the single most crucial hurdle for plaintiffs to pass and allow judges to assess whether cases can be heard on the merits. Congress members' claims of institutional injuries are particularly hard to prove. To establish standing to sue under Article III of the U.S. Constitution, plaintiffs must show that: "(1) they have suffered an injury that is both 'concrete and particularized' and 'actual or imminent,' not 'conjectural' or 'hypothetical'; (2) that the injury is fairly traceable to the conduct of which they complain; and (3) the injury is likely to be redressed by a court decision in their favor. The party seeking to demonstrate standing bears the burden of establishing each element."[7]

Via standing and additional hurdles, judges generally have the institutional right to reject congressional lawsuits before getting to the merits, although the book shows they are often divided amongst themselves about which doctrine to emphasize in the process. We will also see that a vocal minority of judges from the district court level to the Supreme Court believe these cases are indeed justiciable and that the Court has an obligation to take them up.

Either way, the specific arguments that federal courts use to accept and reject cases based on justiciability reveal the judges' own (dis)comfort with the issues at hand and their views of other options for the litigants to resolve their claims. Justiciability is therefore the language judges use to signal their broader views of their own branch's "proper place" in the separation of powers system. Scholars have long argued about why and how courts have developed and utilized these standards regarding member suits specifically—and separation of powers questions more broadly—including law professors[8] and even the research arm of Congress.[9]

This book appreciates and engages these efforts, while asking bigger questions than whether/how/should courts take up these cases. The starting point is the assumption made by the framers that each branch's unique perspective on the same issues will be fed by different electoral timetables, constituencies, and the ever-present human drive for power. "Ambition must be made to counteract ambition. The interest of the man must be connected to the constitutional rights of the place," as said in *Federalist* 51.[10] The use of the word "must"—twice—implies that a healthy separation of powers system requires peaceful but consistent interinstitutional combat. Member lawsuits expose the unevenness of institutional ambition today. Why are members turning to the courts if their own chambers can flex constitutional muscles more directly?

By the same token, what would the Supreme Court—or any court in the federal system—gain by accepting member cases regularly and ruling on the merits? Like other areas of constitutional law that inspire cries of "judicial activism" or "legislating from the bench," separation of powers cases are extremely risky for federal judges. What would happen if the Supreme Court ordered a war unconstitutional and the executive branch did not obey? Or what if it did? These questions go right to the heart of the *countermajoritarian* position of the federal courts in American politics. Alexander Bickel famously said that the Court's fraught place in the political and policy landscape should compel it to find ways of avoiding conflicts, if possible, by utilizing the "passive virtues" of justiciability doctrine. Bickel said the Supreme Court has three choices: "It checks, it legitimates, or it does neither."[11] His point was that all three actions are appropriate, and doing nothing in some cases actually gives it the power to do more in others.

Around the same time, in 1962, the Supreme Court defined the *political question doctrine* (PQD) in a case that was more about federalism than separation of powers. The concept of PQD goes way back to *Marbury*, but in *Baker v. Carr* the Court articulated a specific bundle of questions to assess the appropriateness of its taking a case. With an eye toward avoiding as many "political" questions as possible, judges assessed whether the Constitution granted the power to decide elsewhere. In addition, judges could conclude that they lacked fact-finding capacity. The majority in *Baker v. Carr* added that judges should consider whether, in taking on a case, they risked offending one or the other branch, as well as "the potentiality of embarrassment from multifarious pronouncements by various departments on one question."[12] Although the Supreme Court added that the PQD was not meant to avoid all "political cases," the doctrine's broader implications came under fire for fear that it would cordon off certain types of constitutional questions from review indefinitely, if cemented by repeated precedent.[13]

The PQD was tested again and again in the midst of interbranch warfare in the 1970s and 1980s, leading prominent legal academics to weigh in on its appropriateness. Louis Henkin argued that the PQD erroneously leaves the impression that certain controversies are not, in fact, legitimate constitutional questions. This mistake may encourage the branches to proceed without deeper reflection, including on foreign policy, which was once a routine area of judicial disposition.[14] Jesse Choper went in a different direction, saying that federal courts have a structural specialty to handle individual and group rights claims, while federalism and separation of powers concerns can work themselves out through the regular political process.[15]

Meanwhile, Congress members continued to turn to the courts for help in restraining presidents. After a new round of suits in the late 1970s and early 1980s, Federal Judge Carl McGowan said standing, ripeness, and even the PQD were inadequate to this type of claim. He said that even fully justiciable questions can be ill suited for resolution in the courts when the members had not exhausted their other institutional options. Instead, McGowan preferred *equitable discretion*. "Invoking the court's discretion to deny an equitable remedy when the petitioner could get adequate relief from his fellow legislators seems to be the most satisfying way of resolving these cases. It avoids the difficulties and confusions engendered by the doctrines of standing, political question, and ripeness, and affords the court wide latitude to choose the course that it believes to be most in the public interest under the precise circumstances before it."[16] Of course, the doctrine had its critics, but it added another judicial tool to deflect member cases in a manner that encouraged members to support the Constitution's separation of powers system.[17]

However, the plaintiffs say it is not so simple, as the president's veto is a formidable obstacle to any bills that attempt to curb presidential power—from military campaigns to executive orders on domestic policy. Under these circumstances of deferential courts and congresses, is there any power in U.S. politics that can really stop a president? One answer is public opinion: "The formal institutional constraints that Congress and the courts impose on presidential unilateral action are feeble. As a result, recent scholarship suggests that public opinion may be the strongest check against executive overreach."[18] Yet public opinion is an imperfect vehicle for reining in presidents and inspiring Congress to fight back for a variety of obvious reasons, including its partisan volatility. Voters, like partisans in the branches, may root for their preferred presidents to expand powers and then profess horror when the opposition party's president follows suit. Instead, members of the House and Senate could try to lead public opinion in these areas by being more consistently ambitious in an institutional sense. If Congress stood up for itself, neither the president nor the Supreme Court would have the "final word." The ways that members routinely punt big questions to the court that they can and should answer themselves inadvertently exaggerates judicial power. This book joins a long list of other work that views federal courts, including the Supreme Court, as one of many institutions and arenas to hash out constitutional conflicts—not the last stop.[19]

There is also another alternative to member lawsuits—conventional private plaintiffs allow the courts to take up the same constitutional questions that are raised by congressional litigants, but without some of the justiciability problems. The book contrasts private and public litigation on similar subjects to show federal courts' inconsistent comfort with being part of public policy dialogues. An important separate issue (not taken up by the book) is judicial power to support congressional prerogatives on oversight and investigations. Total judicial restraint across these other areas would certainly increase presidential power.[20]

In addition, on civil rights and liberties claims, federal courts can check presidential power expansion by simply asking whether he has received authority to do what he is doing. Cases on post-9/11 detainee treatment under President George W. Bush, drone strikes under President Barack Obama, and the "travel ban" cases under President Donald Trump all bring legitimate constitutional questions to the court system through high profile injury claims. Whether these private plaintiffs were satisfied or not, the political result of the courts' actions reverberate through the entire electoral system. Regardless of the outcome of a particular case, the policy ball often returns to Congress's court, if it wants it. Courts can scrutinize presidential power any number of ways, but they cannot force members and leaders to take the reins.

Broad constitutional dialogues also take pressure off the courts to "resolve problems," despite having such limited enforcement power. James Bradley Thayer noted over a century ago that the federal courts' "incidental and postponed control" over constitutional violations should cue a "narrow" view of action. In a similar vein, Herbert Wechsler famously advocated a cautious role for the Supreme Court—one that was restrained by an adherence to consistency and "neutral principles," not simply related to "prudential" institutional strategies and policy preferences. While Wechsler cautioned against the courts' becoming a "naked power organ," "courts have both the title and the duty when a case is properly before them to review the actions of the other branches in the light of constitutional provisions."[21]

Just because federal courts are wary of congressional litigation does not mean they are bystanders in presidential power development. There is a long historical record of examples where federal courts have been inclined toward presidential power for a variety of reasons.[22] In short: if the courts take member cases, members risk losing on the merits. Out of pure pragmatism, then, Congress must be willing to step into constitutional controversies head-on.[23]

Layout of the Book

The six chapters of this book review the federal courts' actions across three areas of constitutional law crucial to understanding the separation of powers system: presidential war powers (part 1); House and Senate legislative processes (part 2); and other types of unilateral executive actions at home and abroad, including treaty withdrawals and executive orders (part 3). Each of the three parts contains two chapters: one that examines scholarly treatments and constitutional law regarding private federal court litigation, and one that concentrates on congressional members' lawsuits on the same topic. The three parts are arrayed in a loose chronological order, with some exceptions. War powers come first because the very first congressional lawsuits ever challenged President Nixon's bombing campaigns in Cambodia, as mentioned above. Legislative process lawsuits dominate in the 1980s and 1990s. Part 3 looks at executive orders and treaty withdrawals from the late 1970s through today. One recent member lawsuit on enforcement of the 2010 Patient Protection and Affordable Care Act ("Affordable Care Act") was settled in 2017. As of this writing, two ongoing member lawsuits concern President Trump's alleged acceptance of emoluments through his business interests and his invocation of emergency power to expand the southern border wall.

The chapter pairings are meant to highlight the similarities and differences between private and public litigation on the same topics. Private litigation is necessary when the plaintiffs do not have another way to get direct relief from legitimate injuries related to presidential or executive branch power, but that argument does not apply to Congress. Throughout all chapters, institutional rhetoric and action across all three branches drive the inquiry, with emphasis on judicial rulings and reasoning. All three branches' official words and decisions form the real-world basis of constitutional interpretative change. Public archives, largely available online (with free access, such as the Government Publishing

Office website, National Archives, and Congress.gov), and university subscriptions (e.g., to the HeinOnline and LexisNexis databases) were supplemented with two trips to the Library of Congress to look at special legislative archives that were especially instructive in members' war litigation.

The congressional litigation chapters also include information from my interviews with member-plaintiffs and attorneys of record in their lawsuits.[24] The goal of the interviews was to understand the background of these suits and the plaintiffs' motivations, knowing the high bar to court acceptance of the cases on the merits. Interviews are somewhat out of fashion in political science as a sole method of research, but are very useful as a supplement to other sources, especially when there is no other reliable way to find out why these member-plaintiffs pushed the cases against long odds. The twelve subjects include six former members of Congress (four Democrats and two Republicans), five attorneys of record for member-plaintiffs, and one legislative director for a former member of Congress (also a Republican), who was authorized to speak on the member's behalf. Under the terms of my research proposal to the University of Louisville's Institutional Review Board, the subjects are not listed by name and interviews were not recorded. Although the interviews were extremely helpful for understanding litigants' strategies, partisan context, and policy components of the lawsuits, the official words and actions of Congress, the president, and the Supreme Court drive each chapter.

Part 1: War Powers

War was once a three-branch question. The Constitution's text has remained the same, but Congress and the federal courts have receded from view. The ascendant Cold War executive branch came at Congress's expense, often voluntarily, which indirectly shaped self-imposed judicial restraint. When majorities in Congress repeatedly fail to confront unilateral presidential decisions, federal courts claim to lack an entry point for judgment. So the default assumption now is that presidents have unique and discretionary powers to start military action abroad, with Congress in a supporting role and the courts largely out of sight. In this part of the book, we see that federal court standards on private lawsuits are very different from public lawsuits.

Chapter 1 demonstrates that courts were once comfortable entering into the fray when they have clear congressional guidelines about war authorization (private lawsuits) and when members of Congress press their claims through political as well as legal channels (Cambodia cases). This chapter also demonstrates that federal courts can have a place in war powers conflicts—and they did up through the mid-twentieth century, but only in individual plaintiff cases. Although no federal court has ever ordered a president to stop a war, there was once more comfort in judicial engagement in war-related constitutional questions, at least from the founding generation through the Civil War and beyond; the Cold War changed all three branches' orientations.

Chapter 2 shows the consequence of four decades of congressional and judicial restraint that followed the passage of the 1973 War Powers Resolution. The suits began with four challenges to President Ronald Reagan (on El Salvador, Nicaragua, Grenada, and the Iran-Iraq War), and one each against George H. W. Bush (Persian Gulf War), Bill Clinton (Kosovo), George W. Bush (Iraq), and Obama (Libya). These cases were dismissed for different reasons by the federal courts, citing mootness, ripeness, standing, the political question doctrine, and equitable discretion, usually in some combination, as barriers to adjudication. Upon dismissal, federal courts placed the entire burden to rein in presidential power on supermajorities in Congress, even though prior authorization may not have occurred. This disapproval would ultimately require two-thirds of both chambers to override a presidential veto. In these ways, federal courts normalized the very dynamics the member-plaintiffs were targeting in their suits.

Part 2: Legislative Processes

Congress's legislative process developments expose different kinds of existential institutional questions than war powers. This part concerns Congress's attacks against itself—not presidential assertion of prerogative. Since the mid-1980s, the House and Senate repeatedly delegated enumerated powers to the executive branch and created new legislative processes that require two-thirds or three-fifths votes. These "reforms" were designed to meet policy or partisan goals by attacking simple majority norms and rules. Members say they want to tie their own hands in the national interest.[25] Some members of both chambers opposed to these self-imposed obstacles filed suit in federal court five times to block or alter them. The courts struck down two of the processes. Majorities then regrouped in various attempts to get around the decisions rather than savor regained authority. Congress's determination to thwart its own prerogatives shows the depth of its retreat from the framers' vision of institutional ambition. Lawsuits can be a potent method for members to express frustration but, ultimately, federal courts cannot save Congress from itself.

In these ways, Congress's legislative process changes prompt different kinds of constitutional questions than foreign policy powers. The House and Senate have long tinkered with legislative processes, including member prerogatives, committee powers, party structures, and chamber floor rules. The Constitution says, "Each House may determine the Rules of its Proceedings" (Art. I, Sec. 5) and does not explicitly prevent delegation of power to the executive branch, supermajority chamber rules, or other self-imposed, complex processes. As with the rest of the book project's case studies, there is no political or scholarly consensus that decreases in congressional power in any policy area are even a "problem" to merit special scrutiny. Some scholars argue that congressional delegation of power and complex internal reforms should be studied purely from a strategic party and policy angle, implying they are constitutionally harmless.[26] Others show concern that if Congress repeatedly undermines simple majority rule to fulfill its enumerated legislative powers, there are profound impacts on public policy outcomes and the representative and deliberative goals of the separation of powers system. Recent scholarly consensus shows how federal courts inspire and provoke dialogues on an array of policies and procedures bounce through other branches, states, and elections. In this view, federal court involvement can spur other parts of the political system into action, but cannot and should not be seen as "final."[27]

Chapter 3 shows that even in private litigation cases, the federal judiciary is not always comfortable getting involved. Two takeaways from this chapter are that the federal courts are inconsistent in their interest in legislative process cases (the last delegation of legislative power cases were decided during the New Deal) and that when they do enter these debates they get roundly criticized for it (see debate over the "legislative veto" case *INS v. Chadha* in 1983).

In chapter 4, we compare these private actions to five suits filed by members of Congress against legislative processes. In the 1980s and early 1990s, lawsuits filed by members span the Gramm-Rudman-Hollings deficit-reduction processes of 1985; a base closure commission; supermajority tax increase rules in 1995; the Line Item Veto Act in 1996, which inspired a landmark rejection of member lawsuits except when authorized by the chambers; and the Senate filibuster regarding blockage of the Development, Relief and Education for Alien Minors (DREAM) Act in 2007. Even when the Supreme Court struck down holdings that could have conserved congressional prerogatives, majorities then tried new ways to give up the same power. The determination of both chambers to thwart their own enumerated powers (more often under split-party or Republican control) shows the depth of Congress's retreat from the visions of institutional ambition articulated in the *Federalist*, as Congress takes the initiative to sacrifice institutional power.

Part 3: More Executive Unilateralism

When it comes to such disparate issues as presidential treaty withdrawals and domestic executive orders, the debate echoes an old one between President William Howard Taft's "whig" philosophy of presidential power and Theodore

Roosevelt's "stewardship" model. Are presidents bound by what the Constitution and Congress allow explicitly or by what they disallow? The difference in these perspectives is profound. If presidents are allowed to act only on issues and in ways that Congress authorized previously, no action by Congress means no action by the president. If presidents look at the constitutional question as Theodore Roosevelt did, presidents can do pretty much what they want unless the Constitution and Congress disallow it. Congressional disallowance is especially tricky because presidents can veto any bill that comes to them that is intended to restrict his power. Congress would then have to overcome the sure veto by two-thirds in each chamber. This constitutional question is relevant in one way or another to all the chapters of the book but gets the greatest attention here due to the specifics of the cases at hand.

Chapter 5 demonstrates the sprawling breadth of executive power expansion in the twentieth century through private cases that challenged presidential firings by Woodrow Wilson and Franklin Roosevelt, the landmark "Steel Seizure" case under Harry Truman, financial settlements related to the Iran hostage crisis, the post-9/11 cases of detainee treatment, and the most recent passport case on the U.S. policy toward Israel's capital. In almost all of these private litigation cases, the Supreme Court looked at congressional intention and action to guide their decisions. These precedents help us to understand the most recent legal controversies against President Trump. Wherever federal courts can find Congress's delegation of power, presidents will likely win.

Chapter 6 is equally diverse in the member cases, spanning the "pocket veto" (a rare member suit success story, due to the Court's narrow conception of institutional injury), three cases related to treaty changes/withdrawals, and a case on the Affordable Care Act that was settled recently. All of these cases highlight the way that conventional partisan warfare creeps into legal battles. Like the cases in part 1, the member-plaintiffs in this chapter are attacking opposition presidents for institutional behaviors and constitutional interpretations that they appear to forgive in their own presidents. This partisan dynamic dilutes the power and potential significance of the claim.

The pattern of aggressive presidents and deferential/ambivalent Congresses stretches back decades under both parties' leadership. The "court cure" sought by many members of Congress is fundamentally flawed for many reasons, particularly as it can backfire on members in different ways. Certain justiciability doctrines can legitimize the status quo, which is the opposite of the litigants' intention. Courts can also take up the cases and rule against the members, or for the presidents, taking away constitutional claims for future political engagement. These lawsuits are also unattractive to courts in a time of heightened partisanship when litigants target opposition presidents but not their own. Although the questions these litigants raise are legitimate, they are better suited to more conventional institutional actions.

The Constitution's framers built the separation of powers system to thrive through the branches' engaging with each other on policy principles and powers, not punting to judges. Judges are understandably wary of accepting cases that have long been discredited and that threaten to drag courts even deeper into the political morass. The 115th Congress was one of unified government, while the 116th is divided. Neither party's members nor leaders in Congress have showed sustained interest in holding their own presidents to the constitutional fire. The judiciary cannot provide the institutional ambition that *Federalist* 51 assumed would occur naturally within the House and Senate, especially when the so-called institutional injuries do not offend majorities.

In the famous Steel Seizure case of 1952, the Supreme Court ruled against the President Truman's executive order to nationalize steel mills during a labor dispute that threatened to disrupt production during the Korean War. Justice Robert Jackson's concurring opinion (discussed in chapter 5) formed the basis of the Court's subsequent examination of separation of powers disputes. He warned Congress to be mindful of its powers and assumed federal courts would maintain some interest in supporting fundamental principles of constitutional government. "With all its defects, delays and inconveniences, men have discovered no technique for long preserving free government except that the Executive be under the law, and that the law be made by parliamentary deliberations. Such institutions may be destined to pass away. But it is the duty of the Court to be last, not first, to give them up."[28] This book provides a new perspective on the unraveling of these presumptions.

Part 1
WAR POWERS

1

WAR IS JUSTICIABLE,
UNTIL IT ISN'T

The framers of the Constitution disagreed about the meaning of its war powers clauses as early as George Washington's presidency. Washington's Neutrality Proclamation to keep the United States out of the war between Great Britain and France prompted a series of dueling letters between "Pacificus" (Alexander Hamilton) and "Helvidius" (James Madison) about whether the president had to wait for congressional authorization before declaring a state of nonwar. Washington ultimately decided to wait for legislative authorization.[1] But the United States was unable to stay out of the conflict after all, which triggered the undeclared naval "Quasi War" with France under President John Adams. Three cases related to the Quasi War's constitutionality went to the Supreme Court, all brought by private plaintiffs who claimed economic damages from the skirmishes. The Supreme Court scrutinized the legislative record to make its decisions and, in one of the cases, rebuked President Adams's administration for exceeding Congress's authorization.

These early war cases offer three lessons. First, if the very men who wrote and ratified the Constitution disagreed on war powers, it should be no surprise that later generations argue about them. Second, when federal courts hear conflicts related to war, judges can examine the constitutionality of executive actions if Congress provides a clear record of intent. Third, courts are in a stronger institutional position to resolve private lawsuits that claim specific economic injuries from military actions than they are to resolve public (member) lawsuits that claim vague institutional injuries. Private plaintiffs often have nowhere else to turn other than courts while members of Congress can seek relief from their colleagues.

A summary of private plaintiff lawsuits from the founding period to the early twentieth century demonstrates these points and also contrasts this earlier Supreme Court engagement in war powers conflicts with the first two member cases surrounding the Vietnam War's expansion. Member litigation began during the Vietnam War out of frustration with imbalance of power that took permanent root in the Cold War and then remained in our political culture under new international pressures in the 1990s and after 9/11. These plaintiffs may genuinely want to stop death and destruction, and turn to federal courts because of fecklessness in the House and Senate. But Courts cannot, will not, and should not do Congress's work for it. No amount of member litigation can correct these bipartisan institutional developments. Member litigation is an index of separation of powers dysfunction, not the cure.

Early Constitutional History

Institutionally protective members of Congress are rightfully frustrated. No matter the party in the White House or Congress, presidents after 1950 have ordered offensive military actions abroad before waiting for formal legislative authorization. The intention and text of the Constitution says the opposite. In Article I, Section 8, of the Constitution, Congress has powers to "declare War, grant Letters of Marque and Reprisal, and make Rules concerning Captures on Land and Water; To raise and support Armies, but no Appropriation of Money to that Use shall be for a longer Term than two Years; To provide and maintain a Navy and; To make Rules for the Government and Regulation of the land and naval Forces."

Far from being unilateral, the president's constitutional military authority is drawn from what Congress authorizes, through declarations of war, other forms of authorizing legislation, and policymaking through the annual budget process, which can be supplemented anytime. If there is any special reservoir of war power to be found in the Constitution, James Madison's convention notes suggest that a president can repel sudden attacks on U.S. soil, but that power would not extend to initiating purely offensive actions that begin outside of national territory.[2] Most modern presidents, however, assume or claim much broader discretion from the "executive power" clause (Art. II, Sec. 1) and the phrase that the president "shall take care that the laws be faithfully executed" (Art. II, Sec. 3).[3]

The president's only unilateral foreign policy power in the Constitution is diplomatic: he can recognize foreign countries (stated as "receive ambassadors" in Art. II, Sec. 3). The Senate must consent to nominations of executive branch officials, and it approves treaties with a two-thirds vote (Art. II, Sec. 2). The president's other shared legislative powers can apply to foreign or domestic policy, including the veto (Art. I, Sec. 7) and recommendation of legislation in the State of the Union (Art. II, Sec. 2). Presidents are expressly forbidden from spending money without prior congressional approval: "No Money shall be drawn from the Treasury, but in Consequence of Appropriations made by Law" (Art. 1, Sec. 9). The most important constitutional provision that modern presidents use to justify their decisions to begin new military action is "The President shall be Commander in Chief of the Army and Navy of the United States, and of the Militia of the several States, when called into the actual Service of the United States" (Art. II, Sec. 3). All modern presidents interpret this power broadly—and say that they may order first strikes in foreign territory for the "national interest."[4]

Yet, in *Federalist* 69, Alexander Hamilton described the Constitution's presidential war powers in far weaker terms, saying the "Commander-in-Chief" provision "would amount to nothing more than the supreme command and direction of the military and naval forces . . . while that of the British king extends to the *declaring* of war and to the *raising* and *regulating* of fleets and armies— all which, by the Constitution . . . would appertain to the legislature."[5]

By comparison to the legislative and executive branches, the Constitution's description of the federal courts is short, lacking details on judges' personal qualifications, any reference to judicial review power, and guidance on interpretation. But war and foreign policy powers are expressly described in the Constitution and can be the subject of legislation and interbranch disagreement just the same as domestic economic issues. The framers did not signal that foreign policy cases should be treated differently from others. "The judicial Power shall extend to all Cases, in Law and Equity, arising under this Constitution, the Laws of the United States, and Treaties made, or which shall be made, under their Authority;—to all Cases affecting Ambassadors, other public Ministers and Consuls;—to all Cases of admiralty and maritime Jurisdiction;—to Controversies to which the United States shall be a Party;—to Controversies . . . between a State, or the Citizens thereof, and foreign States, Citizens or Subjects" (Art III, Sec. 2). Marriage, reproduction, education, technology, the environment, and health care are not mentioned in the Constitution but the Supreme Court rules on them. War powers and processes *are* mentioned: why are they off-limits?

Although federal courts have the authority to take up foreign policy and war powers cases, engagement in these issues is neither automatic nor always desirable. Judges can exercise at least some control over the types of cases they hear, especially at the Supreme Court. While Congress can regulate appellate jurisdiction (Art. III, Sec. 2), the courts set their own standards for justiciability and can shape their place in the political system through norms and precedent. Hamilton anticipated in *Federalist* 78 that federal judges will be mindful of their lack of enforcement power in their rulings, even as they have a duty to uphold the

Constitution.[6] While war powers and related processes and policies can be especially fraught for court involvement, no provision in the nation's founding documents implies that judges have any less power or competence to accept these types of cases and in fact courts have decided some important institutional disagreements in this area. So the question among scholars is really the same one as we see among judges—not whether federal judges *can* rule on foreign affairs, but whether they *should*.

Debating Courts and War

In the twenty-first century, the most prominent scholarly debates on war powers in political science focus on the constitutional roles of the president and Congress, not the courts. From assessments of a new "imperial presidency"[7] to defenders of a "unitary executive theory"[8] and their detractors,[9] we know that presidential war power is controversial, regardless of party in the White House. Congressional actions (and inactions) have also received a fresh look, with some studies highlighting House and Senate input prior to presidential war decisions and afterward in the oversight process.[10] Other scholars accuse Congress of abdication on war, or at least deep institutional ambivalence, evidenced by repeated cycles of delegation and regret.[11] A more nuanced view on executive power development uses a lens of institutional virtues to assess constitutional boundaries across a variety of policies.[12] Scholars who are otherwise on different sides of the presidential war powers debates nevertheless agree that courts should stay out.[13]

Yet there was once a lively debate in law and political science on whether and how courts could reinvigorate the Constitution's war powers clauses, before and after the War Powers Resolution (WPR) of 1973. If a court found a presidential-ordered military action a violation of domestic or international law, the president could appeal to Congress for statutory approval.[14] In other words, as John Hart Ely put it, "Courts have no business deciding when we get involved in combat, but they have every business insisting that the officials the Constitution entrusts with that decision be the ones who make it."[15] One lesson from the Vietnam War is that when governmental power goes unchallenged by both other branches, there is little incentive for self-constraint by the president.[16]

Foreign policy was not cordoned off as a blanket political question in *Baker v. Carr*, which concluded that "it is error to suppose that every case or controversy which touches foreign relations lies beyond judicial cognizance."[17] But the federal courts' lack of enforcement power make war powers cases especially tricky. In an article otherwise very critical of the Nixon administration's Vietnam-era military decisions, Alexander Bickel still argued that Congress had the burden to change the war's direction, not the courts. He observed the Supreme Court's capacity to enforce its judgments were limited. "The Court cannot declare the war unconstitutional and then do nothing about it. That would deny its nature as a court of law, sitting to decide cases and see controversies to their resolution. And it is on its nature as such an institution of law that the Court's whole claim to authority rests."[18]

Jesse Choper, meanwhile, said if Congress or the rest of the political system chooses not to resist presidential actions, this consensus may indicate that "no true constitutional violation has occurred. And if they seek to halt what they perceive to be an unconstitutional executive incursion and fail, there is little reason to believe that the Court will succeed when they have not."[19] Choper later updated his argument to say war powers should not be justiciable because they do not involve constitutional individual rights claims. "The judiciary should not intervene in a matter that can be appropriately resolved within the political process. Although the modern presidency is usually perceived as holding the much stronger hand in conflicts between the executive and legislative branches over military affairs, Congress has many effective tools available to express its disagreement."[20] Choper wants federal courts to preserve their institutional power for more vulnerable plaintiffs than politicians.

Louis Fisher and Neal Devins similarly reject efforts to rope the judiciary into war power claims, arguing that courts are "ill equipped" to decide factual conflicts about the initiation of war but for different reasons than Choper. They maintain that congressional majorities have not set up proper constitutional conflicts through regular legislative processes. While they are sympathetic with the argument that presidents often overstep their constitutional bounds on war, "in surrendering its powers to the President, Congress has little reason to expect assistance from the courts . . . unless and until Congress has joined the issue by invoking its institutional powers."[21] And in other work, Fisher repudiates Supreme Court actions that are decidedly "pro-presidential," and the fear of ever-more expansive precedent is reasonable.[22]

At the center of these arguments are three facts of U.S. political and constitutional life. First, in the nuclear age, national security has become synonymous with the president's branch. Second, Congress shrank back as the executive grew in stature, with partisanship often driving Congress's inconsistent defense of its own prerogatives. And third, courts now treat domestic and foreign policy differently, and the precedent wall on the latter grew. "The President is therefore not uniquely granted greater leeway in national security affairs because he is the primordial embodiment of the nation's sovereignty in international affairs, but because he the Executive and as such is the nation's agent in the unique legal realm which comprises the Law of Nations."[23]

When litigation arises about the executive branch's use of power, federal courts cannot be shunted aside for all claims. There is a place for private litigants who have no other place to turn for relief, from habeas corpus claims (discussed in part 3) to economic damages (discussed here and in parts 2 and 3). If their claims hinge on whether the executive branch acted lawfully, courts can trace the line of authority to Congress. The Constitution Project published a report saying as much in 2005: "The federal courts have the constitutional power to decide whether the use of force has been lawfully authorized. That justiciable question should not be confused with the different non-justiciable political questions whether we should go to war or whether Congress must use formal declaration, use-of-force statute, or specific appropriation as the form of authorization. The courts can and have decided the authority question incidentally to deciding the legal effects of the exercise of war powers."[24]

Pre-Vietnam Private Litigation

As mentioned above, interbranch constitutional conflicts on war began within five years of ratification. Most early questions were resolved politically among Congress and the president. Federal courts were also brought in early on, and showed they were capable of weighing in on questions involving the branches' war powers. The Quasi War with France under President John Adams prompted the first federal lawsuits on war powers. The Supreme Court ruled for legislative primacy in offensive war action and for the Court's power to say so. Some of these precedents predate *Marbury v. Madison* (1803) and have never been overturned.[25] The fact that Chief Justice John Marshall articulated a theory of political questions, discussed in the introduction to this book, did not preclude his own competence and interest, or those of his successors, in taking war powers cases. These cases are noteworthy beyond the issues at hand because Supreme Court judges "sometimes spoke against the authority of the president to venture in war-making activities against the express will or the silence of Congress. The fact that some of the earliest of these decisions were written by justices who had been members of the Constitutional Convention or participated in state ratifying conventions lends additional weight to the importance of these early interpretations."[26]

Quasi War litigants were private interests who claimed economic injuries, and to adjudicate the cases federal courts had to decide whether France was an "enemy" of the United States and, in effect, whether the country was legally at war. The ambiguity of the conflict stemmed from the fact that Congress had passed laws authorizing limited military activity, but did not declare war against France formally. Justice Salmon Chase in *Bas v. Tingy* explained that "perfect" war (declared) and "imperfect" (authorized by Congress but not a formal declaration) were the same for the purposes of the private compensation at issue in the case.[27] In *Talbot v. Seeman*, Chief Justice Marshall said the status of U.S. foreign affairs rested with Congress. "The whole powers of war being by the Constitution of the United States vested in Congress, the acts of that body can alone be resorted to as our guides in this inquiry. It is not denied, nor in the course of the argument has it been denied, that Congress may authorize general hostilities, in which case the general laws of war apply to our situation, or partial hostilities, in which case the laws of war, so far as they actually apply to our situation, must be noticed. To determine the real situation of America in regard to France, the acts of Congress are to be inspected."[28]

The third and final Quasi War case concerned a presidential action on a ship capture from a French port that went beyond congressional authorization of captures of ships headed to a French port. In this case, Chief Justice Marshall ruled against the president's orders, saying his "instructions cannot change the nature of the transaction, or legalize an act which without those instructions would have been a plain trespass."[29] This case, *Little v. Barreme*, is often highlighted by scholars who support judicial involvement in war powers cases, at least those brought by private litigants. It is worth noting, as others have, that Marshall himself established the parameters of the political question doctrine a few years earlier in *Marbury*, saying that the Supreme Court should tread carefully when the issue was better suited to the other elected bodies. Yet this case was not deemed to be off-limits by the Supreme Court. As Edward Keynes observes, "While the Court did not question the wisdom of congressional policy, the justices did not hide behind procedural barriers to avoid deciding the legality of the seizure."[30] Michael Glennon notes that "Marshall does not even consider the possibility that the dispute might have constituted a political question, unsuitable for judicial resolution." The takeaway from this seemingly minor case is that the executive branch was not above the law, even in foreign policy, and the Supreme Court could assess the question by examining the legislative record."[31]

Between the Quasi and Civil Wars, federal courts heard several cases on legislative and executive war power. The issues included the authorization for individual actions against foreign governments, where the Supreme Court declared that "it is the exclusive province of congress to change a state of peace into a state of war."[32] Other cases were on habeas corpus petitions regarding men captured in the United States and alleged to be levying war,[33] and property disputes related to war at the beginning of the War of 1812.[34] In these cases, federal court decisions repeatedly endorsed a Congress-centered foreign policy by focusing upon the statutes (or lack thereof) to determine the outcome of the issues. In two cases, the Supreme Court leaned toward more contemporary notions of deference to presidential prerogative or political questions; the earlier concerned federal use of state militia and the latter civil unrest.[35] But soon after, the Mexican American War gave the Supreme Court three additional opportunities to reinforce congressional supremacy on general war powers.[36]

The Civil War tested constitutional separation of powers in at least three significant ways that would echo through war powers cases over a hundred years later. President Abraham Lincoln admitted to going beyond the normal reach of executive power when the rebellion began with Congress out of session. In his famous letter to Congress upon its return in July 1861, he catalogued his actions and his legislative requests for retroactive and future authority. "It was with the deepest regret that the Executive found the duty of employing the war power in defense of the Government forced upon him. He could but perform this duty or surrender the existence of the Government."[37]

Could the president exercise powers that are granted to Congress in the Constitution? These questions are the center of at least nine federal cases on Lincoln's suspension of the writ of habeas corpus beginning in 1861, which is a centuries-old originally common law rule that prisoners have the right to hear charges against them and the reason for imprisonment. Article I, Section 9, of the Constitution, which is the legislative article, says, "The privilege of the writ of habeas corpus shall not be suspended unless when in cases of rebellion or invasion the public safety may require it." Lincoln granted the U.S. military authority to arrest and hold citizens suspected of rebellious activities a month after his inauguration in March 1861, in the face of Virginia secession and the possibility of Maryland's following suit. To prevent that outcome in Maryland and protect communication and transportation to Washington, with Congress out of session, Lincoln ordered General Winfield Scott to arrest potential rebels and hold them in military custody without access to civil courts. John Merryman was arrested near Baltimore in May and received a writ of habeas corpus from Chief Justice Rodger Taney, a Maryland native with southern sympathies and complex judicial baggage stemming from the Dred Scott case of 1857. Taney, who was riding circuit at the time and sitting as a trial judge, concluded Lincoln had the power to suspend the writ, but, famously, Taney's opinion was ignored by Merryman's military jailers. "Lincoln ignored Taney, and that was the end of the federal judiciary's involvement with the suspension of habeas corpus. Neither the Supreme Court nor the lower federal courts dealt with the issue again. The action now passed to the president and Congress."[38]

Congress retroactively ratified most of Lincoln's military actions when it convened in July 1861. The following year both Lincoln and his secretary of war issued additional proclamations suspending the writ, and then in 1863 Congress passed the Habeas Corpus Suspension Act, deferring to Lincoln on the issue for the duration of the war when in his "judgment, the public safety may require it."[39] Federal courts would hear the habeas corpus issue, and the related issue of military trials, several additional times during and immediately after the Civil War.[40]

Another crucial question about the president's prosecution of the Civil War came to a head in the *Prize Cases*. How broadly could the president interpret his own Article II powers, with or without congressional authorization? This litigation by private shipowners questioned the constitutionality of a blockade of southern ports that Lincoln ordered in April, 1861, three months before Congress was in session. Similarly to the habeas corpus writ suspension, Lincoln's actions were retroactively legalized by Congress that summer. Nevertheless, shipowners whose cargo was seized between April and July 1861 sued for damages the following year claiming the president acted unconstitutionally in making the order. In this decision, the Supreme Court narrowly upheld the president's action as well as Congress's retroactive blessing. The 5–4 outcome came while the war was still ongoing in 1863.

Justice Robert Grier delivered the opinion of the Court, which said Lincoln's actions were legitimate because Congress conferred the authority retroactively. He noted Congress had previously delegated authority to other presidents to repel invasions and suppress insurrections—and may have indirectly authorized in advance through other related acts.[41] Justice Samuel Nelson's dissent said that the property claims were valid for actions that occurred between April and July 1861, when Congress acted.[42] Federal courts remained comfortable ruling on war powers cases through the end of the Civil War, including property disputes that required judicial confirmation of the war's official termination.[43] After the Civil War period, federal courts continued to take and rule on cases that related to immigration, property disputes during the Spanish-American War, military criminal justice procedures during overseas occupations, World War I-era domestic economic regulation, and more.[44] Two exceptions involved a foreshadowing of later Supreme Court decisions' deference to presidential actions[45] and a registering of discomfort with judicial involvement in foreign policy.[46]

Three twentieth-century landmark cases before Vietnam brought the Supreme Court back into controversial questions about executive branch powers related to foreign policy but ultimately left a mixed legacy on whether presidents are beholden to congressional intent and action. In a sense, the outcomes of *United States v. Curtiss-Wright Export Company* (1936), *Korematsu v. United States* (1944), and *Youngstown Sheet & Tube Co. v. Sawyer* (1952, which is discussed in chapter 5) all hinged on congressional authorization of power, or its absence, just as previous court decisions did since 1802. In *Curtiss-Wright*, Congress authorized President Franklin Roosevelt to declare and enforce an arms embargo on two warring countries in South America.[47] In *Korematsu*, the Supreme Court upheld the president's executive order for the internment of Japanese Americans, saying in part that it had been authorized by Congress.[48] In the *Curtiss-Wright* case, Justice George Sutherland's controversial dicta brought the "sole organ" doctrine of presidential foreign policy power into the political and legal lexicon. While Sutherland's opinion on behalf of the Court has been criticized as off the constitutional and historical mark,[49] it stood as precedent until the Supreme Court undermined it in the 2015 case *Zivotofsky v. Kerry* (again, discussed in part 3).[50] The Court also overturned the much-maligned *Korematsu* in a case challenging President Donald Trump's travel ban.[51] Regardless of these recent reconsiderations, the Court's twentieth-century legacy in foreign policy cases echoed the deference that Congress granted repeatedly. All three branches demonstrated consensus of what became known as the "two presidencies" thesis. The idea was that the president exerted far more influence and power in foreign policy while often becoming bogged down in interbranch politics in domestic policy.[52]

First-Ever Member Suits

The Cold War brought a new constitutional dynamic that continues through today, marked by presidential assertiveness, congressional ambivalence, and judicial disengagement. While there were controversies regarding Franklin Roosevelt's actions in Europe before the formal declarations of World War II, the Korean War was the first truly presidential war because Harry Truman executed a United Nations resolution to delegitimize and repel Communist forces in the Korean Peninsula without explicit congressional authorization. As Francis Wormuth and Edwin Firmage note, "Until 1950, no judge, no President, no legislator, no commentator ever suggested that the President had legal authority to initiate war."[53] Truman informed congressional leaders of his decision, rather than requesting a formal authorization or declaration. In a nine-page memo describing the meeting, Congress is hardly mentioned.[54] Some scholars argue the Korean War was a startling break with constitutional tradition;[55] others that the United Nations treaty had the force of domestic law and supplemented broad World War II statutes that were still in effect.[56] There is also some evidence that at least one committee chair rebuffed Truman's inquiries on whether a formal legislative action was necessary.[57] There was no doubt the nuclear age brought a new war powers culture.

The Vietnam War was a much longer and politically fraught military action than the Korean War. U.S. involvement in Vietnam spanned six presidencies (Truman to Ford), with formal authorization in the Gulf of Tonkin Resolution in 1964. Despite the nearly unanimous vote on the resolution (arguably based on false information supplied by President Lyndon B. Johnson about the incident), the war's escalation became highly divisive by the Democratic National Convention in Chicago in 1968 and sustained social protests, political division, and court challenges that continued nonstop for over five years. In contrast to a handful of legal questions about Truman's actions in the Korean War (including conscription, private insurance claims, and the Steel Seizure case),[58] over seventy suits were filed during the Vietnam War by novel types of litigants all alleging that its latter phases were unconstitutional, largely because they were not authorized explicitly by Congress. As mentioned earlier, Vietnam-era litigants included soldiers, their families, citizens, taxpayers, and even a state (Massachusetts). The period also saw the first two lawsuits ever filed by members of Congress, discussed below. In many cases, the named defendants in these suits were executive branch department heads or President Nixon himself.[59]

In the first two member cases, pointed judicial disagreement on standing and merits hinged on how Congress expressed its approval and disapproval of presidential actions. Congress did not go to the extremes of its constitutional authority to reject presidential action—from overruling a veto to impeachment.[60] Did the president disobey a law specifically limiting his military discretion or did he expand the methods and geography of a broad authorization? Much of the litigation over Vietnam hinged on whether there were any limitations to presidential enforcement of the 1964 Gulf of Tonkin Resolution or discretion in the administration's authorized spending. The broad delegation of authority in that resolution was a particularly difficult hurdle for lawsuits to overcome, even after Congress repealed it. Scholars later criticized President Johnson's account of the events, and the abrupt creation and passage of the resolution within days.[61] The resolution was approved with unanimous support in the House of Representatives and just two senators opposed.

> *Resolved by the Senate and House of Representatives of the United States of America in Congress assembled,* That the Congress approves and supports the determination of the President, as Commander in Chief, to take all necessary measures to repel any armed attack against the forces of the United States and to prevent further aggression. . . .
>
> Section 3. This resolution shall expire when the President shall determine that the peace and security of the area is reasonably assured by international conditions created by action of the United Nations or otherwise, except that it may be terminated earlier by concurrent resolution of the Congress.[62]

The resolution gave the president vast constitutional and policy responsibility, from reporting and analyzing the incidents to policy evaluation to signaling

the end of war. The lack of specific geographic boundaries in the Tonkin Gulf resolution (similar to the 2001 Authorization for the Use of Military Force) also gave
Johnson's successor, Nixon, a legal argument for expanding the war into Laos and
Cambodia. At time of the Gulf of Tonkin Resolution, Congress had already indirectly supported over 16,000 troops in Vietnam, including 5,000 added in the week
before the incident. By the end of the decade, 550,000 U.S. soldiers were engaged
in various theaters in Southeast Asia under this authority.

All of these issues came to a head in 1973, a year of legislative battles over the
Cambodia bombings, lawsuits and, in the fall, the passage of the War Powers
Resolution over President Nixon's veto. Vietnam had already dominated electoral and institutional conflict for over 5 years. The legal front proved equally
divisive. Federal courts wrestled with a variety of existing justiciability doctrines,
including standing, mootness, ripeness, and political questions. Some judges
went against the dominant view and said that lawsuits involving members of
Congress raised legitimate jurisdictional and constitutional questions on war
powers.

The short- and long-term legacy of this litigation, however, reflected the majority of judges who said that members of Congress already possessed all the
needed institutional wherewithal to check presidential war powers. The litigants
responded by saying they had spent years and an extraordinary amount of legislative power on the issue—to no avail. Indeed, congressional majorities passed
ten major laws spanning 1969 to 1973, including the 1964 resolution's repeal in
1971.[63]

The constitutional question brought by members of Congress on the issue of
Cambodia was whether the bombing was legal after the repeal, as Congress had
not authorized it via separate legislation. The Nixon administration began to
bomb Cambodia secretly in 1969 because it was being used by Viet Cong forces,
along with Laos, to stage attacks against the South.[64] Although the full extent of
"Operation Menu" was not known for several years, news of the attacks leaked
out of the Nixon administration and Congress passed the first "Fulbright Proviso" in 1970, saying any action in these countries must be limited to assisting
the withdrawal of U.S. troops. The two branches tangled over the contours of the
Cambodia operations for the next three years, with Nixon's arguing that his administration could not be micromanaged by Congress.[65] The first case on Cambodia, *Mitchell v. Laird*, was also the first Congress member suit in U.S. history;
it was filed by thirteen House members in 1971 and dismissed on standing and
political question grounds by a district and appellate court, even as the judges
acknowledged there was no direct authorization.[66]

One of the cases that divided the Supreme Court was *Massachusetts v. Laird*
(1970). The Commonwealth passed a law that denied conscription of the state's

citizens, alleging the war was unconstitutional because the 1964 resolution was an incomplete authorization. The case went directly to the Supreme Court under a petition for original jurisdiction but was determined to be nonjusticiable by a vote of 6–3. Justices William O. Douglas, John Marshall Harlan II, and Potter Stewart dissented from the majority's use of political question and standing doctrines, saying that the Court had a long history of taking war questions. "We are asked instead whether the Executive has power, absent a congressional declaration of war, to commit Massachusetts citizens in armed hostilities on foreign soil. Another way of putting the question is whether under our Constitution presidential wars are permissible? Should that question be answered in the negative we would then have to determine whether Congress has declared war. That question which Massachusetts presents is in my view justiciable."[67]

The issue of member litigation was different. Unlike a state, which could influence only a small minority of the House and Senate through elections every two and six years, judges assumed members of Congress had a variety of direct war controls. Congress also has to have the will, expressed through a majority (and even a supermajority if necessary), to defend its prerogatives. Despite expressions of sympathy regarding plaintiffs' standing to the merits of the case, the Supreme Court again decided to sidestep these opportunities to rule President Nixon's expansion of the Vietnam War unconstitutional. Instead, the burden was on Congress to pass disapprovals and remove funding, as well as overcome inevitable presidential vetoes.

Mitchell v. Laird (1971)

Mitchell v. Laird was filed by Representative Parren Mitchell (D-MD) and twelve other members of the House in 1971 against the president, secretaries of state, defense, and the three branches of the military. The plaintiffs alleged that the United States had been engaged in a war in Indo-China (the term then used for Vietnam, Laos, and Cambodia) for seven years after the 1964 Gulf of Tonkin Resolution without obtaining "either a declaration of war or an explicit, intentional and discrete authorization of war," which had the effect of "unlawfully impair[ing] and defeat[ing] plaintiffs' Constitutional right, as members of the Congress of the United States, to decide whether the United States should fight a war."[68] The first demand of the lawsuit was a judicial order to stop the executive branch from prosecuting the war unless, within sixty days, Congress "explicitly, intentionally and discretely authorized a continuation of the war." The second demand was for "a declaratory judgment that defendants are carrying on a war in violation of Article I, section 8, clause 11 of the United States Constitution."[69] A district court dismissed the case on standing grounds.

The court of appeals for the DC circuit examined several issues, some not raised in the district decision, but still agreed to dismiss the case. In the majority opinion, Judge Charles Wyzanski acknowledged that the panel came to the dismissal through different jurisprudential paths. Standing, mootness, and ripeness were not the main issue; the political question doctrine was the fundamental barrier. The judges cited a variety of other options afforded to plaintiffs, including conventional legislation and even impeachment. "We are unanimously agreed that it is constitutionally permissible for Congress to use another means than a formal declaration of war to give its approval to a war such as is involved in the protracted and substantial hostilities in Indo-China. . . . We deem it a political question, or, to phrase it more accurately, a discretionary matter for Congress to decide in which form, if any, it will give its consent to the continuation of a war already begun by a President acting alone."[70]

At the same time, the judges took the position that there are limits to congressional control of presidential war powers. They agreed unanimously that Congress does not have the constitutional right or institutional wherewithal to authorize every type of defensive or emergency military action. Presidents may respond to belligerent attacks or "in a grave emergency" may take military initiative without prior congressional consent. There was no objectively defensive emergency in Cambodia or Laos. Still, the court concluded that "in such unusual situations necessity confers the requisite authority upon the President. Any other construction of the Constitution would make it self-destructive."[71]

The more difficult issue was whether Congress had consented to the war's expansion in supplementary budgets and other forms of legislation. The appellate court also noted that the 1964 resolution had been repealed by the time the case was filed and yet the defendants argued that other types of legislation allowed the war efforts to continue anyway. On this issue and others, the judges showed some ambivalence: Is a congressional vote for funding an implied vote to authorize the actions being funded? Do laws passed by previous Congresses and signed by previous presidents authorize new expansions of that same conflict? The way the three-judge panel wrestled with this issue is as relevant today as it was a half-century ago. On the points below, they were unanimous: "This court cannot be unmindful of what every schoolboy knows: that in voting to appropriate money or to draft men a Congressman is not necessarily approving of the continuation of a war no matter how specifically the appropriation or draft act refers to that war. A Congressman wholly opposed to the war's commencement and continuation might vote for the military appropriations and for the draft measures because he was unwilling to abandon without support men already fighting." The judges said that Nixon inherited a war and while he pledged to wind it down, the court could not judge his military strategy to do so.[72]

An attorney involved in *Mitchell v. Laird*, as well as other Vietnam-era cases, said in an interview for this book that "the courts are not eager to tell Congress [or, by implication, the president] what it can and cannot do" and so hide behind justiciability doctrines. The attorney said the court's inaction was tragic on many levels, including the Vietnam War's failed policies abroad and divisiveness at home. On war, this attorney said, judicial restraint left a fundamentally conservative (in the literal sense of exceedingly cautious) institutional legacy even by judges otherwise known as policy and ideological liberals. The attorney noted, however, that Judge Wyzanski seemed particularly torn by the dilemma: "Lawyers are the only profession in the world where they drive by light of taillight or rear view mirror. They do what has been done before. There is ideally some wisdom in history. Apropos of that, how is it that these judges could foresee only disaster stemming from a judicial ruling on the legality of the [Vietnam] war? But no such disaster occurred after *Youngstown Sheet and Tube*. . . . How is it that the judgment is going to destroy the country? People are very fearful . . . [especially] judges and members in Congress."[73] This response summarizes the precedents that grew from the Mitchell case and the significance that judges place on evidence of direct congressional challenge to the president.

Holtzman v. Richardson/Schlesinger (1973)

In early January 1973, the Paris Peace Accords ended the active U.S. military involvement in Vietnam and, theoretically, should have extinguished the reasoning for the Cambodia operation. However, the Nixon administration continued to conduct air raids, drawing criticism even from previous supporters of the president.[74] This impasse prompted Elizabeth Holtzman (D-NY) to sue both of Nixon's secretaries of defense in 1973 (James R. Schlesinger replaced Eliot L. Richardson when the latter was appointed attorney general that same year). At the time of the first filing in April, a cease-fire was in effect in Vietnam and all American prisoners of war had been returned. In response to the lawsuit, according to a statement of facts in the first [*Richardson*] case, "the Executive has informed Congress that it is prepared to continue its military activities whether or not the Congress appropriates funds for the Cambodian combat operations."[75] Through May and June, the Nixon administration fought with Congress on whether and how the House and Senate could cut off the Cambodia campaign through language in a supplemental appropriations bill. Nixon vetoed the first attempt and, as Congress fell short on the override, they settled on a cutoff date of August 15.[76]

While these legislative battles continued, district judge Orrin Judd heard the case and confirmed that Representative Holtzman "has raised a serious constitutional question dealing with the war-making power of Congress enumerated in

Article I, § 8 of the Constitution. The seriousness of this question has been recognized repeatedly within this circuit. . . . The delicate balance in the relationship
between Congress and the President concerning the power to wage war is a controversy arising under the Constitution and therefore within the jurisdiction of
this court."[77] Judge Judd also cited two prior cases where members of a state legislature were found to have standing, and concluded that "[these] cases, involving state legislatures, are not completely parallel, but a member of Congress should
have an equal right to invoke the jurisdiction of a federal court."[78] He acknowledged the difficulty of members proving an institutional injury but agreed with
standing, saying that as a member of Congress Holtzman was called upon to appropriate funds, raise an army, declare war, and "insure the checks and balances
of our democracy through the use of impeachment." Therefore, he said, she met
the standing test.[79]

Judge Judd ruled in Holtzman's favor, first on jurisdiction/justiciability and
then a month later on the merits in his opinion and order, breaking from the recent *Mitchell* precedent. On the political question doctrine, Judd cited a variety
of cases to show that courts have made and can make determinations about when
states of war and peace exist.[80] In July, after the case's defendant had been switched
to *Schlesinger*, Judd ruled again for Holtzman, providing both declaratory and
injunctive relief. The judgment declared that "there is no existing Congressional
authority to order military forces into combat in Cambodia or to release bombs
over Cambodia, and that military activities in Cambodia by American armed
forces are unauthorized and unlawful" and restrained defendants and their staff
from "participating in any way in military activities."[81] The orders were stayed
until July 27 by a unanimous panel of the U.S. Court of Appeals for the Second
Circuit, allowing both sides to petition with additional documentation.

Meanwhile, on July 1, 1973, Nixon signed the second attempt at a supplemental appropriations after vetoing the first a week before, saying that he could not
abide by the rider that called for an immediate halt to the bombing.[82] The second version denied appropriations for any Cambodian combat activities after
August 15, 1973. This new posture, in combination with previous legislative activities indicating congressional opposition to the new phase of the war, was
cited by Judge Judd in his final memorandum and decision. He consulted and
interpreted over three years of legislation, appropriations, and even cited collo-
quy at length from the *Congressional Record*. Judd concluded that majorities of
the House and Senate were on the record as opposed to the continuing bombing of Cambodia but included the August 15 cutoff date to avoid a veto and a
government shutdown over the budget impasse. "Legislative history as evidenced
through bills that were vetoed is relevant to a judicial inquiry. . . . It cannot be
the rule that the President needs a vote of only one-third plus one of either House

in order to conduct a war, but this would be the consequence of holding that Congress must override a Presidential veto in order to terminate hostilities which it has not authorized."[83]

Between the district and appeals court rulings, the Supreme Court became involved through applications to vacate the stay issued by Judge Judd. In the first round, Justice Thurgood Marshall (in his circuit judge capacity) denied the plaintiff's application. Although he strongly hinted at policy agreement with Holtzman, Marshall favored judicial restraint, concluding, "When the final history of the Cambodian war is written, it is unlikely to make pleasant reading. The decision to send American troops [to Southeast Asia] . . . may ultimately be adjudged to have been not only unwise, but also unlawful." Yet he demurred on justiciability, saying that the Supreme Court's overreaching would compound the problems created by President Nixon's actions: "The proper response to an arguably illegal action is not lawlessness by judges charged with interpreting and enforcing the laws. Down that road lies tyranny and repression. We have a government of limited powers, and those limits pertain to the Justices of this Court as well as to Congress and the Executive. Our Constitution assures that the law will ultimately prevail, but it also requires that the law be applied in accordance with lawful procedures."[84]

Justice Douglas filed a dissent on the procedural issue regarding vacating, but disagreed with Marshall's premise that the court had no place in weighing in on the constitutional question. Douglas veered in a different direction by seeing victims of U.S. military actions as suffering capital punishment without due process. Although he agreed with Marshall that "if the foreign policy goals of this Government are to be weighed, the Judiciary is probably the least qualified branch," he still concluded that courts could take such cases as "the basic question on the merits is whether Congress, within the meaning of Art. I, § 8, cl. 11, has 'declared war' in Cambodia." He challenged the idea that Congress authorized bombings before August 15.[85]

The appeals court heard the case a few days later. Judge Judd's district court opinion was overturned 2–1. The circuit judges ruling against Holtzman were William H. Mulligan and William H. Timbers, with James L. Oakes dissenting (interestingly, all three were Nixon appointees). Judge Mulligan ruled that the complaint was a political question, relying on other Vietnam and Cambodia decisions as precedent. He cited at length Judge Wyzanski's opinion in *Mitchell v. Laird*, as well as nonmember precedents[86] that ruled the continuation of military action in Vietnam despite the repeal of the Gulf of Tonkin Resolution was a debate for the other branches because the court was not competent to access or assess the strategic mission and military assessments behind the administration's decisions.[87] "While we as men may well agonize and bewail the horror of this or any war, the sharing of Presidential and Congressional responsibility particularly at this juncture is a bluntly political and not a judicial question."[88]

The ruling also took specific issue with Judge Judd's characterization of congressional debates and operating law. Judge Mulligan cited appropriations language that cut off funding for Cambodia operations in mid-August, which, in his view, legitimized all action up to then. He also quoted floor debate between Senators William J. Fulbright and Thomas Eagleton that Judd "inadvertently omitted," which implied the senators did not think their amendments could really prevent further bombing. Mulligan concluded that "even if the legislative history were considered it is at best ambiguous and does not clearly support the theory that the Congress did not mean what it said."[89]

Judge Oakes's dissent supported Holtzman's standing as a legitimate plaintiff and Judge Judd's characterization of the congressional position. He acknowledged that authorization and appropriation legislation could be sufficient to show legislative support for the Cambodian operations, but he concluded neither was in effect because Congress (and the public) lacked knowledge of the bombings. He also used precedent quite differently than Mulligan, saying *Da Costa*, *Orlando*, and other Vietnam-era cases actually did reserve judicial consideration if there was a "radical change in the character of war operations." Oakes's position against unlimited executive power is unusually strong and rare in recent decades on war powers litigation. He said the United States was bombing Cambodia despite a cease-fire in Vietnam and the return of prisoners of war. The justiciable question was authorization in light of these events without a "belligerent attack" or "grave emergency" that would make Cambodia a defensive context similar to what was envisioned by the framers of the Constitution for unilateral presidential action. He found no authorization in law or appropriations: "That the Executive Branch had the power to bomb. . . . Whether it had the constitutional authority . . . is another question. . . . I fail to see, and the Government in its able presentation has failed to point out, where the Congress ever authorized the continuation of bombing in Cambodia after the cease-fire in Vietnam, the withdrawal of our forces there, and the return of our prisoners of war to our shores. Accordingly, I must dissent."[90] The Cambodia portion of the Vietnam War ended on August 15, 1973, as negotiated by Congress and President Nixon.

The WPR's passage in November 1973 did not help the cause of member-plaintiffs. In eight such cases afterward, spanning President Reagan (regarding El Salvador, Nicaragua, Grenada, and Kuwaiti tanker flagging), George H. W. Bush (Operation Desert Shield), Clinton (Kosovo), George W. Bush (Iraq), and Obama (Libya), the majority of federal judges did not focus, as Judges Judd and Oakes had, on looking for prior legislative approval but rather for *disapproval* (Desert Shield and Kosovo inspired the deepest disagreement on the issues).

The political question and equitable discretion doctrines were crucial to this new justiciability wall as they stem from judicial discomfort with the substance of the case, not the timing or type of plaintiff. The litigants argued unsuccessfully that the courts could indeed determine constitutionality if they focus on presidential action, not congressional supermajorities' failure to confront. As we will see in chapter 2, these cases highlighted legislative dysfunctions on when, whether, and how to disapprove of presidential unilateralism on war. These lawsuits not only failed, but backfired against members as the justiciability doctrines used by federal courts put the burden on Congress to disapprove rather than the president to wait for prior authorization. The cases also risked the possibility that a federal court would rule definitively in favor of presidential power and against the constitutionality of the War Powers Resolution altogether.

All three branches were engaged in war powers questions—until around 1950. Starting with President Truman's unilateral actions in Korea, Congress began to shrink from the scene for a variety of reasons. As a result, the federal courts also began to shrink. Even as federal judges expressed consensus on the fact that Congress never explicitly authorized the Cambodia bombings, they were divided on what congressional actions counted as support or disapproval. Members of Congress went to extraordinary lengths to express their views. The bloodshed in Cambodia and destabilization of the country for the next generation under the Khmer Rouge should be placed on the Nixon administration, not on the court's narrow shoulders.

In the five decades since this time, under a variety of partisan and policy landscapes, war has continued to be a presidential question, with Congress lightly shaping policy on the sidelines before and after. The stubborn narrative that presidents get to make all decisions concerning who, what, where, when, and why to strike because they are "Commander-in-Chief" persists across all possible partisan distributions in Congress and the White House. Presidents say over and over that they alone have the power to see and act upon the "national interest" and only go to Congress because they are choosing to do so to show the nation and the world that the legislative branch is in support—not because they must do so.

While the Supreme Court has taken up a variety of due process issues raised by detained alleged terrorists since 9/11 (discussed in part 3),[91] there has been no judicial assessment of presidential power to launch offensive operations abroad without explicit congressional consent in modern times. Across the Bush, Obama, and Trump presidencies, members and leaders have criticized the White House (especially from the other party), but the criticism fell far short of regaining control of war policy. U.S. political culture on war reflects the absence of deep policy and/or constitutional dialogues. News accounts now describe congressional war authorization as a "tricky" proposition in an election year, not a constitutional requirement.[92] Small groups of institutionally protective members of Congress are reduced to pleading for inclusion in the decision, even petitioning the Speaker of the House to give floor time to the issue.[93] It is true that partisan strategy often drives both branches' actions, but the "inherent powers of the commander-in-chief" narrative is now a permanent part of our legal and political assumptions. The judiciary cannot undo this constitutional interpretation perpetuated by the other branches alone. The next chapter will trace the eight additional war powers cases that tried to force presidential adherence to the WPR's procedural requirements. Despite its intention, the WPR itself became a symbol of war powers dysfunction because it tried to graft a new process on Congress and the president, without the institutional acceptance of the terms on either side. Presidents did not wait for congressional authorization before initiating war, and Congress did not seriously attempt to force him to wait for it.

SUING TO SAVE THE WAR POWERS RESOLUTION

Ethnic Albanians living in the Serbian province of Kosovo declared independence in 1998. On March 24, 1999, NATO began an air campaign against Serbian targets to support the movement. President Bill Clinton announced the United States' engagement in a national address.[1] On April 7, the president updated congressional leaders, saying, "It is not possible to predict how long [the] operations will continue."[2] The House of Representatives and the Senate quickly debated a variety of bills and resolutions to support or oppose the president; nothing passed both chambers. Five weeks after the bombing campaign began, the House voted on four resolutions on the same day to either authorize or withdrew forces, again yielding no clear direction. In mid-May, seventeen members of the House, mostly Republicans, filed suit in federal court seeking declaratory judgment that President Clinton violated the War Powers Resolution (WPR) of 1973 and the Constitution—and demanded all forces be withdrawn by May 25 unless Congress authorized continuation. The number of House litigants increased to thirty-one members by the time of appeal. A split appeals court concluded Congress's inability to disapprove the bombing was tacit consent for it. Meanwhile, in May alone, 800 U.S. airplanes flew 20,772 air sorties, hitting almost 2,000 Serbian targets.[3]

From the founding of the United States to 1950, war usually proceeded in constitutional order: congressional authorization followed by executive enforcement. Over that century and a half, federal judges adjudicated dozens of war-related disputes raised by private litigants that hinged on executive branch adherence to Congress's prior legislative direction. Today, presidents of both parties order new offensive military actions abroad without explicit congressional consent before or even during the conflict. Although House and Senate majorities eventually support these actions one way or another (including statements in support of soldiers and monetary appropriations), on ten occasions members of Congress (up to 110 at a time) have challenged presidential wars in federal court. Eight suits came after the WPR passed Congress over President Richard Nixon's veto. While unsuccessful, these legal fights reflect a quiet but steady three-branch constitutional revolution on war under both parties' watch and under a variety of foreign policy contexts. If congressional division counts as authorization, fundamental war processes are flipped and the WPR is a dead letter.

These eight post-WPR lawsuits, brought almost exclusively by partisan opponents of the presidents spanning Ronald Reagan to Barack Obama, are symptoms of long-simmering constitutional dysfunction on war and, in various ways, have backfired. From the Cold War through today's "war on terror," presidents say they see, speak, and act for the "national interest." Members of Congress are relegated to voicing support for the troops and funding the cause, lest they be accused of undermining morale and a unified strategy. Members do engage in fierce debate and oversight, but they do not actually control events. Despite all the differences between Democratic and Republican presidents over the past fifty years, and all manner of party arrangements in Congress, these institutional rhythms are consistent. Judges alone cannot force troops from the field, nor pressure presidents to heed Congress and wait for explicit, prior authorization before each new military campaign. Members ask courts to resolve legally the most difficult kind of political work that they must relearn to do for themselves. In addition, members' fluctuations in institutional ambition, largely dependent upon which party is in the White House, does not bode well for long-term constitutional balance on war.

Member Litigation after the War Powers Resolution

At the same time as the *Mitchell* and *Holtzman* cases went through the federal system (discussed in chapter 1), Congress debated and passed the WPR. Its explicit intention was to force interbranch collaboration before and during new military operations abroad. Yet almost every president since its passage has explicitly denied, or implicitly tested, the WPR's constitutionality, beginning with President Nixon's veto.[4] Presidents have since reported around 170 actions as "consistent" with the WPR requirement.[5] Eight lawsuits filed by members of Congress accused presidents of not complying with the WPR and other legal and constitutional requirements for offensive actions, including Reagan (interventions in El Salvador, Nicaragua, Grenada, and the Iran-Iraq War), George H. W. Bush (the Persian Gulf War), Clinton (Kosovo), George W. Bush (Iraq), and Obama (Libya).

While its purpose is clear in its preamble, rebalancing congressional-presidential power over war decisions, the WPR included loopholes and internal contradictions that did little to help restrain presidents or embolden Congresses.[6] Section 2(c) appears to provide clear, limited parameters for new military action, saying the president, as commander-in-chief, can introduce U.S. armed forces into situations of hostilities or imminent hostilities "only pursuant to (1) a declaration of war, (2) specific statutory authorization, or (3) a national emergency created by attack upon the United States, its territories or possessions, or its armed forces."[7] But these presidential restrictions are undermined by sections 3 and 4. In section 3, presidents are required to consult with Congress "in every possible instance" before introducing U.S. forces (of any military branch) into "hostilities or . . . situations where imminent involvement in hostilities is clearly indicated by the circumstances." In section 4 (a)(1), regardless of the extent of consultation, the president must report to Congress within forty-eight hours of the start of a military action if a declaration of war or other legislative authorization had not been passed by both chambers. In section 5(b), if Congress did not vote to approve the action, before or after forces were committed, they must be withdrawn by the president within sixty days, which could be extended to ninety days for special military circumstances. Although section 5(c) also gave Congress power to remove forces by concurrent resolution at any time, this action is now subject to presidential veto. Sections 6 and 7 lay out the expedited legislative procedures to prioritize congressional authorization related to the reported conflict or a withdrawal resolution. Section 8 says that authorization for military force cannot be construed from appropriations bills or treaties, unless accompanied by a separate authorization. Hinting at future litigation, a "separability" clause in section 9 says if any part "is held invalid" then the rest still stands.[8]

Against Presidents Reagan and Bush I

All post-WPR litigation has built on the *Mitchell* and *Holtzman* precedents. First, the cases are dismissed on a variety of justiciability grounds; judges did not rule directly on the legitimacy and application of the WPR. Second, unlike private litigation prior to Vietnam, most judges do not trace presidential action to prior congressional authorization, nor compel reporting under the WPR, but rather reverse the burden to inquire whether there is supermajority disapproval of action in progress. Third, while there is ample evidence of partisanship in the lineup of member-plaintiffs against opposition party presidents, there is no ideological distinction in the constitutional claims made by Democrats and Republicans in either branch. Congress members of both parties assert the same constitutional points, as do presidents of both parties. Judges appointed by presidents of both parties are largely dismissive of the cases.

Crockett v. Reagan (1982)

During a brewing civil war that was destabilizing El Salvador, President Jimmy Carter tried to shore up support for its military government through various forms of assistance beginning in 1979. Although called "nonlethal" aid, the United States sent equipment such as "tear gas grenades, grenade launchers, night vision instruments, image intensifiers, and other riot control and counterinsurgency equipment."[9] An attack on American nuns by a death squad linked to the rightist faction of the junta in December 1980 led Carter to suspend some of the aid pending an investigation. Then, in February and March 1981, newly elected President Ronald Reagan sent thirty-five military advisers to assist the Salvadoran government, in addition to maintaining the nineteen dispatched by President Carter. President Reagan's interest in expanding U.S. influence in El Salvador reflected a hemispheric Cold War strategy. The new secretary of state, Alexander Haig, argued that U.S. interests required supporting the right-wing junta to head off a new Latin America "domino" effect of communist influence emanating from Cuba.[10]

While the legislative-executive wrangling went on for three more years over El Salvador, Crockett v. Reagan was filed early on by opponents in Congress. The lawsuit was the first one to allege violations of the WPR when it was filed in 1981 by twenty-nine House members (all Democrats) who protested the lack of a formal WPR report, among other claims. In a one-of-a-kind response by the president's supporters in Congress, the lawsuit prompted the same number of Republicans (13 senators and 16 House members) and one southern conservative Democrat to file an amicus curiae brief against their colleagues, claiming the original group was going to court too hastily. The allegations by Representative George W. Crockett (D-MI) and colleagues against the administration included violations of the Constitution, the WPR, and a legislative ban on foreign aid and military assistance to any regime alleged to have engaged in extensive human rights abuses. The defendants (President Reagan, Secretary of Defense Caspar Weinberger, and Secretary of State Alexander Haig) argued that the plaintiffs lacked standing, and assistance had been authorized by an act of Congress in 1981.

While not conceding the constitutionality of the WPR, the administration said there were no "hostilities."

Federal district judge Joyce Hens Green dismissed the case, saying federal courts were not institutionally equipped or situated to define the nature of the El Salvador operation. In an interview for this book, a House coplaintiff who had also voted in favor of the WPR in 1973 vehemently disagreed with Judge Green's claim that fact-finding on war was not possible for a judge. The member had visited El Salvador during the early 1980s and said, "It looked like a war to us. " The member added that judges routinely engage in other types of fact-finding.[11] Green dismissed the lawsuit on political question grounds.

First, citing *Baker v. Carr, Mitchell v. Laird,* and *Holtzman v. Schlesinger,* Judge Green said the courts could not assess the facts of the case on which the two sides disagreed: were there "hostilities" in El Salvador or not? Second, she cited *Goldwater v. Carter* (discussed in chapter 6) in her argument that a "constitutional impasse appropriate for judicial resolution would be presented" only if the president ignored a resolution requiring a report per WPR section 5 (b) or withdrawal of the advisers. Green added that "the nature of the fact finding in these circumstances precludes judicial inquiry" but allowed that the WPR was still open for future justiciability.[12] An appeals court affirmed, saying members lack standing without a clear "nullification or diminution of a congressman's vote" shown by bill passage.[13] Defendants prevailed with another pro-presidential precedent.

Sanchez-Espinoza v. Reagan (1983)

In 1979, the Sandinistas, a left-wing guerrilla group, overthrew the Somoza family dictatorship that had ruled Nicaragua since the 1930s. In President Reagan's first term, he issued national security findings and directives to create the "Contras," a counterrevolutionary force. After Congress appropriated money to support the Contras in 1981, the first "Boland Amendment" passed in 1982 (named for Representative Edward P. Boland, D-MA), banning the executive branch from spending any money "for the purpose of overthrowing the government of Nicaragua."[14] Leaked classified memos proved the Reagan administration was not adhering to Boland. In 1983, the House voted to cut off all Contra aid, but a Senate-based compromise allowed $24 million, a fraction of the administration's request. Ultimately, two more restrictive amendments passed the House and Senate in Reagan's first term.

Sanchez-Espinoza v. Reagan was filed in 1983 and focused on adherence to the first Boland Amendment. Twelve members of the House of Representatives (all Democrats) joined over a dozen private citizens of Nicaragua (who alleged damages due to actions of the U.S.-supported Contra rebels) and Florida (who alleged damages due to paramilitary training operations). The suit was filed to protest U.S. paramilitary operations that the plaintiffs alleged violated various neutrality laws, the National Security Act of 1947, the Boland Amendment, WPR, and the Constitution.[15] The plaintiffs said that the judiciary is needed to control executive abuses of power in this case "because Congress has done all it can, namely, pass legislation." District court judge Howard Corcoran dismissed the case as a political question, saying: "A court must take special care, when confronted with a challenge to the validity of U.S. foreign policy initiatives, to give appropriate deference to the decisions of the political branches, who are constitutionally empowered to conduct foreign relations."[16] Judge Corcoran cited *Baker v. Carr*, the Vietnam-era cases, as well as the recent *Crockett* precedent. He also echoed Judge Green, saying the case required fact-finding that is beyond the court's competence: "Were this Court to decide . . . that President Reagan either is mistaken, or is shielding the truth, one or both of the coordinate branches would be justifiably offended . . . and there is a real danger of embarrassment from multifarious pronouncements by various departments on one question. . . . Such an occurrence would, undoubtedly, rattle the delicate diplomatic balance that is required in the foreign affairs arena. . . . It is, therefore, prudent for us to decline to adjudicate plaintiffs' claims at this time."[17]

The appeals court affirmed Judge Corcoran's decision unanimously. Future Supreme Court justice Antonin Scalia delivered the opinion, citing mootness since the appropriations rider at issue in this lawsuit (Boland I) expired in 1983. "Dismissal of this claim is required by our decision in *Crockett v. Reagan*, which upheld dismissal of a similar claim by twenty-nine members of Congress relating to alleged military activity in El Salvador on the ground that the war powers issue presented a nonjusticiable political question."[18] Another future Supreme Court justice, Ruth Bader Ginsburg, filed a concurrence on ripeness grounds, blaming Congress for ambiguities on U.S. support for the Contras. Ginsburg also cited *Goldwater v. Carter*, saying Congress had not thrown down the "gauntlet" by using its own tools, which are more powerful than the federal court's.[19]

Conyers v. Reagan (1984)

October 1983 was an active month for U.S. military engagement. On October 12, President Reagan signed a congressional resolution that spelled out an eighteen-month continuation of U.S. troop presence in Lebanon, ending an interbranch dispute about Congress's role in the deployment. Upon signing, Reagan said it "was not to be used as any acknowledgement that the President's constitutional authority can be impermissibly infringed by statute."[20] The next day, Maurice Bishop, the left-leaning prime minister of Grenada who had seized power in 1979, was arrested by members of his own militia. Bishop was temporarily freed by supporters on October 18 but was assassinated later that day. He was replaced by what Reagan described as a more staunchly pro-Cuban junta. Reagan decided to invade Grenada on October 24 and then announced it the next day, citing the presence of around 1,000 U.S. medical students on the island.

Reagan sent a written report of the invasion to the Speaker of the House, Thomas P. O'Neill (D-MA), and the president pro tempore of the Senate, Strom Thurmond (R-SC), on October 25. The president said the letter was "consistent with" the WPR. He did not mention that troops were going into "hostilities," which would trigger the WPR clock. The House and Senate moved swiftly to approve resolutions to hold the Grenada operations to a sixty-day timetable.[21] Around the same time, Representative John Conyers (D-MI) was the lead plaintiff in a lawsuit filed against the president that challenged his authority to invade Grenada in the first place without congressional authorization. Ten other House Democrats signed onto the suit, most of whom had joined in previous suits, including Parren Mitchell (D-MD).

District judge Green dismissed the suit, citing the member war suit precedents (two before and two after the WPR), including her own *Crockett* decision. She also utilized the novel equitable discretion doctrine theory that said courts should be leery of accepting cases from plaintiffs (especially members of Congress) who have other methods of resolving their disputes. "If plaintiffs are successful in persuading their colleagues about the wrongfulness of the President's actions, they will be provided the remedy they presently seek from this Court. If plaintiffs are unsuccessful in their efforts, it would be unwise for this Court to scrutinize that determination and interfere with the operations of the Congress. . . . The Court must withhold jurisdiction of this matter and exercise judicial restraint."[22]

By the time the case reached the appeals court in 1985, the final noncombat troops were slated to leave Grenada. The appeal was dismissed for mootness unanimously by the three judges, Edward A. Tamm, Patricia M. Wald, and Robert H. Bork. The issue of whether the WPR clock was triggered by "hostilities" was not resolved. In the mission, 18 U.S. soldiers were killed and 116 were wounded; 24 Cuban soldiers were killed and 59 wounded; and Grenadian casualties included 45 killed and 337 wounded.[23] The final suit against President Reagan pivoted away from Central America to the Persian Gulf.

Lowry v. Reagan (1987)

Beginning in 1986 during the Iran-Iraq War, Iranian military vessels around the Persian Gulf threatened Kuwaiti oil tankers. Kuwait reached out to both the Soviet Union and the United States for protection. Upon hearing that Kuwaitis requested the United States to reflag six vessels and the Soviet Union five, the Reagan administration offered to reflag all eleven tankers.[24] In 1987, thirty-seven U.S. sailors were killed by a missile attack on the USS *Stark* in the Gulf by Iraq. In response, the administration augmented a single air craft carrier with eleven warships, six minesweepers, and over a dozen small patrol boats. Secretary of State George P. Shultz submitted a letter on the buildup to speaker of the House Jim Wright (D-TX), but did not mention the WPR or its clock. The administration did not file formal reports after two U.S. ships struck mines in summer 1987, nor when a U.S. fighter plane shot missiles at an Iranian aircraft the U.S. crew perceived as threatening.[25] During this time, military personnel were also receiving "danger pay," reflecting potential "hostilities."[26]

Alleging the presence of "hostilities" and "imminent hostilities," 110 Democratic House plaintiffs filed a federal suit to demand a formal WPR report. In the district court's dismissal of the case, *Lowry v. Reagan*, Judge George H. Revercomb said a "profusion of relevant congressional activity" in response to the president's actions in the Persian Gulf was evidence that this was a matter for the two branches to work out among themselves. The litigants had in fact worried that legislative activity would shift the judicial spotlight from Reagan's actions to Congress.[27] Judge Revercomb cited the equitable discretion and political question doctrines in this particular case: "This Court declines to . . . impose a consensus on Congress. Congress is free to adopt a variety of positions on the War Powers Resolution, depending on its ability to achieve a political consensus. If the Court were to intervene in this political process, it would be acting 'beyond the limits inherent in the constitutional scheme . . .' Judicial review of the constitutionality of the War Powers Resolution is not, however, precluded by this decision. A true confrontation between the Executive and a unified Congress, as evidenced by its passage of legislation to enforce the Resolution, would pose a question ripe for judicial review."[28] On an expedited appeal, the panel affirmed as a political question.[29] Yet, in an encouraging turn for member-litigants, this standard was rejected two years later. However, the implicit threat by Judge Revercomb arises again— bringing lawsuits on presidential compliance with the war powers also provides opportunities for judges to rule with presidents that the WPR itself is an unconstitutional constraint on his powers.

Dellums v. Bush (1990)

On August 2, 1990, Iraq invaded Kuwait. Within a week, the United Nations (UN) imposed economic sanctions against Iraq and, on August 25, the UN Security Council authorized "such measures as may be necessary" to cease and regulate cargo shipping to Iraq. On August 8, President George H. W. Bush announced the deployment of U.S. forces to Saudi Arabia in a live televised speech, saying he "shared [meaning communicated] the decision" with Congress. On August 17, 1990, Acting Secretary of State Robert M. Kimmitt sent a letter to Congress (not mentioning the WPR) saying, "It is not our intention or expectation that the use of force will be required to carry out these operations. However, if other means of enforcement fail, necessary and proportionate force will be employed to deny passage to ships that are in violation of . . . sanctions."[30] On November 8, 150,000 additional troops were sent to the Gulf. Bush sent a second report to Congress over a week later describing the continuing and increasing deployment of forces to the region, but said hostilities were not imminent, in part due to the massive buildup. In this phase, called Operation Desert Shield, around 350,000 U.S. troops were eventually deployed.[31]

In response, Representative Ronald Dellums (D-CA) led fifty-three members of the House and one senator (all Democrats) to file an injunctive suit against the president to prevent his going to war against Iraq without explicit congressional consent. *Dellums v. Bush* was rejected for ripeness by district judge Harold Greene. Judge Greene said it is up to the other branches to parse the diplomatic and military meaning of "war," but at a certain scale, the label clearly applies. He explored the history of member litigation on war and concluded that political question, standing, and equitable discretion precedents *did not* apply here. The hurdle for the members was simply ripeness. Rejecting the administration's argument, Greene implied that there was a door to future litigation if a president's claim of unilateral authority is clearly out of line with the Constitution: "If the Executive had the sole power to determine that any particular offensive military operation, no matter how vast, does not constitute war-making but only an offensive military attack, the congressional power to declare war will be at the mercy of a semantic decision by the Executive. Such an 'interpretation' would evade the plain language of the Constitution, and it cannot stand . . . here the forces involved are of such magnitude and significance as to present no serious claim that a war would not ensue if they became engaged in combat, and it is therefore clear that congressional approval is required if Congress desires to become involved."[32] The ripeness challenge came from the fact that U.S. troops had not yet engaged Iraq. The judge noted that only around 10 percent of Congress's membership signed onto the suit, implying that a majority-sanctioned suit might have a better chance at being heard on the merits.[33]

Within a month of the federal opinion, on January 8, 1991, President Bush sent a request to the congressional leadership to pass legislation that supported military enforcement of UN Resolution 678, which called for member nations to use force to expel Iraq from Kuwait if it did not withdraw by January 15, 1991. The Authorization for the Use of Military Force (AUMF) passed with party-line votes in the House (250–183) and Senate (52–47) and said explicitly that the legislation was complying with section 2 of the WPR. Bush's signing statement on January 14 said none of the debates, nor even the resolution, was interpreted as threatening to his "constitutional authority to use the Armed Forces to defend vital U.S. interests or [acknowledging] the constitutionality of the War Powers Resolution."[34] Days later, Bush reported the beginning of combat operations "consistent with" the WPR.[35]

Member Litigation after *Raines v. Byrd*

The landmark case on Congress members' standing in court came in 1997 (discussed in more depth in part 2). Senator Robert C. Byrd (D-WV) sued to prevent the Line Item Veto Act of 1996 from taking effect. Although the district court sided with Byrd on both justiciability and substance, the Supreme Court reversed on the former, saying members cannot claim an institutional injury stemming from a loss of political power (the Court declined to rule on the merits of the suit). The majority opinion, like the war powers precedents, emphasized that Congress has legislative options to recover power. However, the Court found the act unconstitutional the following year on presentment grounds once private interests claimed injury. The *Raines* case also proves that private interest litigation can succeed where members cannot.

Campbell v. Clinton (1999)

The Republican Congress did not consistently protect its institutional prerogatives through the presidency of Bill Clinton. It granted President Clinton item veto power but did not explicitly authorize (nor disapprove of) military action in Somalia, Iraq, Bosnia, and Haiti in his first term.[36] In Clinton's second term, however, his military orders related to Kosovo inspired a congressional lawsuit in the final year of the administration. As noted above, in 1998–1999 a move for independence by ethnic Albanians in the Serbian province of Kosovo brought a new wave of conflict and, in 1999, a joint U.S./NATO military response. The story of U.S. action in Kosovo is similar to previous cases discussed here, despite a partisan switch in both branches.

Judge Greene implied in *Dellums* that member-plaintiffs would have standing if they voted against a specific engagement abroad that proceeded anyway. That theory was tested in the spring of 1999. On March 24, the NATO air campaign began against targets in Serbia. Clinton announced the action in a national address and submitted a report two days later to Congress, saying it was "pursuant to my constitutional authority to conduct U.S. foreign relations and as Commander in Chief and Chief Executive" and the report was "consistent with the War Powers Resolution." Secretary of Defense William Cohen told the Senate Armed Services Committee: "We're certainly engaged in hostilities, we're engaged in combat."[37] During the fifth week of strikes, on April 28, 1999, the House voted on multiple resolutions the same day that ultimately neither declared war, authorized the campaign, nor withdrew forces. The Senate, however, did pass an AUMF. Then, on May 21, 1999, the president signed an emergency supplemental that funded the operation.[38]

Representative Tom Campbell (R-CA) and over twenty fellow members, almost all Republicans, filed a complaint on May 19, seeking declaratory judgment that President Clinton had violated the WPR and the Constitution. The suit also demanded that "no later than May 25, 1999, the President must terminate the involvement of the United States Armed Forces in such hostilities unless Congress declares war, or enacts other explicit authorization, or has extended the sixty day period."[39] The suit was dismissed by district court judge Paul Friedman who reviewed the congressional actions and concluded that the "plaintiffs have failed to establish a sufficiently genuine impasse between the legislative and executive branches to give them standing. The most that can be said is that Congress is divided about its position on the President's actions in the Federal Republic of Yugoslavia and that [Clinton] has continued . . . in the face of that divide."[40]

The appeals court upheld the district court but was divided on reasoning. The panel offered four opinions among the three judges (an opinion for the court and three concurrences). The panel's opinion was written by Judge Laurence Silberman who said the congressional votes were not sufficiently "nullified" by the president's actions for an injury. The three judges then went in different directions. In his separate concurrence, Judge Silberman said the appellants' claim of "hostilities" in Yugoslavia does not lend itself to resolution, even if it appears to be true: "Appellants cannot point to any constitutional test for what is war." Judge Raymond Randolph emphasized the principles of standing and mootness. He looked at the totality of the House votes on April 28, saying they were "not for naught" because Clinton had not introduced ground troops, which he might have done if the full war declaration had passed. Judge David S. Tatel offered the most sympathetic reading of the member-plaintiffs complaint. Although he agreed with the majority that the standing problems were too severe, overall he said war is justiciable: "Since the earliest years of the nation, courts have not hesitated to determine when military action constitutes 'war.'"[41]

In separate interviews for this book, a Republican House member and staffer for a different Republican member involved in *Campbell* expressed frustration about both parties' inconsistencies on war powers. They said the lawsuit was designed to bring public attention to Congress's "lack of will" to confront President Clinton on war. "Republicans pride themselves as constitutionalists. Democrats pride themselves as learning lessons from Vietnam." Yet "war brings . . . institutional disinterest."[42] As we saw at the opening of this chapter, President Clinton continued the line of argument that all presidents share: he has the institutional capacity *and* the constitutional authority to commit U.S. troops to war unilaterally. This time, mostly Republicans tut-tutted.

Doe v. Bush (2003)

Despite campaigning against Bill Clinton's "nation building," and promising a "humble foreign policy" in 2000,[43] President George W. Bush's presidency was built on post-9/11 foreign interventions. However, the Iraq War suit is unlike the previous ones because the Congress debated and passed a resolution authorizing President Bush to decide when or if to invade. A dozen Democratic House members focused on the latter in a lawsuit saying that it is unconstitutional for Congress to delegate away the war powers that are enumerated in Article I. Because the nub of their argument focused on a passed and signed resolution and President Bush waited until the AUMF was in place to invade, this case had less promise for the plaintiffs than the others discussed here.[44] This case had the weakest argument going into federal court; the AUMF question received a vote, albeit in a charged 9/11 atmosphere a month before the 2002 midterm. Bush never conceded that he needed an AUMF, but asked for a display of unity.

Just weeks before the invasion began, the House members, joined by twenty private plaintiffs (active military and their families) tried to prevent the AUMF's execution. They made two somewhat contradictory constitutional claims: Congress delegated too much war power and what they granted to President Bush was not a green light for invasion. Judge Joseph Tauro agreed with the defendants and dismissed the case as a political question, saying there was no clear conflict between the political branches. Tauro said, "There is a day to day fluidity in the situation that does not amount to resolute conflict between the branches—but that does argue against an uninformed judicial intervention."[45] Circuit judges Sandra Lynch, Conrad Cyr, and Norman Stahl dismissed the case on ripeness rather than the "murky" political questions.[46] The previous year, however, the Bush administration got a separate member suit dismissed on political question precedent regarding treaty abrogation (discussed in part 3).[47]

Kucinich v. Obama (2011)

Like President Bush's flip from candidate to president, President Obama's war powers interpretations changed dramatically from 2007 to 2011.[48] During the "Arab Spring" revolts in 2010–2011, street protests in Benghazi, Libya, began to turn toward regime change and the ouster of longtime dictator Colonel Muammar Qadhafi. The UN Security Council passed two resolutions that together condemned violence against civilians, encouraged member nations to place asset freezes and travel bans on the Libyan leadership, endorsed the travel bans already being put into place by the Arab League and other regional organizations, introduced a no-fly zone, and authorized member states through regional organizations to use "all necessary measures" to protect civilians. Operation Odyssey Dawn was a multinational coalition led by the United States in response to the second UN resolution; Operation Unified Protector was the NATO operation that "responded to the UN call" by enforcing an arms embargo as well as the no-fly zone. On March 31, NATO assumed command for all international operations in Libya.[49]

The constitutional question through these months was whether President Obama needed explicit authorization from Congress to engage in this offensive military action abroad. The president and his administration argued that he possessed unilateral authority, bolstered by treaty obligations.[50] Echoing the Kosovo situation, Congress neither authorized nor banned action. The mission began on March 19; the president reported to Congress two days later that he "directed U.S. military forces to commence operations to assist an international effort authorized by the United Nations." The strikes will be "limited in their nature, duration, and scope. . . . I am providing this report as part of my efforts to keep the Congress fully informed, consistent with the War Powers Resolution. I appreciate the support of the Congress in this action."[51] Without any supportive action in Congress, Obama asserted that the UN can "authorize" members' military campaigns (which the WPR specifically denies in section 8), and said, "It is U.S. policy that Qaddafi needs to go.[52] The administration took the position that the mission was not "war" in a constitutional sense that required congressional authorization. Nor did Obama acknowledge explicitly that he was bound to a withdrawal clock under the WPR.[53] However, when the sixty-day clock expired on May 20, the president wrote to leaders to express support for a resolution passed in the Senate that would authorize the mission. The House did not pass it. A few days before the ninety-day clock expired on June 19, the White House said there were no "hostilities" without U.S. casualties.[54]

Meanwhile in Congress, several House actions indicated interest in holding the president to the WPR. First, House Concurrent Resolution 51 was introduced by

Dennis Kucinich (D-OH), who would soon be the lead plaintiff in the member lawsuit), which said, "Pursuant to section 5(c) of the War Powers Resolution. . . . Congress directs the President to remove the United States Armed Forces from Libya by not later than the date that is 15 days after the date of the adoption of this concurrent resolution." The resolution failed on the floor 148–265, with bipartisan groups on both sides of the question; the "yea" votes had 87 Republicans and 61 Democrats and the "nay" votes had 144 Republicans and 121 Democrats. Second, on June 3, Speaker John Boehner himself sponsored House Resolution 292, which banned ground troops and passed on a party-line vote. Third, on June 15, Boehner wrote to warn the president he was about to violate the WPR. The fourth major House action of the month came when Representative Alcee Hastings (D-FL) sponsored a resolution to authorize the mission, which failed 123–295, with only eight Republicans voting "aye." Finally, Representative Tom Rooney (R-FL) sponsored a resolution to defund the NATO mission, which also failed 180–238.[55] These last two (seemingly contradictory) votes took place on the same day.

In the middle of this active month, ten members of the House of Representatives (two Democrats and eight Republicans) filed suit against President Obama on June 15, 2011. The complaint noted that "the Obama Administration had yet to ask Congress for specific funding [for military action in Libya]" nor sought "a declaration of war from Congress or even congressional approval for [the military action]." Information from the Department of Defense estimated spending around $550 million in the first ten days of the military engagement, paid for with reallocations.[56] Nevertheless, district judge Reggie Walton agreed with the defendants and the case was dismissed in mid-October. Judge Walton rejected the members' standing to sue as legislators and taxpayers. Citing several previous member lawsuits, he said that the alleged injuries to these ten plaintiffs are not separate from those that may have been suffered by the other 425 members of the House.[57]

Therefore, what Kucinich et al. claimed was an "institutional injury," which had been dismissed as a standing category in *Raines v. Byrd* (see part 2). If an institutional injury characterizes the situation, then it should be endorsed by the body, which was precisely what Judge Rosemary Collyer noted in a later suit on enforcement of the Affordable Care Act, *House v. Burwell* (discussed in part 3). The next issue was whether a legitimate conflict arose from the president's actions in light of congressional votes. Specifically, did Obama "nullify" any particular congressional action, including the defeat of the authorization bill on June 24? Judge Walton endorsed the Obama administration's view: "The President's actions, being based on authority totally independent of the June 24, 2011 vote, cannot be construed as actions that nullify a specific Congressional prohibition."[58] The decision came on October 20, 2011. The NATO campaign ended on October 31. Kucinich did not file an appeal. The tenth member war suit failed to disrupt the new order, as did a private suit by an Army captain.[59]

As federal courts are accused of activism on many policy fronts, members' war questions meet restraint. Whatever the motivations of federal judges who have formed these multilayered barriers around war powers, the consistency of the judicial position defies ideological polarization on other issues and transcends change on the bench, majority control of the House and Senate, the occupant of the White House, and even the foreign policy zeitgeist.

All three branches and both parties have contributed to our nation's flipped understanding of constitutional war. After-the-fact public criticism, oversight hearings and investigations, and party switches in the White House and Congress have not changed this dynamic. Even when presidents seek and receive authorizations for the use of military force, presidents push the outer limits of their constitutional power. The two AUMFs after 9/11 were written to punish the terrorists and their accomplices as well as preempt future terrorism by invading Iraq. Three presidents have utilized these two legal bases for expanding war well beyond the stated intentions of the AUMFs. We are living in the longest war authorization in U.S. history. The most recent pivot in presidential interpretation of the AUMFs concerns the fight against the so-called Islamic State of Iraq and al-Sham (ISIS). President Obama began this campaign in August, 2014, and President Donald Trump is continuing it by leaving hundreds of troops in Syria, even as he declared victory against the terror group in early 2019.[60] According to the Department of Defense, Operation Inherent Resolve cost an average of $13.6 million per day for a total of over $14 billion through 2017.[61]

Despite repeated cries of "lawlessness" against the last three presidents on war powers, Congress members have not yet pursued a lawsuit on the ISIS actions, or other expansions of the "war on terror." Various members of the House and Senate proposed revoking or replacing the AUMFs of both 2001 and 2002, with nothing coming out of committee during the Bush, Obama, or Trump administration (thus far).[62] But there is renewed interest in these issues over the past two years as the public learned about the repeated expansions of these two AUMFs to cover over a dozen countries, in addition to Syria, outside their original targets of Afghanistan and Iraq. First, four U.S. service members were killed by an ambush in Niger in 2017. Our military presence in West Africa, under the auspices of the 2001 AUMF, caught even members of Congress by surprise.[63] Second, the brutal killing of journalist Jamal Khashoggi in Istanbul, Turkey, in 2018 led many members of Congress across both parties to question the close connections we have with Saudi Arabia, whose government appears to be connected to the murder.

In 2019, Congress passed a resolution to reduce the U.S.'s role in assisting the Saudi-led military campaign fighting Houthi rebels in Yemen. The rare rebuke on the ever-expanding AUMFs of 2001 and 2002 was related to the Khashoggi story, the unfolding humanitarian crisis in Yemen as the civil war rages on, and, undoubtedly some war fatigue by the public and members of Congress. The Senate voted 54–46 in favor of the joint resolution, with 7 Republicans joining the majority. The House voted 247–175, with 16 Republicans in favor. President Trump vetoed the joint resolution, saying it attempted to weaken his constitutional authority over foreign affairs. He also rejected the idea that providing logistical assistance to Saudi Arabia constituted "hostilities."[64]

As of this writing, the Trump Administration reported active US military involvement in Afghanistan, Iraq, Syria, Yemen, Somalia, Libya, and Niger. The statutory basis of these actions, according to an Administration report, is the fact that the 2001 and 2002 AUMFs contain "no geographical limitation on where authorized forces may be employed." The report goes on to say that in addition to these laws passed in the wake of 9/11, "the Constitution provides authority for the use of military force in certain circumstances even without prior authorization of Congress."[65] The Constitution says no such thing. This framework comes from the War Powers Resolution. Like the 2001 and 2002 AUMFs, the War Powers Resolution is a legislative action. If Congress wants to change the direction of U.S. military operations around the world, its members would have to confront their own institutional contributions to today's endless wars.

Part 2

LEGISLATIVE PROCESSES

LEGISLATIVE PROCESSES ARE
CONSTITUTIONAL QUESTIONS

Soon after his inauguration in 1933, President Franklin Roosevelt and large Democratic majorities in Congress began to pass major industrial reforms that touched
almost every sector of the national economy during the Great Depression. Many
of these policies suffered repeated setbacks as parts of the New Deal were challenged successfully in a closely divided Supreme Court over the next four years.
Corporate litigants asserted one or two fundamental constitutional questions.
First, can the national government control private economic activities previously
regulated by states (if at all)? Second, can Congress delegate its legislative authority to the executive branch to determine the new administrative rules? Two landmark decisions that said Congress had indeed delegated unconstitutionally to the
president were never overturned by the Supreme Court, even as a majority of justices shifted on the first question beginning in 1937.[1]

Are there any constitutional limits to how Congress conducts its legislative
business internally, or with the executive branch, as they forge public policy? If
so, should the federal judiciary help to determine those boundaries? In addition
to delegation of rulemaking, these questions are central to a variety of legislative
processes, including the legislative and line-item vetoes, base closing commissions,
the Senate filibuster, and more. The Constitution says that the House and Senate
can determine their own rules and procedures (Art. I, Sec. 5). Nevertheless, private interests (discussed in this chapter) and members of Congress (chapter 4)
have alleged that certain process arrangements violate the separation of powers
system, legislative prerogatives, and principles of majority rule. Private litigants
pursue these claims by emphasizing economic and/or regulatory damages from

the law's implementation, while members claim institutional injuries and loss of individual-level legislative power.

In both sets of cases, we see clashing normative guidelines about the role of the federal courts in broader separation of powers development. First is the non-delegation doctrine, which says that Congress should not delegate legislative power that has been granted to it by the Constitution. Proponents of this view say the federal judiciary is necessary to help mark these constitutional boundaries when Congress is not protective of its most fundamental legislative turf.[2] Second is the political question doctrine, which says that federal courts should avoid taking on certain kinds of separation of powers controversies that can be better fought by the elected members of the branches themselves, allowing the court to save institutional capital for other areas of jurisprudence.[3] In this latter view, courts should allow the chambers of Congress to negotiate new processes with each other and the executive branch to keep up with modern legislative workloads and policy pressures.[4]

Private litigants can often press these claims more successfully than members of Congress who are on the losing side of a floor debate. The larger question is whether courts, through activity or restraint on these types of cases, are helping the separation of powers system achieve its goals. The Constitution is more than a procedural map of how to achieve policy outcomes—it sets out a complex system of institutional and electoral differences to foster representation and deliberation. In the modern administrative state, spanning foreign and domestic policy, Congress behaves in ways that would be shocking to the framers as members and leaders argue again and again that their own institution cannot and should not control policy details. The House and Senate built the modern presidency through transfers of legislative power to the newly ascendant and all-encompassing executive branch. Members, of course, retain the right to oversee and criticize presidents and agencies for what they do with the delegated authority. But judges cannot force Congress to want power back.

Constitutional Theory and Separation of Powers

Key *Federalist* papers explain the Constitution's theory of separation of powers. Different branches and chambers will (ideally) see the same policy questions differently through their unique local, state, and national purviews. These differences can be aired through institutional processes and (again, ideally) resolved through deliberation, moderation, and compromise. Many structural differences designed by the framers across the institutions remain largely intact, including different constituencies, methods of election and appointment, as well as terms of office. These institutional differences can lead to policy differences that are expressed by the chambers and branches through shared legislative, executive, and judicial powers. Even though the framers had a vision of natural and healthy intra- and interinstitutional conflict, members themselves sometimes opt to smooth out legislative processes through delegation of power and automatic processes, while at other times complicate the lawmaking process by introducing new barriers that require supermajorities to overcome.

These issues have received attention from other institutional scholars, with disagreement over whether anti-majority processes in Congress rise to the level of an institutional and/or constitutional problem. Some argue that congressional delegation of power and complex internal reforms should be studied purely from a strategic party and policy angle, implying they are harmless to Congress, or even a positive indicator of its ability to overcome complex collective action problems and thus better secure its representative and legislative goals.[5] Others argue that if Congress repeatedly sabotages its constitutionally granted legislative powers, there are profound impacts on public policy outcomes and a balanced separation of powers system.[6] Either way, federal courts' comfort with these types of questions seems to have shifted over time. The Supreme Court took a handful of delegation of powers cases in the late 1800s through the mid-1900s. Legislative processes then returned to the Court's radar in the 1980s and 1990s. In both sets of cases, federal judges wrestle with their own proper role.

Delegation of Power Cases

The nondelegation doctrine asks under what circumstances Congress can and cannot give away legislative prerogatives spelled out in Article I. *J. W. Hampton, Jr. & Co. v. United States* ruled that common sense allows Congress to delegate at least some power to the executive as it cannot be held to minute decisions on administrative matters that may vary in the future.[7] The key test was whether Congress intended the delegation of a core constitutional power and provided some guidelines to the executive branch. Seven years later, despite ostensibly meeting those criteria, *Panama Refining Co. v. Ryan* disallowed delegation of legislative power to the president on oil shipment controls and famously struck down one part of the wide-ranging New Deal-era National Industrial Recovery Act (NIRA).[8] Another NIRA case, *Schechter Poultry Corp. v. United States* struck down legislative delegation of power to industrial groups to make and enforce rules with presidential cooperation.[9] The legacy of these latter two cases, both decided in 1935, is very different from the more famous interstate commerce dramas from the New

Deal. *Panama* and *Schechter* were never explicitly overruled and yet these cases did not restrain Congress from delegating legislative power to the executive branch over the following decades. The question did not go away, but the jurisprudence did, leaving the nondelegation doctrine "moribund."[10] These issues are as relevant as ever to contemporary controversies in administrative discretion.[11]

Field v. Clark (1892) and *J. W. Hampton, Jr. & Co. v. United States* (1928)

While not the first case to focus on a specific congressional delegation of power,[12] *Field v. Clark* concerned the legislative processes surrounding the creation of the Tariff Act of 1890, also known as the McKinley Tariff, and its transfer of rulemaking power to the executive branch and Republican president Benjamin Harrison. This act, among other things, repealed the previous Tariff Act of 1883 to allow the president to determine the extent of trade duty reciprocity with other nations on certain products—and then adjust import tariffs accordingly. The appellants included the Chicago department store Marshall Field, arguing that the legislative process was incomplete because certain steps were missing from the final enrolled bill and that the law delegated excessive authority as the new rates were not explicitly included in the law.

Justice John Marshall Harlan wrote the opinion for the Supreme Court, saying, "That Congress cannot delegate legislative power to the president is a principle universally recognized as vital to the integrity and maintenance of the system of government ordained by the constitution."[13] But the holding said that the enrolled bill was constitutionally passed. Specifically, on section 3, Justice Harlan said, "Congress cannot delegate legislative power to the President is a principle universally recognized as vital to the integrity and maintenance of the system of government ordained by the Constitution. The Act of October 1, 1890, in the particular under consideration, is not inconsistent with that principle. It does not in any real sense invest the President with the power of legislation."[14]

Chief Justice Fuller and Justice Joseph Lamar concurred on the congressional procedures part of the holding, but dissented on the "Reciprocity Provision" and whether the legislation in question had delegated enumerated constitutional authority to the president: "We think that this particular provision is repugnant to the first section of the first article of the Constitution of the United States, which provides that 'All legislative powers herein granted shall be vested in a Congress of the United States, which shall consist of a Senate and House of Representatives.' That no part of this legislative power can be delegated by Congress to any other department of the government, executive or judicial, is an axiom in constitutional law, and is universally recognized as a principle essential to the integrity and maintenance of the system of government ordained by the Constitution. The legislative power must remain in the organ where it is lodged by that instrument."[15]

Over three decades later, a similar constitutional question on which branch should set tariff rates reached the Supreme Court. The law at issue this time was the Tariff Act of 1922, which again delegated to the executive branch the power to decide and implement customs duties on imports. The explicit goal of the law was to adjust importation rates to equalize (meaning raise) the cost of producing articles abroad that were also made in the United States at a more expensive rate.[16] Importer J. W. Hampton, Inc., was charged a duty on the chemical compound barium dioxide that was two cents per pound higher than the amount set in the statute. The company challenged the discretion utilized by then-president Calvin Coolidge in a rate-setting proclamation. The company's argument was twofold: that section 315 of the Tariff Act delegated excessive power to the president and that the tariff was a form of protectionism that exceeded the Congress's constitutional power to tax for revenue purposes only.

Citing the *Field v. Clark* precedent, the Supreme Court concluded that if Congress lays down "an intelligible principle" for carrying out the delegation, the transfer of power is constitutional. "This conclusion is amply sustained by a case in which there was no advisory commission furnished the President—a case to which this Court gave the fullest consideration nearly 40 years ago."[17] And on the policy issue of protective trade regulation the Court said, "So long as the motive of Congress and the effect of its legislative action are to secure revenue for the benefit of the general government, the existence of other motives in the selection of the subjects of taxes cannot invalidate congressional action."[18]

Ongoing controversies surrounding presidential power to change trade and tariff policy, in part by circumventing the conventional legislative process, echo many of these arguments almost a century ago. In the 1980s and 1990s "fast track" legislative procedures allowed presidents to expand or extend free trade agreements by speeding the proposal through the House and Senate with minimal deliberation and opportunity for changes in committees and on the floors. In the early 2000s and today, more protectionist-leaning presidents can use power delegated by Congress in 1962 to change tariffs unilaterally—with hardly any legislative process at all. Either way, traditional congressional prerogatives are sacrificed for administrative efficiency.[19]

Panama, Schechter, and *Yakus* (1933–1944)

As mentioned above, Franklin Roosevelt took office in March 1933 with the benefit of a landslide electoral victory and supermajorities of Democrats in both chambers of Congress. The first year of the New Deal agenda included the NIRA, passed in June. It had three broad components: fair trade through industrial regulations, labor organization support through the creation of the National Labor Relations Board, and the Public Works Administration. The first set of judicial rulings on the NIRA concerned regulation, specifically agricultural and petroleum processes. *Panama Refining Co. v. Ryan* and *A.L.A. Schechter Poultry Corp.. v. United States* cases set back the administration's policy goals and a new constitutional vision of an unfettered executive. In the long run, as we will see in part 3 of the book, the executive branch expanded exponentially nonetheless. More restrictive decisions were largely ignored.[20]

In an 8–1 case, with Justice Benjamin Cardozo dissenting, the Supreme Court said in *Panama Refining Co. v. Ryan* that Congress had not given sufficient clarity to the executive branch when attempting to delegate power to it. Section 9(c) of the NIRA stated, "The President is authorized to prohibit the transportation in interstate and foreign commerce of petroleum and the products thereof produced or withdrawn from storage in excess of the amount permitted to be produced or withdrawn from storage by any State law or valid regulation or order prescribed thereunder, by any board, commission, officer, or other duly authorized agency of a State. Any violation of any order of the President issued under the provisions of this subsection shall be punishable by fine of not to exceed $1,000, or imprisonment for not to exceed six months, or both."[21] Section 10 allowed the president to issue an executive order to the secretary of the interior, which Roosevelt did on July 14, 1933. The order included "full authority to designate and appoint such agents and to set up such boards and agencies as he may see fit, and to promulgate such rules and regulations as he may deem necessary."[22]

Chief Justice Charles Evans Hughes's majority opinion focused on the breadth of this delegation of power, which Congress passed willingly. "Section 9(c) is brief and unambiguous . . . It does not qualify the President's authority. . . . It establishes no criteria to govern the President's course. It does not require any finding by the President as a condition of his action. The Congress in § 9(c) thus declares no policy as to the transportation of the excess production. So far as this section is concerned, it gives to the President an unlimited authority to determine the policy and to lay down the prohibition, or not to lay it down, as he may see fit. And disobedience to his order is made a crime punishable by fine and imprisonment."[23] The chief justice added, "The question whether such a delegation of legislative power is permitted by the Constitution is not answered by the argument that it should be assumed that the President has acted, and will act, for what he believes to be the public good. The point is not one of motives, but of constitutional authority, for which the best of motives is not a substitute."[24]

Justice Cardozo's dissent said that standards were indeed present in the act. "My point of difference with the majority of the court is narrow. I concede that, to uphold the delegation, there is need to discover in the terms of the act a standard reasonably clear whereby discretion must be governed. I deny that such a standard is lacking in respect of the prohibitions permitted by this section when the act, with all its reasonable implications, is considered as a whole. What the standard is becomes the pivotal inquiry."[25] The Connally Hot Oil Act of 1935 rewrote the offending section of the NIRA and was held constitutional when challenged in court.

Earlier in 1935, the A.L.A. Schechter Poultry Corporation was convicted of criminal industrial violations under the Live Poultry Code, passed in 1934 as part of the NIRA. Section 3 of the NIRA was particularly controversial because it delegated to the President the power to write and enforce "codes of unfair competition." Roosevelt's regulatory actions in the poultry industry included wages, hours, and the condition of chickens shipped across state lines. Schechter was charged with selling "unfit chickens," among other NIRA violations.[26] The company lost at the district and appellate levels, but won in the Supreme Court in a narrow decision. The Court said there was no clear "intelligible principle" in the delegation and that the charge was too broad in the first place. Further, the commerce clause was not applicable because the company's actions in question were largely performed intrastate in New York.

Building on the *Panama* decision a few months earlier, the Supreme Court was unanimous, with the decision written by the Chief Justice Hughes. By detailing the intrastate activities related to the chicken trade and invoking the Tenth Amendment, which says that powers not delegated by the Constitution to the federal government are reserved to the states, Hughes said, "Powers of the national government are limited by the constitutional grants. Those who act under these grants are not at liberty to transcend the imposed limits because they believe that more or different power is necessary."[27] But the key constitutional offense in this legislation, according to the chief justice, was the lack of "intelligible principles" in the statute. "The Congress is not permitted to abdicate or to transfer to others the essential legislative functions with which it is thus vested. We have repeatedly recognized the necessity of adapting legislation to complex conditions involving a host of details with which the national legislature cannot deal directly . . . [however,] Section 3 of the Recovery Act is without precedent. It supplies no standards for any trade, industry or activity. It does not undertake to prescribe rules of conduct to be applied to particular states of fact determined by appropriate administrative procedure. Instead of prescribing rules of conduct, it authorizes the making of codes to prescribe them . . . [and] is an unconstitutional delegation of legislative power."[28]

In this way, *Panama* and *Schechter* contrast with two other important FDR-era delegation cases. *United States v. Curtiss-Wright Export Company* upheld the delegation of power from Congress to the president to declare and enforce an arms embargo in South America, and is discussed in other parts of the book because of its wide use as a precedent on executive foreign policy power. *Yakus v. United States* case is less well known, but it marked a new era where the nondelegation doctrine began to disappear from federal court jurisprudence.

Yakus concerns wartime delegation of domestic regulatory and economic power. Instead of being an abrupt departure from *Schechter* and *Panama*, the law in this case included more regulatory details. The constitutional question concerned the Emergency Price Control Act of 1942, which was passed soon after the declarations of war against Germany and Japan and delegated wartime commodity controls to an administrator in the Office of Price Administration. The goal of the act was to control inflation in specific products. With a 6–3 split, the Supreme Court majority offered five related arguments in defense of the act: the delegation was narrow to a specific outcome and time frame, Congress "preserved" its legislative function in outlining this scope, Congress has price fixing powers to set the parameters of the policy, Congress need not choose the least available type of delegation to meet the constitutional threshold, and the standards for the practice of price controls were included in the act so that public and even legal scrutiny would be able to ascertain whether the powers were utilized appropriately. The case resulted from the conviction of private violators of the act.

Chief Justice Harlan Fiske Stone wrote for the majority, saying this act was unlike the one at issue in the *Schechter* case, which he described as lacking standards. Delegation of power with additional details is permissible. Stone went on to explain that the Constitution "does not demand the impossible or the impracticable. It does not require that Congress find for itself every fact upon which it desires to base legislative action, or that it make for itself detailed determinations which it has declared to be prerequisite to the application of the legislative policy to particular facts and circumstances impossible for Congress itself properly to investigate."[29]

In dissent, Justice Owen Roberts (who was previously the key to the "switch in time that saved nine," turning the Supreme Court toward approval of New Deal legislation) argued that delegation of power standards should be the same in peacetime and war.[30] "But if the court puts its decision on the war power, I think it should say so. The citizens of this country will then know that, in war, the function of legislation may be surrendered to an autocrat whose 'judgment' will constitute the law, and that his judgment will be enforced by federal officials pursuant to civil judgments, and criminal punishments will be imposed by courts as matters of routine."[31]

Looking at these issues from a judicial perspective, scholar Cass Sunstein makes two points about the so-called death of the nondelegation doctrine by midcentury.

First, he argues that federal courts do indeed scrutinize agency rulemaking to balance congressional grants of power with individual and corporate rights in many cases. Second, Sunstein says that the nondelegation doctrine is not an appropriate or practical use of judicial institutional powers, and concludes, "There is no plausible case for a broad-scale revival of the nondelegation doctrine. A reinvigoration of the conventional doctrine would pose serious problems of judicial competence, and it would not be a sensible response to any of the problems and pathologies of the modern administrative state."[32]

New Wave in the 1980s

While the judiciary retreated from reviewing rulemaking aggressively after the 1930s, a landmark decision in 1983 brought the Supreme Court back into debates about intra- and interinstitutional arrangements. Throughout the twentieth century, Congress and the president tinkered repeatedly with legislative and oversight processes to keep up with the myriad political, policy, and workload pressures of modern governance. The main questions surround several experiments in legislative processes and whether the federal courts have the practical insight and institutional comfort to weigh in. Champions of judicial restraint in separation of powers questions turn to the *INS v. Chadha* case as one example of misdirected Supreme Court power. The Court was roundly criticized for a formalistic and rigid view of separation of powers that did not take into account the realities of twentieth-century governance.

INS v. Chadha (1983)

The legislative veto was a one- or two-house administrative oversight capability that seemed to invert the branches' constitutional places. The process is associated with administrative growth under the New Deal, but actually began in 1929, when President Herbert Hoover asked for a broad delegation of power from Congress for an executive branch reorganization, subject to congressional approval afterward. In 1932, the bill passed, including provision for a one-house veto of executive branch reorganization made pursuant to the law. In 1939, Congress granted FDR authority to reorganize the executive branch, this time including a two-house veto into the law.[33] In 1949, Harry S. Truman also signed a reorganization bill that included a one-house veto provision. As the legislative veto expanded into other policy areas, presidents derided congressional "micromanagement," but saw legislative vetoes as preferable to waiting for new prior agency authorizations.[34]

According to data in the *Chadha* case, an estimated 300 legislative vetoes had been built into around 200 laws beginning in 1932, the vast bulk of which were passed between 1970 and 1975 (an era with over 160 provisions in 89 laws). "Members were drawn to the constitutionally suspect legislative veto in the early 1970s because it provided them an easy way to give public expression to growing public distrust of the federal government's executive and regulatory powers. . . . And in those situations where they were intent on exercising real control over delegated authorities, members were clearly not in need of any constitutional innovations."[35] The legislative veto concept is also similar to the rhythms of the war powers cases discussed in chapter 2. Congress is allowing president to act, reserving power to rein in if need be—but also allowing the president to bear responsibility for any mistakes and/or bad political consequences flowing from presidential decisions made pursuant to the laws (at least where Congress declined to exercise legislative veto).

The types of vetoes varied. It is worth exploring some distinctions between the one-house, two-house, and committee vetoes. The institutional logic of the one-house legislative veto was that it takes both chambers to agree to legislation in the first place, so it makes sense that one house can block before or after the fact. However, this logic does not apply for the more controversial committee veto, which implies a committee could have blocked an initial authorization. In some cases, legislation can pass even without a committee's approval (although it is not necessarily common). Even proponents of the one-house veto do not extend the argument to the committee versions.[36] The two-house veto, by contrast, is the highest hurdle for legislative oversight of agencies and puts Congress in the greatest disadvantage. In any of these forms, some scholars say that the power of the legislative veto has been overblown because Congress has so many other legislative and oversight tools that in some ways better connect representation of constituencies and institutional power.[37]

Even if this is true, for our purposes, *INS v. Chadha* is still important as a rare landmark of Supreme Court institutional formalism, which means the Court saw walls between branches rather than flexible fences (the other example is the member suit three years later, *Bowsher v. Synar*, discussed in chapter 4). According to Neal Devins and Louis Fisher, in *Chadha* the Supreme Court "encouraged the belief that Congress existed for the sole purpose of passing legislation, with no opportunity to influence the implementation of a bill once it had been enacted. The Court's abstract opinion failed to describe how the executive and legislative branches actually interact and overlap in practice."[38]

The details of the case are complex. Jagdish Chadha had remained in the United States after his student visa had expired in 1972 and was informed of his qualification for deportation by the Immigration and Naturalization Service (INS) in

1973. Section 244(c)(2) of the Immigration and Nationality Act of 1965 allowed either house of Congress to pass a resolution that could invalidate the decision of the attorney general to allow a deportable "alien" to remain in the United States. An immigration judge suspended Chadha's deportation in June 1974, utilizing hardship and "good character" provisions in the act, and reported the suspension to Congress, as required. Days before the legislative window closed in December 1975, the House of Representatives passed a resolution in four days to veto the suspension, and deportation proceedings began again.[39]

Chadha tried to argue for the unconstitutionality of the legislative veto to the immigration judge unsuccessfully and an appeal to the Board of Immigration Appeals was dismissed. The Ninth Circuit appellate court held the veto unconstitutional. The Supreme Court took the case, even though Chadha and parts of the executive branch were pleased with the appellate court's decision. This aspect of the case brings back the issue of whether standing is applied consistently or, rather, if courts simply take the cases they want to hear on the merits. But as the INS wanted to deport him, it had the standing to appeal. "An agency's status as an aggrieved party under § 1252 is not altered by the fact that the Executive may agree with the holding that the statute in question is unconstitutional."[40]

Chief Justice Warren Burger wrote the opinion for the majority, which was joined by Justices William Brennan, Thurgood Marshall, Harry Blackmun, John Paul Stevens, and Sandra Day O'Connor. Justice Lewis Powell concurred and Justices Byron White and William Rehnquist dissented, the latter concentrating narrowly on severability of the veto provision from the rest of the act. Burger's opinion began by dismissing the standing, political question, and other justiciability questions surrounding the case. Burger emphasized bicameralism and presentment standards in the Constitution that, he argued, required both houses of Congress and the president to be engaged in lawmaking. "We see therefore that the Framers were acutely conscious that the bicameral requirement and the Presentment Clauses would serve essential constitutional functions. . . . The legislative power of the Federal Government [will] be exercised in accord with a single, finely wrought and exhaustively considered, procedure."

What was more controversial about the opinion was Burger's formal demarcation of the boundaries of the branches. "The Constitution sought to divide the delegated powers of the . . . Government into three defined categories, Legislative, Executive, and Judicial, to assure, as nearly as possible, that each branch of government would confine itself to its assigned responsibility. The hydraulic pressure inherent within each of the separate Branches to exceed the outer limits of its power, even to accomplish desirable objectives, must be resisted. . . . In purely practical terms, it is obviously easier for action to be taken by one House without submission to the President; but it is crystal clear from the records of the Convention, contemporaneous writings, and debates that the Framers ranked other values higher than efficiency." Burger went on to say that the values of deliberation outweighed its frustration: "With all the obvious flaws of delay, untidiness, and potential for abuse, we have not yet found a better way to preserve freedom than by making the exercise of power subject to the carefully crafted restraints spelled out in the Constitution."[41]

Justice Powell's concurrence rested on two important differences with Chief Justice Burger. First, he argued the legislative veto is more offensive as a judicial power exercised by Congress in this kind of immigration proceeding—rather than as an executive power. "When Congress finds that a particular person does not satisfy the statutory criteria for permanent residence in this country, it has assumed a judicial function in violation of the principle of separation of powers." Second, although Powell agreed the legislative veto should be overturned in this instance, he expressed trepidation about the outsized consequence of its blanket elimination on hundreds of statutes. "The breadth of this holding gives one pause. . . . Congress clearly views this procedure as essential to controlling the delegation of power to administrative agencies. One reasonably may disagree with Congress' assessment of the veto's utility, but the respect due its judgment as a coordinate branch of Government cautions that our holding should be no more extensive than necessary to decide these cases."[42]

Justice White's dissent took up a similar line of reasoning, starting with the unprecedented breadth of the case. He also listed the landmark acts that would be adversely impacted by the decision, such as the War Powers Resolution (WPR) of 1973 and certain impoundment provisions of the Congressional Budget and Impoundment Control Act of 1974, among others. He said without the legislative veto, Congress would have to choose between not resolving problems because of the details needed in legislation or delegating more power to unelected administrators. "The prominence of the legislative veto mechanism in our contemporary political system and its importance to Congress can hardly be overstated. It has become a central means by which Congress secures the accountability of executive and independent agencies."[43] Justice White added, "The apparent sweep of the Court's decision today is regrettable. The Court's Art. I analysis appears to invalidate all legislative vetoes, irrespective of form or subject. . . . Courts should always be wary of striking statutes as unconstitutional; to strike an entire class of statutes based on consideration of a somewhat atypical and more readily indictable exemplar of the class is irresponsible."[44] White touches on a key question of this book and indirectly explores the other side of the argument. He asks whether the Supreme Court has the constitutional authority to make this type of decision and implies "yes." However, he questions whether the Supreme Court should have ruled as broadly as it did and answers "no."

Unsurprisingly, in the wake of *Chadha*, power rocked back and forth between the branches on small-bore questions related to the now-defunct legislative veto, and the case provoked scholarly criticism as well. A variety of formal and informal agreements between committees and agencies allowed the legislative veto to continue in effect, despite critical rhetoric from presidents—even the committee version of the veto.[45] The Congressional Review Act, an alternative passed in 1996 by Congress to expedite legislation disapproving certain types of agency rules within a specific time frame, does not overcome the constitutional hurdles of regular legislation, which requires presidential signature or veto override.[46] Some critics think the Supreme Court misunderstood the history and purpose of the legislative veto, leaving unintended consequences behind. Devins and Fisher argue that "the predictable and inevitable result of *Chadha* is a system of lawmaking that is now more convoluted, cumbersome, and covert than before. In many cases, the Court's decision simply drove underground a set of legislative and committee vetoes that used to operate in plain sight."[47]

Other criticism of *Chadha* extends into the realm foreign affairs, pointing out the decision impacted the War Powers Resolution, Arms Export Control Act, Nuclear Non-Proliferation Act, National Emergencies Act, and International Emergency Economic Powers Act. Congress may only disapprove of an executive act under these laws by passing a joint resolution that would be subject to a veto. As Harold Hongju Koh remarks, "The president may consequently make numerous major foreign-policy decisions under the cloak of congressional approval when in fact he possesses support from only the thirty-four senators [or 146 House members] needed to sustain his veto against an override."[48]

There is no question that the Court suffered a backlash, at least in legislative and scholarly circles. The next two major separation of powers decisions showed a retreat from a rigid view of the branches' wall and relationship with each other. Koh concludes that "in both cases [discussed below] the Court's opinion eschewed *Chadha*'s formalistic approach in favor of a more flexible, functional separation-of-powers analysis that would permit a broader interbranch sharing of powers."[49]

Morrison v. Olson (1988)

This case concerned the constitutionality of Title VI of the Ethics in Government Act of 1978. This landmark and far-reaching law was a legislative reaction to President Nixon's "Saturday Night Massacre" firing of the independent special Watergate prosecutor in 1973. The act authorized the attorney general to convene a "special division" court, which could then choose to appoint an independent counsel to investigate high-ranking government officials accused of federal crimes.

During such an investigation, the counsel had specific reporting obligations to Congress. The specific incident leading to the challenge of the law began in 1982 with a House investigation into the Department of Justice (DOJ)'s actions regarding information requested of another agency by two subcommittees. The House was displeased that the DOJ advised President Reagan to invoke executive privilege regarding documents that the House wanted from the Environmental Protection Agency (EPA) regarding "Superfund" environmental cleanup enforcement. Theodore Olson worked for the attorney general's office in the Office of Legal Counsel and was accused by the House Committee of giving false testimony, along with two other officials in the DOJ who were accused of interfering in the House's EPA investigation. In 1983, the EPA released some of the documents. After a two-year investigation by the House Judiciary Committee, focused on DOJ testimony and various EPA documents still withheld, the House requested that the attorney general appoint a special prosecutor to investigate Olson's actions before the committee in testimony, as well as two other DOJ officials related to the documents.

After two additional years of tussles between the attorney general, the special division, and the House regarding the scope of the investigation, in 1987 special prosecutor Alexia Morrison secured a grand jury subpoena for documents against Olson and two other DOJ officials. The three moved to quash the request, arguing the Ethics Act was unconstitutional on various grounds related to the appointment and powers of the special prosecutor. These arguments against the act won at the district level, but that decision was reversed on appeal. Soon after, the Supreme Court upheld the Ethics in Government Act 8–1. Chief Justice Rehnquist delivered the opinion, joined by Justices Brennan, White, Marshall, Blackmun, Stevens, and O'Connor. Justice Antonin Scalia dissented and recent appointee Anthony Kennedy did not participate.

Rehnquist reviewed the constitutional convention's notes on any limitations to Congress's authorizing interbranch appointments, as well as court precedent, and concluded, "In this case, however, we do not think it impermissible for Congress to vest the power to appoint independent counsel in a specially created federal court. We thus disagree with the Court of Appeals' conclusion that there is an inherent incongruity about a court having the power to appoint prosecutorial officers."[50] Likewise, the opinion does not find constitutional offenses in the "Special Division" powers. The Supreme Court did not "view this provision as a significant judicial encroachment upon executive power or upon the prosecutorial discretion of the independent counsel."[51]

The next question was whether the special prosecutor's independence violated principles of separation of powers by limiting the conventional prosecutorial powers by the president and executive branch. The majority found no fault with

Congress's design for appointment of the office, or removal for cause by the attorney general. "Time and again we have reaffirmed the importance in our constitutional scheme of the separation of governmental powers into the three coordinate branches. . . . The system of separated powers and checks and balances established in the Constitution was regarded by the Framers as 'a self-executing safeguard against the encroachment or aggrandizement of one branch at the expense of the other.' . . . We have not hesitated to invalidate provisions of law which violate this principle. On the other hand, we have never held that the Constitution requires that the three Branches of Government 'operate with absolute independence.' The Act does give a federal court the power to review the Attorney General's decision to remove an independent counsel, but in our view this is a function that is well within the traditional power of the judiciary."[52]

Justice Scalia began his dissent by explaining the different types of authority granted to each branch in the Constitution and his view of the symbolic and substantive importance of the case. "That is what this suit is about. Power. The allocation of power among Congress, the President, and the courts in such fashion as to preserve the equilibrium the Constitution sought to establish . . . can effectively be resisted."[53] The lengthy dissent in this case and *Mistretta v. United States* (discussed next), shows Scalia was very protective of executive and judiciary prerogatives within the separation of powers system. Chapter 4 will show that this institutional protectiveness does not extend to Congress in relation to the item veto and base closure cases, where it seems to sabotage its powers. In this way, Scalia was wary of the Court's involvement in these decisions, but his approach should also signal concerns for anyone who thinks the Court's forays into interbranch workings automatically help to balance branch power. Although Scalia implies the Court will continue to protect legislative prerogatives, we see in the coming chapters a more mixed record on that point. "The utter incompatibility of the Court's approach with our constitutional traditions can be made more clear. . . . Once we determined that a purely legislative power was at issue, we would require it to be exercised, wholly and entirely, by Congress."[54]

Scalia's objections aside, this case was one of nine uses of the special prosecutor in its first decade. Ultimately, there were a number of investigations before Congress allowed the law to expire in 1999, the year after President Bill Clinton's impeachment, which was pursued by the House of Representatives with evidence gathered by special prosecutor Ken Starr. As noted in a Congressional Research Service report on the history of self-investigations within the executive branch, there remains an inherent authority by attorneys general to appoint special counsels even without congressional authorization, as seen before, during, and after the law's existence, including the recently completed special counsel investigation of President Donald Trump.[55]

Mistretta v. United States (1989)

Justice Scalia's concern about the Court's maintaining institutional integrity across the branches hit home in the next case. In 1984, the U.S. Sentencing Commission was created in the Sentencing Reform Act and housed as an independent body in the U.S. judiciary. The goal of the act and commission was to reduce disparities in federal criminal sentences and improve predictability of release dates for the executive branch's parole planning. Another goal was to shift away from traditional deference given to sentencing judges and parole officers regarding who was fit for rehabilitation and whether inmates needed to remain imprisoned or under supervised release. "Under the indeterminate sentence system, Congress defined the maximum, the judge imposed a sentence within the statutory range (which he usually could replace with probation), and the Executive Branch's parole official eventually determined the actual duration of imprisonment."[56] The commission was mandated to report to Congress annually.[57]

John Mistretta was charged under the new commission's guidelines and argued against its constitutionality on several grounds: delegation of legislative power, placing the commission in the judiciary, and authorizing the president to appoint and remove commissioners (seven total, at least three federal judges, all confirmed by the Senate, and a mix of parties). The district court in Missouri rejected these arguments, saying the commission has quasi-executive status. After this outcome, Mistretta pleaded guilty, received an eighteen-month sentence, three years' probation, and then appealed to the Eighth Circuit. Due to the "imperative public importance" of the issue, and disarray at the lower courts on sentencing more generally, the Supreme Court took the case.

As in most other separation of powers cases in this book, there was no predictable ideological quality to the judicial lineup. Justice Blackmun wrote the majority opinion and was joined by Chief Justice Rehnquist and Justices White, Marshall, Stevens, O'Connor, Kennedy, and Brennan in all but one part. Justice Scalia filed a dissent. Blackmun's opinion begins by quoting heavily from a 1983 Senate report that accompanied the legislation and explained that the sentencing commission was the preferred alternative to even stricter sentencing dictation by Congress or the looser model of an advisory sentencing body. He describes the remaining discretion given to judges and how the sentencing guidelines included variations and ranges.[58]

Blackmun begins by explaining the "nondelegation doctrine" and rejecting its use in this case. He cites the "intelligible principle" test of *Field v. Clark*, *Hampton v. United States*, and *Yakus v. United States*, among others, saying "our jurisprudence has been driven by a practical understanding that, in our increasingly complex society, replete with ever-changing and more technical problems, Congress simply cannot do its job absent an ability to delegate power under broad general directives."[59] After acknowledging the outliers of *Panama* and *Schechter*, also discussed above, Blackmun recites the longer history of allowing various kinds of congressional delegation in the twentieth century, saying, "In light of our approval of these broad delegations, we harbor no doubt that Congress' delegation of authority to the Sentencing Commission is sufficiently specific and detailed to meet constitutional requirements."[60] He details the specificities of the guidelines on types of crimes as well as the type of defendant background information that is and is not a factor of the discretionary range available to judges.

Trying to reconcile this case with prior court formalism, in *Chadha* and elsewhere, Blackmun also argued that separation of powers principles were not violated in the creation of the commission and praised the Court's past pragmatism (discussing cases in this and the next chapter). "In adopting this flexible understanding of separation of powers, we simply have recognized Madison's teaching that the greatest security against tyranny—the accumulation of excessive authority in a single Branch—lies not in a hermetic division between the Branches, but in a carefully crafted system of checked and balanced power within each Branch."[61] Blackmun added: "It is this concern of encroachment and aggrandizement that has animated our separation of powers jurisprudence and aroused our vigilance against the 'hydraulic pressure inherent within each of the separate Branches to exceed the outer limits of its power.' Accordingly, we have not hesitated to strike down provisions of law that either accrete to a single Branch powers more appropriately diffused among separate Branches or that undermine the authority and independence of one or another coordinate Branch."[62]

The related issue of authorizing the housing of the commission in the judiciary was also straightforward to Blackmun. "Our approach to other nonadjudicatory activities that Congress has vested either in federal courts or in auxiliary bodies within the Judicial Branch has been identical to our approach to judicial rulemaking: consistent with the separation of powers, Congress may delegate to the Judicial Branch nonadjudicatory functions that do not trench upon the prerogatives of another Branch and that are appropriate to the central mission of the Judiciary."[63] The fact that Congress dictated the commissioners' composition passed muster too: "Rather, judicial participation on the Commission ensures that judicial experience and expertise will inform the promulgation of rules for the exercise of the Judicial Branch's own business—that of passing sentence on every criminal defendant. To this end, Congress has provided, not inappropriately, for a significant judicial voice on the Commission."[64]

By contrast, Justice Scalia explained his disapproval of the discretion and variation allowed within the sentencing framework. Building on his *Morrison* dissent, he said, "I dissent from today's decision because I can find no place within our constitutional system for an agency created by Congress to exercise no governmental power other than the making of laws."[65] Congressional delegation is often appropriate, but the issue is the degree: "By reason of today's decision, I anticipate that Congress will find delegation of its lawmaking powers much more attractive in the future. If rulemaking can be entirely unrelated to the exercise of judicial or executive powers, I foresee all manner of 'expert' bodies, insulated from the political process, to which Congress will delegate various portions of its lawmaking responsibility. . . . The only governmental power the Commission possesses is the power to make law; and it is not the Congress.[66]

Undermining his later defense of the line-item veto (discussed in chapter 4), Scalia concluded in *Mistretta* that experimentation in separation of powers should be limited. He is often more accommodating for expanded presidential powers (seen in parts 1 and 3) but he does not defend Congress when it shifts policy power to the president. Yet he concludes in this case that "in the long run, the improvisation of a constitutional structure on the basis of currently perceived utility will be disastrous."[67] Member-plaintiffs make a similar point.

There is a voluntary component to Congress's delegation of power and related changes in the legislative process that makes this area of litigation more complex than war powers. Part 1 demonstrated that congressional authority for presidents to begin military activity was a straightforward judicial question until the post-World War II era. Judges largely upheld presidential actions when there was clear prior authorization and struck them down when it was lacking, with some exceptions. Member lawsuits, beginning with Vietnam-related unilateral actions ordered by President Nixon, attempted to bring attention to new institutional dynamics on war. Judges concluded across a forty-year span that House and Senate majority disapproval was needed to prove a live constitutional controversy over presidential war. Whether one agrees or disagrees with these decisions, there is a certain logic to each era, although no real left-right ideological patterns. Here we see there is no ideological or institutional rhythm to delegation of power and legislative process cases.

Sometimes federal courts were hands-off and other times hands-on. The most obvious conclusion from this chapter is that judges appear to want some kind of toehold in the area of legislative processes and delegation of power without taking the full plunge regularly. In activist cases, such as *Chadha*, Chief Justice Burger said, "The presence of constitutional issues with significant political overtones does not automatically invoke the political question doctrine. Resolution of litigation challenging the constitutional authority of one of the three branches cannot be evaded by the courts simply because the issues have political implications."[68]

Chapter 4 will explore the frustrations of member-plaintiffs who argue that federal courts should strike down legislative processes that take away power from simple majorities. Congress's repeated attacks on its own institutional prerogatives and enumerated constitutional powers contribute to our presidency-centered political culture. The separation of powers system was not designed to foster intra- and interbranch conflict for its own sake, but as a means of structuring diverse ideas into government and incentivizing deliberation and compromise between local, state, and national perspectives. Unfortunately for those who advocate a strong judicial correction for imbalances in power, we see in the next chapter that when members of Congress actually win their cases, the reaction of colleagues is to undercut the ruling.

COURTS CANNOT UNKNOT CONGRESS

Under President Ronald Reagan's national budget leadership, annual deficits jumped by hundreds of billions and, by the end of his two terms, the gross national debt had tripled from roughly $1 trillion to $3 trillion. As political pressure surrounding fiscal policy mounted by the mid-1980s, Congress responded with new experiments in legislative processes rather than tackling the problem head-on—the U.S. government was spending too much and taxing too little. In two "Gramm-Rudman-Hollings" reforms in the mid-1980s, Congress mandated across-the-board spending cuts if annual deficits did not meet targets spelled out in advance via a new process called sequestration. The controversial new processes never worked as planned, and the U.S. Supreme Court declared a major part of the procedural change unconstitutional. Congress passed a new version, but the deficit continued to climb. Through the 1990s, Presidents George H. W. Bush and Bill Clinton worked with opposition Congresses on a new approach, using a new set of budget-making steps in the House and Senate to force Congress and the President to make hard decisions on revenue and appropriations. Deficits (not debt) were eliminated in 1998. By early 2001, however, the 1990s-era processes had expired and the branches returned to free-spending ways while also slashing taxes, despite war and recession. Today, there is renewed attention paid to these issues as the gross national debt stands at around $22 trillion.[1]

One lesson is that some legislative process reforms are gimmicks that will never work as planned, while others result from serious reflection about how institutional strengths and weaknesses influence outcomes. For almost any area of public policy, the House and Senate can smooth the lawmaking path or they can throw additional obstacles in the way. There is also the question of constitutionality: Do some novel methods of passing bills or granting legislative authority to other entities rob House and Senate members and majorities of fundamental power? Federal courts assessed this question from different perspectives across five congressional member cases. While members' claims prevailed in one case, over time private litigants achieved more success in attacking legislative process than members of Congress. As with war powers, individual or corporate economic injuries are easier to demonstrate than institutional injuries. Members are often dismissed in court with the assumption that they are sore losers who are trying to convince judges rather than their legislative colleagues. And, ironically, even when a handful of members get their way and the legislative process is thrown out in court, others in the House and Senate try to get around the decision with new legislative processes that mimic the one held unconstitutional.

Ultimately, members and leaders of the House of Representatives and the Senate have to decide for themselves how to use the lawmaking process to represent their constituents and party agendas. Some want Congress in control while majorities are often content to delegate to the executive branch, even under conditions of divided government, or use the legislative process as an obstacle course that few bills can possibly complete. Federal courts may be an avenue for frustrated members of both chambers to express themselves, but judges are often hesitant to substitute their own perspectives on the constitutionality of specific process changes for that of the legislative majority that approved the "reform."

Member Cases on Legislative Processes

This chapter emphasizes five complex legal tangles that resulted in mixed outcomes for the member-litigants. First is the deficit-reduction case (*Bowsher v. Synar*) surrounding the 1985 Balanced Budget and Emergency Deficit Control Act, known after its sponsors as the Gramm-Rudman-Hollings Act (GRH), where plaintiffs ostensibly won back power but Congress opted to delegate again. Second, a multiplaintiff suit against executive enforcement of a base-closing commission decision that required supermajorities to override (*Dalton v. Specter*). This case highlights the risk that Congress takes when it delegates power away and does not have an easy mechanism to regain control over processes and outcomes. Third is Democratic House members' unsuccessful suit against their own chamber's rule that mandated a supermajority in order to raise taxes (*Skaggs v. Carle*). Fourth, the landmark challenge of the 1996 Line Item Veto Act that has been used by later courts to more readily dismiss member standing, even as the item veto itself is ruled unconstitutional by private plaintiffs the next year (*Raines v. Byrd*). Fifth and finally is a hybrid group of House members and private organizations against the Senate filibuster, which stopped the "Dream Act" (*Common Cause v. Biden*). The suit failed, yet the Senate endures continual political pressure to change its rules, now from Republicans.

Bowsher v. Synar (1986)

Deficit spending inspired congressional budget reform in the 1970s and 1980s, but with very different institutional goals that reflected the place of Congress in each era. The 1974 Congressional Budget and Impoundment Control Act acknowledged that Congress was predisposed to high federal spending due to committee fragmentation and members' desire to assist constituencies. But in an era of an ascendant, revived Congress against an "imperial presidency," the 1974 reforms were majority-friendly, Congress-centered solutions that also reined in presidential impoundment power. The 1974 Budget Act gave the House and Senate information tools in the form of the Congressional Budget Office (CBO), new House and Senate Budget Committees and ambitious processes to bring the whole in line with the parts (resolutions and reconciliation).[2]

The 1985 GRH reform was a very different type of response to budget deficits. This time, the goal was to take power away from House and Senate majorities (and the president's own spending agenda) through a rigid deficit-reduction timetable from fiscal years 1986 to 1991. A new process, the above-mentioned sequestration, would perform across-the-board spending cuts to qualified discretionary spending items to meet the annual ceilings. These and other enforcement procedures of the act were part of a contentious compromise between the different chambers and passed in a rush as a rider to a "must-pass" debt ceiling increase. Under the compromise, if CBO and the executive branch's Office of Management and Budget (OMB) estimated that the deficit of a given year would exceed the preset limit (plus a small cushion), they would transmit their overall and program estimates to the comptroller general (CG). The CG would report to the president which federal discretionary funds would be sequestered (equally divided between defense and nondefense, with some social programs exempt). The president would issue the sequestration order, which may not change the CBO/OMB estimates or the CG's order. Congressional committees responsible for the programs could then opt to lead congressional action to make needed changes to avoid the across-the-board cuts and report to the CBO/OMB directors again. If that did not happen the president would issue his final order to eliminate the excess spending to comply with the deficit ceiling.[3]

The change to the majority-friendly 1974 legislative processes was especially controversial, with opponents arguing the delegation of power generally, and specifically to the CG, made GRH constitutionally suspect. The CG is head of the congressional spending "watchdog" known as the Government Accountability Office (then called the General Accounting Office). He or she is nominated by the President from a list of three recommended by the Speaker of the House and the president pro tempore of the Senate. The CG position is explicitly described as "non-partisan and non-ideological." The successful nominee required confirmation by the Senate but was removable at the initiative of Congress in two ways: impeachment/conviction or by joint resolution of Congress at any time for "permanent disability, inefficiency, neglect of duty, malfeasance, or a felony or conduct involving moral turpitude." The joint resolution could be vetoed by the president and subject to override by a two-thirds vote of both Houses.[4] Anticipating legal challenges to the CG's role in GRH, the House-Senate conference committee included expedited judicial review and a fallback process in case the federal courts declared the sequestration process unconstitutional.

At the insistence of Representative Mike Synar (D-OK), the law said that any member of the House or Senate or other person adversely affected under the sequestration action could bring the case before the DC district court "for declaratory judgment and injunctive relief on the ground that any order that might be issued pursuant to section 252 violates the Constitution."[5] In addition, the district court's order could be reviewed by appeal directly to the Supreme Court, and "it shall be the duty" of both courts to expedite the cases as much as possible. If the process was declared unconstitutional, the law's fallback procedure was for the CBO/OMB directors to report to a Temporary Joint Committee on Deficit Reduction, composed of the entire House and Senate Budget Committees. The joint committee would report an expedited resolution to be executed by the president.[6]

As expected, Representative Mike Synar, eleven other members, and the National Treasury Employees Union filed suit in December 1985. The district court handed down its opinion in *Synar v. United States* the following February. In a break from recent federal court decisions on member standing to sue presidents on war powers, the three-judge district court panel took note of section 274 of the act and dispensed with the normal "prudential" dismissal of congressional litigants.[7] A *per curium* opinion by Antonin Scalia (circuit judge of the U.S. Court of Appeals for the DC Circuit), Norma Holloway Johnson (DC district judge), and Oliver Gasch (DC senior district judge) upheld the members' standing on "institutional injuries" stemming from GRH's override (in effect) of prior legislation through the sequestration process that did not conform to Article I, Section 7, of the Constitution and thus conferred standing, despite a long and complex history of similar cases previously: "Under the law of this Circuit, which recognizes a personal interest by Members of Congress in the exercise of their governmental powers . . . specific injury to a legislator in his official capacity may constitute cognizable harm sufficient to confer standing upon him."[8]

On the delegation of power question, the three-judge panel held that since the role of the CG was an unconstitutional violation of the separation of powers structure, the question of whether the act violated the "delegation doctrine" did not need to be settled. The court added that the delegated power was not so broad that it violated previous administrative law precedent, nor did it sufficiently "undo" previous legislation. The court said GRH clearly delegated broad authority, but "compared with the cases upholding administrative resolution of such issues, the present delegation is remote from legislative abdication. Through specification of maximum deficit amounts, establishment of a detailed administrative mechanism, and determination of the standards governing administrative decision making, Congress has made the policy decisions which constitute the essence of the legislative function."[9]

Instead, the constitutionally offensive part of GRH was the CG's executive function in light of Congress's removal powers, which made him a legislative agent in the eyes of the panel. Since a legislative agent is precluded from actions of "an executive nature," the CG lacks necessary independence in this set of responsibilities. However, although it sidestepped the delegation question, the court argued its ruling served a similar purpose. Noting that the Supreme Court has rarely struck down legislation on delegation grounds in 200 years, the possibility of the same outcome has not been a "credible deterrent against the human propensity to leave difficult questions to somebody else. The instances are probably innumerable, however, in which Congress has chosen to decide a difficult issue itself because of its reluctance to leave the decision—as our holding today reaffirms it must—to an officer within the control of the executive branch."[10]

In July 1986 the Supreme Court affirmed in *Bowsher v. Synar*. The majority opinion, written by Chief Justice Warren Burger, held that the "separation of powers doctrine" precluded the CG's role in the sequestration process. Burger's majority opinion in *Bowsher* was joined by Justices William Brennan, Lewis Powell, William Rehnquist, and Sandra Day O'Connor. They affirmed each part of the district court's holding, concluding that the CG's being "answerable only to Congress would, in practical terms, reserve in Congress control of the execution of the laws. The structure of the Constitution does not permit Congress to execute the laws; it follows that Congress cannot grant to an officer under its control what it does not possess."[11] Relying heavily on the decision a few years earlier in *INS v. Chadha*, discussed in chapter 3, the majority opinion said the strict separation of powers doctrine was designed to prevent legislative usurpation of executive power, which is ironic considering the claim of unconstitutional delegation of legislative power alleged by the member-plaintiffs. Instead, the majority repeated a controversial claim from *Chadha* by saying that there were, in effect, bright lines between branches that federal courts were competent to determine.[12]

Justice John Paul Stevens's concurrence, which was joined by Thurgood Marshall, focused less on the removal question and more on the delegation issue of whether the CG could make nationally binding public policy that was not obeying Article I, Section 7. "It is not the dormant, carefully circumscribed congressional removal power that represents the primary constitutional evil. . . . Powers assigned to [the CG] under the Gramm-Rudman-Hollings Act require him to make policy that will bind the Nation; and that, when Congress, or a component or an agent of Congress, seeks to make policy that will bind the Nation, it must follow the procedures mandated by Article I of the Constitution—through passage by both Houses and presentment to the President."[13]

In separate dissents, two justices marveled at their colleagues' rejection of GRH's novel policy and procedural experiment. Justice Byron White called the majority's holding on separation of powers principles "distressingly formalistic" and scoffed at the removal power being so important as to compromise the CG's independence.[14] Separately, Justice Harry Blackmun also criticized the majority's emphasis on the removal provision for the CG, which had never been used, more than the law at issue: "Rarely if ever invoked even for symbolic purposes, the removal provision certainly pales in importance beside the legislative scheme the Court strikes down today—an extraordinarily far-reaching response to a deficit problem of unprecedented proportions."[15]

Notably, all the opinions approved the fallback option, in which Congress would make the spending cuts internally through a special process. In the wake of the *Bowsher* decision, Congress had several options for saving GRH: take enforcement power away from the CG and give it to a legitimately "executive officer," change the removal law, or permanently utilize the pro-Congress fallback. Congress chose the first option and passed the Balanced Budget and Emergency Deficit Control Reaffirmation Act in 1987. This act made it so that the executive branch's OMB issued the sequester order, instead of the CG. A now-Democratic majority chose to delegate to Reagan's GOP-run budget arm.[16]

Dalton v. Specter (1994)

In the same spirit of GRH, Base Realignment and Closure Commissions (BRAC) were established as a complex institutional solution to a perceived national policy crisis caused by members and majorities. Congress authorized and executed five rounds of BRAC spanning 1988–2005. This history is often touted as a legislative reform success story that solved a vexing collective action problem.[17] However, delegation of power in Congress is not an elegant, efficient strategy when members simultaneously support the process and then fight against the outcomes when bases in their own districts are targeted. This messy delegation-regret-delegation cycle is evident in all five rounds of the BRAC process.[18] *Dalton vs. Specter* brings up a similar question to *Bowsher*: Should federal courts intervene in Congress's various internal "reforms?"

The BRAC process was complex and somewhat changeable round to round, but it represented the first real attempt in decades to close arguably unneeded and expensive military installations. Here is how it worked in most rounds: First, the House and Senate recommended potential commissioners to the president. His nominations to fill the eight slots were then subject to confirmation by the Senate. Second, the secretary of defense submitted closure criteria to the commission, which Congress could disapprove. Third, the Department of Defense sent closure recommendations to the BRAC, which held hearings and conducted base visits. Fourth, the commission forwarded its recommendations within three months to the president, who could accept or decline the entire list within two weeks. If he accepted them, the closures and realignments were certified and sent to Congress. Otherwise he could return them to the commission with suggested modifications; BRAC then had a month to submit a new report. Finally, once the final list is sent to Congress, the House and Senate would have forty-five working days to consider and pass a joint resolution of disapproval. If passed, it would likely be vetoed by the president, but the disapproval could prevail with two-thirds vote. In other words, supermajorities were needed to stop the BRAC process once started.

Perhaps unsurprisingly, the process was controversial in each round. Members fought the panel's nominations and ultimate outcomes with additional battles over appropriations to fund the commission's work, various attempts at delaying and/or canceling a round, closure criteria, local protests against the list, and public criticism of the executive branch and the commissioners. The disapproval process was invoked symbolically but never completed. Throughout the five rounds of BRAC, it was a curious fact that many members of Congress voted for the process to begin, but then became vocally critical and resistant when a base in their state or district was threatened. Senator Arlen Specter (R-PA) took this posture one step further by filing a lawsuit to prevent the closure of a large Philadelphia naval facility in the second BRAC.

President Bush I's secretary of defense, Richard Cheney, proposed a list of base closures in early 1990. After congressional pushback to these particular targets, the next three rounds passed together as one part of an annual defense authorization bill in 1991. Members of the House and Senate would have to vote to begin the next three BRACs in the same large bill that lays out proposed defense department projects and spending authority.[19] The proposed new BRAC procedures responded to criticism of the first round and allowed more public and member input. President Bush nominated as chair a former member of the House, Jim Courter (R-NJ). Secretary Cheney published his new list of thirty-one major bases, twelve smaller ones, and detailed reduced operations at over two dozen more. In two days of hearings before the commission, 150 lawmakers representing thirty states made their cases to save local installations. The commission rejected closure of two naval facilities that the secretary recommended, but concurred with the closure of the Philadelphia Naval Shipyard. Once the House version of a disapproval resolution died on the floor 364–60, the Senate's version, sponsored by Senator Specter, was dropped.[20]

In addition to the constituent pressures expressed via Congress, a separate issue was whether the navy gave the commission reliable information, which was a concern from the first round as well. This issue was the ostensible reason for the suit, which ultimately included dozens of other elected figures of Pennsylvania, New Jersey, and Delaware (senators, House members, governors, and attorneys general), the City of Philadelphia, and shipyard workers' unions in their joint lawsuit. The plaintiffs alleged that the secretaries of defense and the navy violated the BRAC process by withholding information pertinent to their decisions, or sending information not available to the Government Accounting Office and public, failing to apply the final criteria and force-structure plan evenhandedly to all installations, and by failing to implement record-keeping and internal controls. The employees and union also filed a due process claim. The first round of the suit targeted Henry Garrett, secretary of the navy under Bush I; the name of the case changed in 1994, when John Dalton was secretary of the navy under Bill Clinton.

District court judge Ronald Buckwalter ruled against the plaintiffs on two counts. First, the Administrative Procedure Act (APA) of 1977 precludes judicial review of agency actions if the authorizing law specifically excludes it or if there is evidence of congressional intent against review in the legislative history. Judge Buckwalter cited the authorizing legislation's conference report, which said that the criteria and closure process were not subject to judicial review.[21] Second, after summarizing *Baker v. Carr* (1962), he said the political question doctrine stands on its own in this case: "I believe that it would be impossible to undertake judicial review of the decision on base closures made by the duly elected representatives of this country without expressing a lack of the respect due those branches of government."[22]

The court of appeals reversed in part, saying the actions of the commission and secretary of defense were reviewable insofar as compliance with the law itself, which was not expressly and completely precluded by the conference report.[23] "In this context, it is important to note that while Congress did not intend courts to second-guess the Commander-in-Chief, it did intend to establish exclusive means for closure of domestic bases. . . . Congress did not simply delegate this kind of decision to the President and leave to his judgment what advice and data he would solicit. Rather, it established a specific procedure that would ensure balanced and informed advice to be considered by the President and by Congress before the executive and legislative judgments were made."[24] Appellate judges Walter Stapleton and Joseph Scirica agreed with the district court that Congress did not intend for court review of the whole process, but said that the specific focus of the plaintiffs is indeed reviewable: "While it is not the role of the courts to disturb policy decisions of the political branches, the question of whether an agency has acted in accordance with a statute is appropriate for judicial review."[25]

Future Supreme Court justice Samuel Alito concurred in part and dissented in part. His opinion on judicial review under the APA was narrower than the majority, citing the fact that Congress had had so much difficulty closing bases before the BRAC process. Reviewing the same passage in the conference report, he acknowledged its ambiguity on judicial review but decided that it is not in the spirit or letter of the law itself: "I conclude only that judicial review of base closing and realignment decisions is conceptually inconsistent with the innovative scheme enacted by Congress. This analysis, reinforced by the legislative history, leads me to the conclusion that base closing decisions are not reviewable under the APA."[26]

The Supreme Court first vacated and remanded back to the court of appeals in light of a recent case that had a similar claim under the APA.[27] The appeals court was unmoved by the new case, with the prior division affirmed by the three judges.[28] Then the Court reversed, saying, "The Court of Appeals erred in ruling that the President's base closure decisions are reviewable for constitutionality. Every action by the President, or by another elected official, in excess of his statutory authority is not ipso facto in violation of the Constitution, as the Court of Appeals seemed to believe. On the contrary, this Court's decisions have often distinguished between claims of constitutional violations and claims that an official has acted in excess of his statutory authority."[29]

In a complicated set of concurrences, the justices were unanimous on two points emphasized by Chief Justice Rehnquist's majority opinion (joined by O'Connor, Scalia, Anthony Kennedy, and Clarence Thomas—the latter three were new additions since *Bowsher*): the challenge is a statutory claim, rather than a constitutional claim, and the action at issue was discretion delegated expressly by the law by Congress to the president. Justices Blackmun, David Souter, Ruth Bader Ginsburg, and Stevens agreed that the president acted within the discretion given to him. If Congress did not want the closures, there was the disapproval process, which still required supermajorities. The outcome of the *Dalton vs. Specter* was therefore mixed for the congressional plaintiffs. In the short term, members' standing was not a focus of the case and the political question doctrine was not automatically invoked in all three levels. However, the fact that Congress agreed to the elaborate process doomed Specter's petition in spirit, if not in the literal focus of the case. Meanwhile, Congress agreed to three more BRAC rounds though 2005. Over the past decade, however, members of both parties and chambers in Congress have balked at reviving the BRAC process for a new round of closures requested by the Department of Defense.[30] By refusing to authorize new automatic processes on base closures, members and leaders are reverting to a pre-1980s posture by opting to protect their constituents and preserve their institutional powers.

Skaggs v. Carle (1997)

The BRAC case did not directly question the constitutionality of supermajority rules that Congress imposed on itself. Rather, Senator Specter alleged that the executive branch failed to comply with the process. But it did not escape the federal courts' notice that Congress came up with the complex mechanism that resulted in the litigation. The next process-centered lawsuit asked the federal court to decide if a very different set of internal rules changes could mandate supermajorities for certain types of policy votes on the House floor. The broader question was whether "silences" in the Constitution implied that regular legislation required simple majorities.[31] This longstanding constitutional controversy arises when members use legislative process changes specifically to enact or thwart public policies.

In 1994, the "Republican Revolution" midterm election brought new party majorities to the House and Senate. Newt Gingrich, then minority whip in the House, was the public face and strategist behind the "Contract with America," which was a set of ten policy and eight procedural promises if the party won.[32] *Skaggs v. Carle* focused on the subsequent House rules change that required "a three-fifths majority vote to pass a tax increase." The goal for the 104th Congress was to make tax increases less likely by requiring a supermajority for passage.

House Rules XXI(5)(c) and XXI(5)(d) were adopted in January 1995. Under the first rule, "no bill or joint resolution, amendment, or conference report carrying a Federal income tax rate increase shall be considered as passed or agreed to unless so determined by a vote of not less than three-fifths of the Members voting." And Rule XXI(5)(d) says, "It shall not be in order to consider any bill, joint resolution, amendment, or conference report carrying a retroactive federal income tax rate increase."[33] This rule marked "the first time in history that the House has purported to alter the number of votes required to make a bill law."[34] Controversies over the proposed rules prompted seventeen law professors to write an open letter to Speaker Gingrich, which then inspired a reply in defense of the supermajority rule by two other law professors.[35]

The controversy centered on a tension between two constitutional clauses related to legislative affairs and processes. Article I, Section 5, says, "Each House may determine the Rules of its Proceedings." Article I, Section 7, Clause 2, meanwhile, says, "Every Bill which shall have passed the House of Representatives and the Senate, shall, before it become a Law, be presented to the President of the United States."[36] The question is whether the House and Senate can set rules for themselves to determine the meaning of "passed." Fifteen members of the House brought suit against Clerk of the House Robin Carle in February 1995; twelve more joined in June, with six citizens and a private organization, the League of Women Voters. The complaint argued that regular lawmaking, including retroactive provisions, was a majoritarian process. In a short decision, federal district judge Thomas Penfield Jackson ruled for dismissal by invoking the equitable/remedial discretion doctrine.[37]

On appeal, the three-judge circuit panel was split. Chief Judge Harry Edwards dissented from the majority opinion by Stephen Williams and Douglas Ginsburg. Ginsburg's opinion said that member standing was neither automatically granted nor denied based on lack of the rules' use.[38] "Vote dilution is itself a cognizable injury regardless whether it has yet affected a legislative outcome. We do agree, however, that the appellants' alleged injury depends upon their assertion that Rule XXI(5)(c) in fact renders the votes of 218 Members inadequate to pass legislation carrying an income tax increase. If the votes of 218 Members are still sufficient in practice to pass such legislation, then Rule XXI(5)(c) has not caused the vote dilution that would establish their injury for the purpose of standing under Article III."[39]

In other words, 218 determined House members could waive or change the rules, if desired, and then pass the tax change bills. But the member-appellants argued that it was too difficult to waive the supermajority rule without the help of the Rules Committee, which of course is dominated by the majority party. However, Clerk Carle said that the rule had indeed been waived on several occasions. "However complicated the procedures for suspending Rule XXI(5)(c) may seem, therefore, they do not appear in practice to prevent a simple majority from enacting an income tax increase."[40] The retroactive rule, however, had not yet been tested. "Before repairing to the courts, therefore, we think it only appropriate for those who would object to the Rule first to test its meaning by pursuing in the House a retroactive Federal income tax rate increase. If they are ruled out of

order merely for speaking their minds, or for any other act even arguably pro-
tected by the first amendment, then they can document their injury and assert
their standing to sue," affirming Judge Jackson's decision.[41]

In a strong and lengthy dissent, Chief Judge Edwards rejected standing and
equitable discretion hurdles for the member-plaintiffs, saying, "If Congress is allowed to employ the rulemaking clause to impose new supermajority requirements beyond those already stated in the Constitution, the potential for mischief
is great." As examples, Judge Edwards asked whether the House could enact a
nine-tenths rule, effectively giving California exclusive power over legislative outcomes, or if the Senate could adopt a supermajority rule for presidential nominations. He invoked founding documents and all nonwar precedents on member standing. "I think it is clear that the Framers never intended for Congress to
have such unchecked authority to impose super-majority voting requirements
that fundamentally change the nature of our democratic processes. It is for this
reason that I find House Rule XXI(5)(c) to be an unconstitutional exercise of Congress's rulemaking power."[42] Citing member-plaintiff precedents, Edwards said
that where standing exists, the equitable discretion doctrine is not appropriate.
Standing is conveyed by the potential for vote dilution.[43] "By granting itself the
power to change the number of votes required to enact a bill into law, the House
violated the command of the presentment clause, which requires that all bills that
receive the vote of a majority of a quorum of each House be presented to the President. The House's action conflicts with the intent of the Framers and Supreme
Court precedent. Allowing this Rule to stand permits Congress to use the rulemaking clause as a tool to redefine its relationship to the executive, a result that
should not be countenanced by this court."[44]

In interviews, two member-plaintiffs from the House cited Edwards's point
that these types of cases were equally important to constitutional balance of power
as war powers cases and should be justiciable. Ideally, Congress should not impose supermajority requirements excessively, so lawsuits provide an avenue for
members to invoke the Constitution in a new arena if normal legislative efforts to
protect majority rule fail.[45] It appears that after three flips of majority control,
since 1995, in the current 116th Congress, the Democratic majority jettisoned the
supermajority tax rule upon returning to power.[46]

Raines v. Byrd (1997)

In addition to making the internal rules behind *Skaggs v. Carle*, the 104th Congress also passed the Line Item Veto Act in 1996, provoking two additional rounds
of lawsuits. The Supreme Court finally put its foot down after three decades of
member suits that were largely swatted away at the district and appellate

levels. The landmark ruling that curtailed member suits' potential did not focus on the merits of the Line Item Veto Act, leaving that question to private plaintiffs who filed suit once the new power was used by President Clinton. In the private case, the Supreme Court declared the Act unconstitutional.

The background of the Line Item Veto Act is similar to the rules changes at issue in *Skaggs*, namely that the Republican Contract with America made very specific promises to change specific fiscal policies as well as related legislative processes. Yet this act was not a "true" item veto, which would allow the president to slice items off an appropriations bill and then sign into law. The goal was to reverse the pro-Congress 1974 impoundment processes and replace it with "enhanced rescission" procedures. The spirit of the 1974 reform was to allow presidents to propose delaying, canceling, or reducing appropriations after they are passed but before the money is dispersed. These presidential proposals would need a positive vote by the House and Senate to go into effect. If Congress did nothing, the appropriations were unaffected. The 1996 act reversed the burden in this process. Presidents could make the reduction or cancellation requests, which would go into effect unless Congress passed a disapproval bill. The disapproval would (like with the base closure process) be vetoed and necessitate a two-thirds override in the House and Senate. So, under the 1996 law, if Congress did nothing, the reductions would take effect.[47]

Unlike BRAC, but like GRH, judicial review was built into the Line Item Veto Act. Any person "adversely affected" could bring suit in the DC district court, with direct appeal to the Supreme Court. Senator Robert C. Byrd (D-WV), along with three other senators and two House members, filed to prevent the item veto's first use in January 1997, saying it violated Article I, Sections 7 and 8 (presentment and enumerated power).[48] District court judge Thomas Penfield Jackson ruled against standing in *Skaggs v. Carle*, but said that the members of Congress had standing here and the suit was appropriate for judicial review. He cited several cases that the DC circuit had accepted with member litigants, while acknowledging they were not upheld by the Supreme Court. "Plaintiffs' votes mean something different from what they meant before, for good or ill, and plaintiffs who perceive it as the latter are thus 'injured' in a constitutional sense whenever an appropriations bill comes up for a vote, whatever the President ultimately does with it."[49] He mentioned a possible "sword of Damocles" effect of the power on Congress, as well as new presidential leverage against specific members.

Judge Jackson then turned to the merits. The defendants argued that the item veto was merely a new iteration of the century-old practice of presidential impoundment. Jackson was unpersuaded and ruled the Line Item Veto Act unconstitutional on presentment and delegation of power grounds: "The Court agrees with plaintiffs that, even if Congress may sometimes delegate authority to im-

pound funds, it may not confer the power permanently to rescind an appropriation or tax benefit that has become the law of the United States. That power is
possessed by Congress alone, and, according to the Framers' careful design, may
not be delegated at all."[50] Citing *Chadha*, he added, "Repeal of statutes, no less
than enactment, must conform with Art. I." The Line Item Veto Act "hands off
to the President authority over fundamental legislative choices. Indeed, that is its
reason for being. It spares Congress the burden of making those vexing choices
of which programs to preserve and which to cut."[51]

Per the law's judicial review provisions, the district court's decision was appealed directly to the Supreme Court. The majority opinion was written by Chief
Justice Rehnquist, and was joined by Justices O'Connor, Scalia, Kennedy, Thomas,
and Ginsburg. The majority began with a statement of institutional humility to
explain the justiciability dilemma: "In the light of this overriding and time-
honored concern about keeping the Judiciary's power within its proper constitutional sphere, we must put aside the natural urge to proceed directly to the merits of this important dispute and to 'settle' it for the sake of convenience and
efficiency. Instead, we must carefully inquire as to whether appellees have met
their burden of establishing that their claimed injury is personal, particularized,
concrete, and otherwise judicially cognizable."[52] Furthermore, the Court was
not moved by the plaintiffs' argument of an institutional injury. The lawsuit was
not sanctioned by the chambers and if the majorities were unhappy with any
president's use of the power, they could repeal it or exempt additional types of
spending.[53]

Justice Souter's concurring opinion, which Justice Ginsburg joined in part, also
emphasized the fraught nature of judicial involvement in inter- and intrabranch
disputes. While acknowledging that a private plaintiff would fare better on standing and the same question could be heard on the merits, these justices also show
institutional discomfort in getting involved. "The virtue of waiting for a private
suit is only confirmed by the certainty that another suit can come to us. The parties
agree, and I see no reason to question, that if the President 'cancels' a conventional
spending or tax provision pursuant to the Act, the putative beneficiaries of that
provision will likely suffer a cognizable injury."[54]

Justices Stevens and Breyer issued separate dissents, with both agreeing the
case was adversarial and proved standing prior to presidential use of the item
veto. Justice Stevens cited *Baker v. Carr* in arguing for members' standing, saying,
"The impairment of [their] constitutional right has an immediate impact on their
official powers" and therefore also violates presentment on the merits.[55] Stevens
concluded, "[given] the fact that the authority at stake is granted by the plain and
unambiguous text of Article I, it is equally clear to me that the statutory attempt
to eliminate it is invalid."[56] Justice Breyer explained why he favored standing,

which was not because the law builds in expedited judicial review: "Congress . . . cannot grant the federal courts more power than the Constitution itself authorizes us to exercise. . . . Thus, we can proceed to the merits only if the 'judicial power' [in Article III allows]."[57] Breyer also relied on the official-litigant landmark case *Coleman v. Miller*, saying "Constitution does not draw an absolute line between disputes involving a 'personal' harm and those involving an 'official' harm."[58]

As predicted by both sides, soon after *Raines v. Byrd* private plaintiffs launched a suit against the item veto due to specific presidential cancellations that Congress did not attempt to override with a disapproval bill. One suit was filed by the City of New York, two hospital associations, one hospital, and two unions representing health care employees, all of which alleged financial injuries from a rescission. The other suit was filed by the Snake River Farmers' Association of Idaho potato growers.[59] District court judge Thomas Hogan consolidated the cases and ruled against item veto on presentment grounds, saying it was "curious" that the defendants said the law was simply an expanded version of existing presidential powers. "The laws . . . that emerged after the Line Item Veto are not the same laws that proceeded through the legislative process, as required. . . . Once a bill becomes law, it can only be repealed or amended through another, independent legislative enactment, which itself must conform with the requirements of Article I. Any recessions must be agreed upon by a majority of both Houses of Congress."[60]

On another expedited appeal to the Supreme Court, this time agreeing with the district court, Justice Stevens wrote the majority opinion, joined by Chief Justice Rehnquist, and Justices Souter, Thomas, and Ginsburg, with Kennedy in part. Relying on *INS v. Chadha*, Stevens said there are two main differences between the president's traditional veto power and the item veto. First, a traditional return of a bill takes place before it becomes law. Second, the traditional veto entails an entire bill and the item veto only a part. On the issue of whether the new process is merely an extension of traditional presidential impoundment power, Stevens adds that impoundment does not allow the president to change the text of the law, unlike the current action. Stevens added the majority did not act "lightly" nor judge the "wisdom" of the law; nor was it is necessary to weigh in on the broader question of how the law impacted balance of power between the branches. Only a constitutional amendment could save the item veto.[61]

Justice Scalia filed a part-concurring and part-dissenting opinion, which Justices O'Connor and Breyer joined in part. He argued that presentment was satisfied prior to the president's use of the item veto. Acknowledging the gravity of the delegation of power issue, Scalia said the extent of power shift was not sufficient to strike on these grounds. He especially disagreed with Stevens on the technical nature of the item veto: "Insofar as the degree of political, 'law-making' power conferred upon the Executive is concerned, there is not a dime's worth of difference between Congress's authorizing the President to *cancel* a spending item, and Congress's authorizing money to be spent on a particular item at the President's discretion. And the latter has been done since the Founding of the Nation."[62]

Justice Breyer's dissent emphasized the disapproval process built into the law and said, unlike traditional delegation of power controversies, in this case the recipient is an elected figure—the president—who will be judged (or his party's successor) for his actions by voters. "I recognize that the Act before us is novel. In a sense, it skirts a constitutional edge. But that edge has to do with means, not ends. . . . They represent an experiment that may, or may not, help representative government work better. The Constitution, in my view, authorizes Congress and the President to try novel methods in this way."[63]

Although short-lived, this "experiment" showcased two sides of Congress that are often in tension: a drive to protect constituents and, counterintuitively, a drive to shed institutional power. First, while the Line Item Veto Act was still in effect, President Clinton did successfully rescind around $600 million (a tiny fraction of total appropriations) but Congress fought to override additional cuts. In 1997, for example, Congress disapproved of Clinton's canceling a $290 million military construction package and then overrode the president's veto of the disapproval. Potentially facing similar opposition, the administration backed away from a separate veto threat on a federal retirement system appropriation.[64] Second, in an echo of the GRH reboot after *Bowsher*, congressional committees tried twice (but ultimately unsuccessfully) to pass new versions of the item veto power to give more budget power to the next two presidents. These moments once again exposed somewhat curious institutional compulsions to shed power to the president—even during downturns in presidential popularity (George W. Bush in 2006) and under conditions of divided government (Barack Obama in 2012).[65]

Until a new reform passes, the branches must live with the simple-majority-friendly rescission processes established in 1974. Ironically, since the Line Item Veto Act's demise, members have been far more active in using rescission than the presidents.[66] In fact, despite the anti-Congress frenzy that drove the budget reforms in the 1980s and 1990s, there was never any evidence that presidents were more fiscally responsible in their own budget proposals.[67]

Unlike these types of policy-heavy process controversies, the Senate filibuster is not about which branch sees the national interest more clearly. Rather, it is about the virtues and vices of supermajority rules—on almost any policy topic that may come to the floor of the Senate.

Common Cause v. Biden (2012)

The filibuster and other dilatory legislative processes have a long and controversial history in both chambers of Congress. In early years, the "previous question" motion allowed simple majorities to cut off debate. The Senate dropped that rule in 1806, but the first filibuster did not occur there until 1837. In 1890, House Speaker Thomas Reed ordered a series of rules that curbed dilatory tactics. In 1917, under pressure from President Woodrow Wilson, the Senate adopted a rule that set debate cloture with two-thirds (cloture rules did not exist before). Only fifty-eight cloture motions were recorded in the Senate from 1917 through 1969. In 1975, cloture was lowered to three-fifths of members, present or not (sixty senators). But filibusters and cloture motions were still not routine until the 21st century, when both parties increased their use. The record of cloture motions, votes, and successful outcomes ticked steadily upward through the 1970s, 1980s, and 1990s, from the single digits to reaching a peak in the 113th Congress (2013–2014) of 253 cloture motions filed, 218 votes on cloture, and cloture invoked 187 times.[68]

In addition to the policy and partisan dimensions of these actions, the use of the filibuster is constitutionally controversial because it creates an effective supermajority hurdle for legislation to reach the White House. The most recent member lawsuit on legislative processes challenged the Senate's use of the filibuster in 2010 and targeted two standing Senate Rules: XXII and V. Rule XXII requires sixty votes (three-fifths) on motions to proceed or close debate on bills and presidential nominations. This rule also demands sixty-seven votes (two-thirds) to proceed with or close debate on proposed changes to Senate rules. Rule V prevents the Senate from amending rules by majority vote.[69] The filibuster lawsuit invoked *United States v. Ballin* (1892) to argue that while the Senate is free to make its own rules, the rules cannot conflict with other parts of the Constitution.[70]

The plaintiffs in this case focused on two pieces of legislation that passed the Democratic House, and President Obama promised to sign them. Even though Democrats held a majority in the Senate as well, they did not meet the sixty-vote threshold to sustain cloture against Republican filibusters. The Development, Relief and Education for Alien Minors Act (DREAM Act) was a set of immigration reforms that would protect illegal immigrants brought to the United States as children from detention and deportation. It passed the House and had fifty-five committed senators.[71] Another bill passed by the House and stopped by a Republican filibuster was the Democracy Is Strengthened by Casting Light on Spending in Elections Act (DISCLOSE Act), a campaign finance reform measure, which was supported by fifty-nine senators.[72] In the lawsuit, four House members and several private plaintiffs (potential "Dreamers" and private group Common Cause) asserted policy and electoral arguments against the filibuster not only because they supported bills that had majorities of committed votes in the Senate, but their own elections could be harmed by these actions.

The main point of contention was whether the Constitution's text implicitly calls for majority rule in regular legislative business, and supermajorities only as indicated. The complaint further argued that the filibuster harms all three branches because the Senate's use of filibusters and other dilatory tactics creates the opportunity for delays and withdrawals of executive and judicial nominations. The plaintiffs asserted that the filibuster is far more pernicious to the Constitution than GRH, the legislative veto, and item veto, all of which were overturned in prior Supreme Court decisions (*Chadha*, *Bowsher*, and *Clinton*). In their motion to dismiss, defendants in the Senate (outside of Biden, who was named due to his title as President of the Senate) drew upon Senate history and traditions, as well as previous cases filed and dismissed against the filibuster.[73] They invoked standing, the political question doctrine, and the Constitution's "speech and debate" clause (Art. I, Sec. 6, Cl. 1), which the defendants said restricts judicial interference with routine legislative matters.

Federal judge Emmet Sullivan largely agreed with the defendants in his memorandum. He acknowledged the controversy caused by the filibuster and the power of even threatening such action. But Sullivan rejected the plaintiffs' standing and claim of injury. Also, under the political question doctrine, he argued judicial interference would demonstrate a "lack of respect for the Senate as a coordinate branch of government. . . . While the House Members have presented a unique posture, the Court is not persuaded that their alleged injury—vote nullification—falls into a narrow exception enunciated by the Supreme Court in *Raines v. Byrd*. . . . The Court is firmly convinced that to intrude into this area would offend the separation of powers on which the Constitution rests. Nowhere does the Constitution contain express requirements regarding the proper length of, or method for, the Senate to debate proposed legislation."[74]

On appeal, DC circuit judges Henderson, Randolph, and Williams agreed with the district court. The opinion by Judge Randolph begins by acknowledging that the contemporary filibuster is not necessarily a physical act of speech, but a procedural action that does not actually bring the chamber to a halt. The Senate's procedures allow for parallel legislative tracks in which business continues on certain bills, while others are "filibustered." Randolph also implied that the contemporary lack of "physical commitment" may be part of the common use of the filibuster. The appellate court also took issue with the target of the litigation. Although President of the Senate Joseph Biden was the defendant, it was the senators themselves who both filibustered and failed to invoke cloture successfully.

"What defeated the DREAM and DISCLOSE bills was legislative action, activity typically considered at the heart of the Speech or Debate Clause. . . . In short, Common Cause's alleged injury was caused not by any of the defendants, but by an 'absent third party'—the Senate itself."[75]

An attorney involved in the filibuster case said their arguments were much stronger than those presented in *Skaggs v. Carle*. The *Skaggs* case "was not wrongly decided" as there was a majority-based backup in the form of committee discharge petitions, as well as the fact (pointed out by the court in *Skaggs*) that the majority can amend or suspend House rules. Neither of these points is true in the Senate. In addition, the attorney said, the federal courts ignored at least three Supreme Court cases that rejected the political question doctrine to examine various state and national internal processes. It seems court deference (for any institutional reason) on Article I, Section 7, is harder to overcome than on Section 8.[76] Meanwhile, citing the filibuster and other delays, President Obama's administration issued a series of executive actions to, in effect, put the DREAM Act into place. These actions by President Obama, and President Trump's attempts to undo them, triggered additional litigation that is still ongoing.[77]

Meanwhile, over the past five years, the Senate filibuster has been dramatically curtailed by recent majority leaders when the White House was held by the same party and frustrated by minority party senators that prevented executive branch and judicial nominations from going forwards. There is no simple-majority mechanism for senators on their own to easily dismantle filibuster rules; it is the majority leaders who have utilized the "nuclear option," so dubbed because Senate minority protections—and existing institutional culture—would be destroyed and unlikely to return. Filibusters were indeed eliminated for executive branch and lower federal court judge nominations under Harry Reid (D-NV) in 2013 and then again regarding Supreme Court justices under Mitch McConnell (R-KY) in 2017. These changes were driven by partisan and presidential pressure, not to preserve majority rule for its own sake. Putting aside the short- and long-term consequences of these actions, elected politicians were responsible for changing the Senate's norms. If the legislative filibuster is jettisoned too, the Senate would become a majority-friendly institution, like the House—but by choice, not due to the decision of federal judges.[78]

As the framers of the Constitution were keenly aware, processes and rules influence legislative outcomes. The Constitution explicitly requires supermajorities for the House and/or Senate to make certain decisions especially difficult and, therefore, rare (explained in *Federalist* 49, 58, and 73). Examples include Senate removal of a president from office after House impeachment (Article I, Section 3), expelling a member of Congress (Article I, Section 5), presidential veto overrides (Article I, Section 7), Senate approval of treaties (Article II, Section 2), and constitutional amendment proposals to go to states (Article V), all of which require a two-thirds vote in one or both chambers. As this chapter shows, federal courts have said additional internal rules changes requiring supermajorities for action are also within Congress's institutional rights.

In recent decades, partisan conflict within Congress and between the branches has received a lot of attention, while two types of more complex, ongoing institutional dysfunction lurk below the surface. One type of deeper dysfunction is highlighted here and occurs when members and leaders of Congress repeatedly attack their own branch's prerogatives across several policy fronts by imposing or increasingly utilizing a variety of legislative process obstacles. The five cases in this chapter demonstrate that, win or lose, member-plaintiffs ask legitimate constitutional questions when they challenge such actions in federal lawsuits. But these questions can and should be answered by the members in their respective institutions. Federal judges cannot single-handedly bring the separation of powers system into better balance, even when they rule for the plaintiffs. Institutionally protective members must also convince their colleagues not to diminish congressional authority in the first place.

Members have also sued, with less success, to challenge presidential unilateralism spanning Richard Nixon to Donald Trump. Unlike the legislative process cases, these conflicts involve actions by presidents without explicit prior or even retroactive authority by majorities. A recently settled House-sanctioned lawsuit against a spending provision in the 2010 Patient Protection and Affordable Care Act surprised many observers by clearing district courts on procedural and merit grounds.[79] It is still true that the federal court system cannot provide the institutional ambition that *Federalist* 51 assumed would occur naturally within the House and Senate. But there is a difference between alleged executive usurpation of power and self-inflicted institutional wounds. Sometimes it seems all three branches are working against Congress.

Part 3

MORE EXECUTIVE UNILATERALISM

SILENCE IS CONSENT
FOR THE MODERN PRESIDENCY

President Donald Trump's first executive order after taking office in 2017 temporarily banned travel to the United States from several Muslim-majority nations that he deemed security risks. The Immigration and Nationality Act (INA) of 1952 gave the president power to "suspend the entry of all aliens or any class of aliens" when he "finds" that their entry "would be detrimental to the interests of the United States." An amendment to the law passed by Congress in 1965 changed some immigration quotas and added anti-discriminatory language, but kept this vast delegation of power. Citing the law, the Supreme Court upheld the order in a 5–4 vote. The majority's opinion did not argue that such a power is inherent to the presidency in the Constitution. The basis was the INA, which "exudes deference to the President in every clause."[1] Trump's other controversial orders on tariffs, environmental regulation, and the declaration of a national emergency to build a southern border wall also utilized similarly broad authorizations passed decades ago. After (or while) fighting the president in court, opponents of these actions could turn to Congress to tighten the laws. Another alternative is to elect a new president who will use executive branch powers just as robustly, but in a different policy and partisan direction.

Federal courts are not the most effective venue to rebalance power between the executive and legislative branches, despite getting pulled into this position on a host of policy issues regularly. In these cases, judges must trace presidential power to one of only two sources of authority: the Constitution and/or acts of Congress. If neither supports the challenged actions, via enumerated or implied powers, presidents will lose in court. But court rebukes of presidents are rare, as when the Supreme Court said that President Harry Truman could not order his secretary of commerce to seize and run privately owned American steel mills in the midst of a labor dispute that could impact wartime production. The Court's majority deferred to Congress, which had considered and rejected this type of presidential power before Truman's action.

Part 3 of this book makes two main points on executive branch unilateralism when challenged in court. First, private litigants are often more successful than member-plaintiffs because private plaintiffs can more easily gain standing through proven injuries from the action at issue. Second, in both types of cases, the court looks to Congress for signs of approval or disapproval. The Supreme Court has never endorsed the "inherent powers" theory of the presidency. Rather, time and again, the Court says Congress holds the keys to presidential power by authorizing and/or disapproving its use. The latter argument is more controversial, however, because it conflates congressional silence or division with consent. However, if Congress did lodge its disapproval in new law, it would probably be vetoed by the president, thus requiring a two-thirds majority to override. Even without citing controversial theories, federal courts do tip the scales when they put the entire burden on Congress to stop an action rather than on the executive branch to wait for authorization in the first place.

In different ways, the federal legislature and judiciary enable imbalanced power as modern presidents of both parties test constitutional boundaries for policy leadership. President Barack Obama said as much in 2014: "Some [economic measures] require Congressional action, and I'm eager to work with all of you. But America does not stand still—and neither will I. So wherever and whenever I can take steps without legislation to expand opportunity for more American families, that's what I'm going to do."[2] Congress often cries foul in these moments, but members and leaders do not often follow through to press for their policy preferences by using and defending institutional power. Under both unified and divided government, congressional members and leaders bemoan presidential overreach and respond with finger wagging and attempting oversight, rather than consistently using individual, committee, and chamber power to at least co-lead national public policy. Again and again, for a variety of reasons, presidential unilateralism is often supported by all branches through overt approval or tepid opposition, and often driven by electoral and partisan motivations either way.

Constitutional Development and Private Litigation

The Constitution does not sketch out the powers assigned to all branches to the same degree, with many institutional processes and shared authorities purposefully left open by the framers. But there is a set of founding assumptions within these arrangements: officeholders are obliged to respect the Constitution (seen in their oaths of office), and each branch would want to protect its own prerogatives through checks and balances animated by different electoral orientations and timelines. *Federalist* 51 says each office holder may use constitutional "means" to advance personal motives (power) and policy (government outcomes). However, over the twentieth and twenty-first centuries, we have seen the presidency continue to grow, with the support of Congress because "political pressures can sometimes overwhelm the natural tendency of elected officials to fight to protect the constitutional prerogatives of their office."[3]

The framers also designed the executive branch to be more unified and hierarchical than the other branches, which structured "energy" to support the president in ways that could never be possible in the more politically diverse and fragmented legislature and judiciary. This energy was not used consistently in U.S. history to eclipse Congress until the 20th century. Before then, presidential overstepping often "triggered a response by the legislative branch, determined to regain control."[4] Most pre-modern presidents demonstrated a "whiggish" bent, largely preferring congressional primacy. Abraham Lincoln alone articulated the "prerogative" style of going outside existing law and constitutional walls in the existential crisis of the Civil War. A handful of other presidents before and after Lincoln attempted to push constitutional boundaries less successfully. Not until Theodore Roosevelt, Woodrow Wilson, Franklin Roosevelt, and Truman did presidents articulate a modern view that advocated permanent presidential leadership spanning domestic and foreign policy, with Congress as an irritating afterthought. These new executive theories were helped by a president-centered popular and media culture, congressional hyperpartisanship, and aggressive executive branch lawyers.[5]

In the twenty-first century, George W. Bush revived a controversial argument that said the president had "inherent" power as a "unitary" institution, especially on national security after 9/11. These phases meant that the president could do what he pleased, essentially, with minimal interference from Congress and the courts. This controversy occupied scholars and legal pundits for years.[6] Historically judicial decisions on executive power rarely invoke this constitutional theory to rule for presidents. One exception to this rule concerned the issue of which branch had the right to fire executive branch officials. This constitutional silence inspired decades of wrangling between all three branches on the limits of a "unitary" executive.

Removal Power (1926–1935)

The Constitution explains the two-step executive branch appointment process, but says nothing about whether, how, or why such appointees can be removed. This question did not get attention at the constitutional convention, despite a clear record of debate over the appointment power.[7] The issue arose immediately in the first Congress as the House and Senate authorized the creation of a Department of Foreign Affairs. Even members of the constitutional convention who were then involved in this interpretation question fell into different camps, unable to provide a unified answer about what the Constitution intended. Some former constitutional delegates invoked *Federalist* 77, where Hamilton wrote, "The consent of [the Senate] would be necessary to displace as well as to appoint."[8] During George Washington's administration, the House of Representatives voted 29–22 in favor of excluding the Senate from the removal decision. The Senate was equally divided on the question, leading Vice President John Adams to break the tie in the Senate, giving Washington the power to remove cabinet secretaries.[9]

Between this controversy and the Supreme Court's first major ruling on removal over a century later, there were two landmark political clashes over removal, among many minor skirmishes. First, Andrew Jackson was censured by the Senate (expunged four years later) for firing the treasury secretary in 1833 for noncompliance with Jackson's order to remove U.S. deposits from the national bank, as well as for not turning over requested material to the Senate on the issue.[10] Second, with the 1867 Tenure of Office Act, Congress tried to prevent President Andrew Johnson from firing anyone requiring Senate confirmation for appointment. The Senate majority wanted to protect the secretaries of state, treasury, war, navy, interior, the postmaster general, and attorney general from Johnson's meddling. In particular, Secretary of War Edwin M. Stanton was appointed to the position by Lincoln and ultimately opposed much of Johnson's policy program. His suspension and firing was one impetus for Johnson's impeachment (Stanton refused to leave office pending a Senate vote on the issue and then resigned three months after the firing, in May 1868). These interbranch fights on removal continued through Ulysses S. Grant's and Grover Cleveland's tenures. Congress ultimately repealed the Tenure of Office Act in 1887.[11]

A new version of this question came to the Supreme Court under President Woodrow Wilson. In 1876, Congress and President Grant enacted a law that said three classes of postmasters "shall be appointed and may be removed by the President with the advice and consent of the Senate." In those days, the "postmaster of a town was one of the plum patronage positions, a reward for party loyalty and a job one could expect to hold for only as long as one's party or faction remained in power."[12] Frank Myers was appointed by Democratic president Wilson in 1917 as a first-class postmaster in Oregon. Around three years into the term, Wilson requested his resignation as Myers had become repeatedly embroiled in local politics, and then fired him when he refused to step down. Myers sued for the lost salary that he would have been paid through the full term, arguing that the Senate had not approved of his removal. The lower court of claims tried to avoid the issue by saying Myers waited too long to sue. When appealing to the Supreme Court, Myers's estate continued the case after his death and ultimately lost in 1926.[13]

The case provoked the justices to look at constitutional convention notes on the removal power. The chief justice, former President William Howard Taft, whom Wilson had defeated in 1912, wrote a majority opinion joined by four other Republican-appointed justices. In dissent were James McReynolds and Louis Brandeis, both Wilson appointees, and Oliver Wendell Holmes Jr. Taft, who had previously expressed a limited view of presidential power during and immediately after his own time in office, offered a broad defense of presidential removal. He said it was the framers' intention to avoid the weaknesses of the Articles of Confederation through robust executive power that should not be "blended" with legislative power and that "the power of removal is incident to the power of appointment, not to the power of advising and consenting to appointment."[14] The majority invoked "unitary" theory to say the 1876 law was unconstitutional, as well as the Tenure of Office Act of 1867, had it not been already been repealed. Justice Holmes's dissent said "the duty of the President to see that the laws be executed is a duty that does not go beyond the laws or require him to achieve more than Congress sees fit to leave within his power."[15] Justice Brandeis concluded, "The purpose [of separation of powers] was not to avoid friction but, by means of the inevitable friction incident to the distribution of the governmental powers among three departments, to save the people from autocracy."[16] These removal arguments are not necessarily significant for their own sake, but rather as "proxy debates" on constitutional interpretations of presidential power.[17]

These questions came back to the court within a decade of the *Myers v. United States* decision. One of the federal agencies created during Wilson's presidency was the Federal Trade Commission, established in 1917. The commission had five members and the law allowed no more than three at a time from the same party. Any of them could be removed by the president for cause, such as "inefficiency, neglect of duty, or malfeasance in office."[18] As in contemporary times, there was a tension between the business community and the regulators on the commission. Republican president Calvin Coolidge appointed William E. Humphrey, a defender of business. President Herbert Hoover, also a Republican, appointed Humphrey to a second term, and he was confirmed in 1931. In Franklin Roosevelt's first year in office, two vacancies allowed him to appoint pro-regulation commissioners, who joined the remaining three (a moderate Republican, a Democrat, and Humphrey). FDR asked Humphrey for his resignation and was refused, so the president fired him in October 1933. Like Myers, Humphrey sued for his back salary and the case continued after his death later in the year.

The court of claims asked the Supreme Court to clarify two questions: Did the establishing act limit dismissals to cause, as specified above? If yes, were such limits on presidential power constitutionally permissible? The Supreme Court answered "yes" and "yes." The Supreme Court's unanimous decision against FDR was a surprise to the administration, which considered the case a "slam dunk" in light of *Myers*.[19] Justice George Sutherland wrote the opinion, which emphasized Congress's intent to minimize presidential influence through set terms and partisan balance. "We conclude that the intent of the act is to limit the executive power of removal to the causes enumerated, the existence of none of which is claimed here."[20] The majority did not repudiate *Myers*, saying instead that "the office of a postmaster is so essentially unlike the office now involved that the decision in the *Myers* case cannot be accepted as controlling our decision here."[21] The issue is the "character of the office." The postmaster, he said, is a purely executive function, whereas Federal Trade Commission commissioners had quasi-legislative and judicial functions. Further, these ends are purposefully separate from executive power by design. But he acknowledged the two decisions together stand uneasily as precedent.[22] Today, the *Humphrey's Executor v. United States* precedent is still in effect and has been used as recently as 2018 as a test for Supreme Court nominees' views of executive branch power.[23]

Steel Seizure Landmark (1952)

Like the appointment and removal power, executive orders are specific institutional actions that support a president's broader policy goals. A renewed interest in executive orders over the past two decades is part of a scholarly pivot to examining formal executive power. Some scholars use executive order as a generic term that includes such actions as Washington's Neutrality Proclamation and Lincoln's Emancipation Proclamation. According to some counts, around 15 percent of executive orders are "significant policy changes."[24] These orders and proclamations can be legitimate and powerful tools for presidents to carry out their interpretation of the Constitution and existing law through branch agencies and offices. Executive orders and proclamations should be published in the *Federal Register*. Sometimes, agency memoranda substitute for official orders, as seen in the immigration-related prosecutorial discretion memos issues by Obama's Department of Homeland Security, which faced protracted litigation from states.[25] In whatever form, direct executive actions must have congressional or constitutional authorization, but neither need be explicit. Judicial scrutiny is not automatic, but when federal courts hear these cases, precedent leans toward the executive branch. The Steel Seizure Case is an exception, but its famous rebuke of presidential authority has softened with time.

This separation of powers story began with a private domestic steel production labor dispute in December 1951. After two federal offices tried to intervene without coming to a settlement, on April 4, 1952, the affected unions called for a strike effective April 9. President Truman, alarmed at the potential war-related effects of an interruption to steel manufacturing, issued Executive Order 10340—Directing the Secretary of Commerce to Take Possession of and Operate the Plants and Facilities of Certain Steel Companies, on April 8.[26] In his order, Truman cited the ongoing Korean War as a "national emergency" that related directly to the breakdown of collective bargaining talks between the steelworkers' union and owners.

On April 9, the day after the order was issued, members of the House rose to "congratulate" the president on his order. Representative John McCormack (D-MA), later Speaker of the House, said Truman used his "inherent executive powers vested in the President under the Constitution, acting during an emergency, and for the common welfare." Truman had made a "clear case" and public opinion was "overwhelmingly in favor" of the action.[27] In the Senate, some Republicans called for an investigation and others debated the order's relationship to broader wartime presidential power in the shadow of World War II. Some Republicans wondered aloud if Democrats would remember their support of Truman when a Republican was in the White House.[28]

Steel companies filed suit immediately to prevent Secretary of Commerce Charles W. Sawyer's takeover of the mills. The case went first to two district courts. In the first, district judge Alexander Holzoff disagreed with the Department of Justice's wide interpretation of "executive power" in times of "national emergency," saying it meant something more narrow—"the power to execute statutes." Judge Holtzoff dismissed the request, assuming the companies would pursue their Fifth Amendment "takings" argument to the court of claims or as a civil suit in district court.[29] The next district judge to hear the case was David A. Pine, who issued an injunction against the takeover, rejecting the Department of Justice's "inherent, implied, or residual" presidential emergency powers argument, as well as the government's argument that the president was "accountable to the country," not the judiciary, which only had the power to determine just compensation under eminent domain.[30] At the end of April 1952, Judge Pine ruled with the plaintiffs in a strongly worded opinion. "There is no express grant of power in the Constitution authorizing the President to direct this seizure. There is no grant of power from which it reasonably can be implied. There is no enactment of Congress authorizing it. On what, then, does defendant rely to sustain his acts?"[31] The temporary injunction was stayed by the DC circuit court of appeals (sitting en banc), and the Supreme Court heard the case soon after.

At the Supreme Court, Truman lost 6–3, with several concurring opinions. Justice Hugo Black wrote for the majority, with Felix Frankfurter, William O. Douglas, Robert Jackson, Harold Burton, and Tom Clark submitting concurrences. Stanley Reed, Fred Vinson, and Sherman Minton were the dissenters. Justice Black first summarized the events and noted that Congress took no formal actions between Truman's messages on April 9 and 21. Black also noted that an amendment authorizing such power was rejected during consideration of the Taft-Hartley Act of 1947.[32] Then, he rejected the three main provisions of the government's argument about Article II, saying authority is not to be found in the executive power, take care, or commander-in-chief provisions. Black concluded by saying, "The Founders of this Nation entrusted the lawmaking power to Congress alone in both good and bad times. It would do no good to recall the historical events, the fears of power, and the hopes for freedom that lay behind their choice. Such a review would but confirm our holding that this seizure order cannot stand."[33]

Justice Frankfurter began his concurrence by hinting that Justice Black's opinion lacked theoretical nuance and sufficient appreciation for separation of powers flexibility. After reviewing the legislative history of the Taft-Hartley Act, he concluded, "To find authority so explicitly withheld is not merely to disregard in a particular instance the clear will of Congress. It is to disrespect the whole legislative process and the constitutional division of authority between President and Congress."[34] Frankfurter continued, "It is not a pleasant judicial duty to find that the President has exceeded his powers, and still less so when his purposes were dictated by concern for the Nation's wellbeing, in the assured conviction that he acted to avert danger."[35]

Justice Douglas likewise separated the potential exigency of the situation from the question of the president's constitutional authority. While acknowledging the deliberate and plodding pace of legislative processes, he said, "The emergency did not create power; it merely marked an occasion when power should be exercised. And the fact that it was necessary that measures be taken to keep steel in production does not mean that the President, rather than the Congress, had the constitutional authority to act."[36] He expressed worry about Truman's precedent. "We pay a price for our system of checks and balances, for the distribution of power among the three branches of government. It is a price that today may seem exorbitant to many. Today, a kindly President uses the seizure power to effect a wage increase and to keep the steel furnaces in production. Yet tomorrow, another President might use the same power to prevent a wage increase, to curb trade unionists, to regiment labor as oppressively as industry thinks it has been regimented by this seizure."[37]

Justice Jackson's landmark concurrence began with a philosophical reflection on his own experience with presidential power, having served as solicitor general and attorney general under Franklin Roosevelt from 1938–1941, immediately prior to his appointment to the Supreme Court. Jackson's main point was that "presidential powers are not fixed but fluctuate depending upon their disjunction or conjunction with those of Congress."[38] Jackson then offered an admittedly over-simplified (but still often cited) tripartite analysis of presidential power:

> 1. When the president acts pursuant to an express or implied authorization of Congress, his authority is at its maximum, for it includes all that he possesses in his own right plus all that Congress can delegate. In these circumstances, and in these only, may he be said (for what it may be worth) to personify the federal sovereignty. If his act is held unconstitutional under these circumstances, it usually means that the Federal Government, as an undivided whole, lacks power. A seizure executed by the President pursuant to an Act of Congress would be supported by the strongest of presumptions and the widest latitude of judicial interpretation, and the burden of persuasion would rest heavily upon any who might attack it.

> 2. When the President acts in absence of either a congressional grant or denial of authority, he can only rely upon his own independent powers, but there is a zone of twilight in which he and Congress may have concurrent authority, or in which its distribution is uncertain. Therefore, congressional inertia, indifference or quiescence may sometimes, at least, as a practical matter, enable, if not invite, measures on independent presidential responsibility. In this area, any actual test of power is likely to depend on the imperatives of events and contemporary imponderables, rather than on abstract theories of law.

> 3. When the President takes measures incompatible with the expressed or implied will of Congress, his power is at its lowest ebb, for then he can rely only upon his own constitutional powers minus any constitutional powers of Congress over the matter. Courts can sustain exclusive presidential control in such a case only by disabling the Congress from acting upon the subject. Presidential claim to a power at once so conclusive and preclusive must be scrutinized with caution, for what is at stake is the equilibrium established by our constitutional system.[39]

Jackson placed the seizure in the third category, saying it went against Taft-Hartley. Presidential power was therefore at lowest ebb; Truman needed to find some constitutional basis to show the statutory restriction was impermissible. Jackson added that the history of congressional delegation of domestic economic power in wartime includes over 100 instances, and there was no doubt that Congress could do the same here. Still, "the claim of inherent and unrestricted presidential powers has long been a persuasive dialectical weapon in political controversy."[40]

The three dissenters (Chief Justice Vinson and Justices Reed and Minton) filed one opinion. They detailed U.S. action in Korea and related defense procurement statutes, as well as the labor-management impasse. Next, they discussed the key differences between Articles I and II in the Constitution, quoting the need for "energy in the executive" from *Federalist* 70. They also said that, in this case, President Truman had no intention of "unlimited executive power. . . . History bears out the genius of the Founding Fathers, who created a Government subject to law but not left subject to inertia when vigor and initiative are required."[41] Despite these objections by the dissenters, and the analysis of Justice Black's opinion and the other concurrences, Justice Jackson's framework has become the benchmark of Supreme Court analysis in separation of powers, although the type of case is still rare in courts.

One lesson from *Youngstown Sheet & Tube Co. v. Sawyer* is that policy actions by the executive branch considered "unilateral" must be separated into "implied" and "inherent" arguments. Implied power stems from a prior grant of authority while inherent power arguably stems from the Constitution's structure of the office. Executive agreements are a related area of implied foreign policy that presidents argue are often carrying out existing treaties and legislation previously approved by the Senate and/or Congress. Contemporary arguments about inherent authority come in post-9/11 legal controversies (discussed below), but they are not novel. One example is the U.S. recognition of Soviet Russia in 1933 following the 1917 Russian Revolution. The coincident Litvinov Assignment led to two landmark cases that approved executive actions in international relations, even those not formally ratified as treaties by the Senate or authorized by Congress as a whole. The issue in both cases included private claims, including takings under the Fifth Amendment.[42]

In *United States v. Belmont* (1937), a unanimous Supreme Court said an agreement entered into by the president under his own authority between the United States and Soviet Union allowed the former to assist the latter's seizure of assets held in a New York bank on behalf of a private Russian company that had been nationalized by the Soviets. The company fought the seizure through the protection of U.S. banking laws. The Court said that "governmental power over external affairs is not distributed, but is vested exclusively in the national government. And in respect of what was done here, the Executive had authority to speak as the sole organ of that government. The assignment and the agreements in connection therewith did not . . . require the advice and consent of the Senate."[43]

The Supreme Court affirmed this position in a subsequent case, *United States v. Pink*, where Justice Douglas offered an even more expansive reading of presidential power to negotiate and implement policy related to the same recognition agreement. "The powers of the President in the conduct of foreign relations included the power, without consent of the Senate, to determine the public policy of the United States with respect to the Russian nationalization decrees. . . . Objections . . . are to be addressed to the political department, and not to the courts."[44] But, fifteen years later, the Supreme Court also held that executive agreements could not confer power "on the Congress, or on any other branch of Government, which is free from the restraints of the Constitution."[45]

Explicit restraints proved hard to find in the case discussed next, *Dames & Moore v. Regan*, which became a broad pro-presidency landmark. The Supreme Court said, "We have in the past found and do today find Justice Jackson's classification of executive actions into three general categories analytically useful,"[46] but this case also reimagined Jackson's categories in a way that proved to be more helpful to presidents than he may have intended.

Dames & Moore v. Regan (1981)

In November 1979, President Jimmy Carter interpreted the International Emergency Economic Powers Act (IEEPA) to declare a national emergency in response to the Iranian hostage crisis and ordered the Treasury secretary to freeze and further regulate Iranian assets in the United States, including suspension of a variety of legal processes. To implement the Algerian Declaration release agreement, on January 19, 1981, Carter signed ten related executive orders to, among other things, terminate all ongoing private legal proceedings against Iran, nullify all attachments and liens on Iranian property, repatriate $8 billion in Iranian assets attached to court claims, and redirect lingering litigation between U.S. nationals and Iran to binding arbitration in the Iran-U.S. Claim Tribunal. The funds and hostages were released by both countries on January 20, which was President Ronald Reagan's Inauguration Day. President Reagan issued an executive order ratifying Carter's suspensions of claims in early February.[47] In pursuit of owed funds by the Atomic Energy Organization of Iran, U.S. firm Dames & Moore challenged new Treasury secretary Donald Regan's enforcement of Carter's 1981 executive orders and release agreement. This firm, and others, brought cases under the Foreign Sovereignty Immunities Act of 1976.

Citing conflicting lower court rulings and the U.S. government's fear that it could be held in breach of the agreement, Justice William Rehnquist wrote the relatively short, expedited 8–1 decision.[48] The case was argued on June 24, 1981, and decided on July 2. Justice Rehnquist began his opinion by saying the "questions presented by this case touch fundamentally upon the manner in which our Republic is to be governed," but then explained the narrowness of the ruling. "Perhaps it is because it is so difficult to reconcile the foregoing definition of Art. III judicial power with the broad range of vitally important day-to-day questions regularly decided by Congress or the Executive, without either challenge or interference by the Judiciary, that the decisions of the Court in this area have been rare, episodic, and afford little precedential value for subsequent cases."[49] But the case's expansive reading of presidential authority and its promotion of the controversial issue of congressional "acquiescence" combined to create an important precedent that impacted later cases.[50]

Using Justice Jackson's tripartite framework, Rehnquist first concluded that the nullification of attachments and transfer of Iranian assets was within the "plain language" of the IEEPA authorization, meaning the first category of presidential power, and provided some court precedent for this interpretation. At the same time, Rehnquist acknowledged evidence that Congress did not intend the law to give these specific nullification powers while still viewing this part of the executive action within Jackson's first category of authorization.[51] More controversial was the Court's argument upholding suspension of claims portion of the opinion. Rehnquist said the support was not directly authorized by the IEEPA, so the second "zone of twilight" category was more appropriate. He cited "the looser sense of indicating congressional acceptance of a broad scope for executive action in circumstances such as those presented in this case."[52] The Court did not cite any prior situations that were similar to these specific actions. "We conclude that the President was authorized to suspend pending claims pursuant to Executive Order No. 12294. . . . In light of the fact that Congress may be considered to have consented to the President's action in suspending claims, we cannot say that action exceeded the President's powers. . . . Just as importantly, Congress has not disapproved of the action taken here. Though Congress has held hearings on the Iranian Agreement itself, Congress has not enacted legislation, or even passed a resolution, indicating its displeasure with the Agreement. . . . Quite the contrary, the relevant Senate Committee has stated that the establishment of the Tribunal is 'of vital importance to the United States.' We are thus clearly not confronted with a situation in which Congress has in some way resisted the exercise of Presidential authority."[53]

In this portion of the opinion, Rehnquist also drew upon three cases for precedent, which together argued that *absence of disapproval by Congress* is a constitutional standard, echoing the outcome of war powers cases filed by members of Congress in part 1 of this book.[54] Therefore, he upheld a sweeping and unprecedented presidential power to terminate and transfer certain legal proceedings from U.S. courts. Rehnquist effectively promoted a category-two claim to category one, through an implied delegation of power. As Harold Hongju Koh notes, "By so holding, [Rehnquist] followed the dissenting view in *Youngstown*, which had converted legislative silence into consent, thereby delegating to the president authority that Congress itself had arguably withheld."[55] In a somewhat tortured conclusion, the Court denied the takings argument by *Dames & Moore* as not ripe for review, but said the firm could still pursue its legal argument about the suspension through the court of claims under the Tucker Act.

Legal scholarship after the case emphasized the pragmatic needs of the moment and the unlikelihood of the Supreme Court's unraveling a sensitive executive agreement so soon after the fact. If the Court had invalidated these claims months later, the order "could have done considerable damage to the President's ability to deal with sovereign nations."[56] However, this deference has been folded into other landmark precedents. According to Rebecca D'Arcy, "The result has been the codification of a distorted understanding of congressional delegation and a limitless field of executive action in the context of a unilaterally proclaimed 'national emergency.'"[57] If any congressional act can be linked, even tangentially, by the executive branch or the courts, then it appears to be safe. Koh argues that the immediate context of the *Dames* decision is understandable within the atmosphere of public relief that the hostage crisis was over. "Yet by finding legislative 'approval' when Congress had given none, Rehnquist not only inverted the Steel Seizure holding—which had construed statutory nonapproval of the president's act to mean legislative disapproval—but also condoned legislative inactivity at a time that demanded interbranch dialogue and bipartisan consensus."[58]

Detainee Treatment Post-9/11 (2004–2008)

Fifty years after *Youngstown*, a new combination of wartime pressure, domestic law, and constitutional interpretation of executive power was front and center after 9/11. An immediate controversy surrounded the capture and prosecution of noncitizens on President George W. Bush's orders. The Bush administration argued that "inherent" constitutional powers, with or without congressional authorization, provided the legal foundation for the "war on terror," including military commissions/tribunals.[59] Congress also empowered the president in a broad, resolution within a week of the attacks. "[The law] authorizes the President to use all necessary and appropriate force against those nations, organizations, or persons *he determines* planned, authorized, committed, or aided the terrorist attacks on September 11, 2001, or harbored such organizations or persons, in order to prevent any future acts of international terrorism against the

United States by such nations, organizations, or persons."[60] The central questions going to federal courts included the scope of power delegated by Congress to the executive branch to hold, charge, and try the detainees, and the role of the judiciary in processing these novel habeas corpus claims. When the president's position was rejected by the court, Congress came back to support him and also tried to stop further federal court involvement in these types of cases.[61]

The first case of three handed down the same day, *Rasul v. Bush* (2004) challenged unlimited detention without charges and asked whether federal courts had statutory jurisdiction to review habeas corpus petitions filed by fourteen noncitizens held in Guantanamo Bay, Cuba. The district court said it did not have jurisdiction, and the appeals court upheld that interpretation. The Supreme Court recognized that the captures were pursuant to the Authorization for Use of Military Force (AUMF) passed in September 2001, but also ruled that Guantanamo was an extension of U.S. territory (under U.S. control), and even noncitizens have the right to federal court review pursuant to habeas statutes in place. The majority opinion by Justice John Paul Stevens traced the judiciary's role in reviewing such petitions to the Judiciary Acts of 1789 and 1867, and distinguished this case from others that concerned noncitizens held abroad by the United States in non-U.S. territories who did not contest the allegations against them and were processed by military tribunal.[62] Within two months, the Pentagon established the Combatant Status Review tribunal in Guantanamo.[63]

Hamdi v. Rumsfeld (2004) concerned a U.S.-born Saudi who was transferred from Guantanamo to a naval base in Norfolk, Virginia. His having citizenship status and situs (now being held in the United States) complicated the administration's argument for indefinite detention without charges or access to an attorney. The district court demanded more government details on the situation than the Bush administration was willing to give. On appeal, the Fourth Circuit sided with the government with a deference to the "political branches" to determine the definition of an enemy combatant. In a complex decision, a plurality of the Supreme Court agreed that Hamdi possessed constitutional rights as a U.S. citizen to challenge his detention, but were split on whether Hamdi's detention was authorized by Congress in the 2001 AUMF.[64] Four justices would have required the Bush Administration to either bring charges in civilian courts or release Hamdi (and he was released, in fact—with no hearing). Four other justices said limited hearing in military tribunal could be permissible and two joined them. Congress's response to *Rasul* and *Hamdi* attempted to take the issue away from federal courts. The Detainee Treatment Act (DTA) utilized Congress's constitutional power to control appellate jurisdiction by stripping all U.S. courts of jurisdiction to hear the Guantanamo detainees' claims, among other key details. The Supreme Court, however, did not stop reviewing these claims.[65]

Padilla v. Rumsfeld also concerned a U.S. citizen, but one who was arrested on U.S. soil after returning from Pakistan in 2002. José Padilla was first charged as a material witness in the 9/11 attacks, but then declared an enemy combatant who conspired to set off a "dirty bomb" inside the United States. Padilla was held in a brig in a Charleston, South Carolina, naval base. As an alleged terrorism conspirator rather than a traditional military actor, his detention was controversial. District judge Michael Mukasey ruled that the president had authority under the AUMF to order the detention of an American citizen, arrested here, as an enemy combatant. Mukasey also deferred to the president's "controlling political authority" to detain combatants by reducing the evidence threshold. The Second Circuit ruled against the president's unilateral labeling and detention system, using *Youngstown* as a guide, by saying the AUMF did not meet the Non-Detention Act's standard of conferring legislative approval. "We agree that great deference is afforded the President's exercise of his authority as Commander-in-Chief. . . . We also agree that whether a state of armed conflict exists against an enemy to which the laws of war apply is a political question for the President, not the courts. . . . But when the Executive acts, even in the conduct of war, in the face of apparent congressional disapproval, challenges to his authority must be examined and resolved by the Article III courts."[66] The Supreme Court sidestepped the question on merits. Instead, it ruled in a 5–4 decision that Padilla's case named the wrong defendant (he should have named the brig commander, not the secretary of defense) in the wrong district (he should have filed in South Carolina, not New York).

In 2006, the Supreme Court heard the case of *Hamdan v. Rumsfeld* saying that Congress did not intend to strip jurisdiction from cases already pending. This challenge to the Bush administration concerned the military commission that was organized to try Salim Ahmed Hamdan, a Yemeni, on conspiracy charges. Hamdan's requested judicial review of his status under the Geneva Convention (conspiracy did not violate traditional laws of war) and challenged the rules of the military commission system, such as inability of the defendant to review evidence against him. Taking a different perspective than the district and appellate courts, the Supreme Court said federal courts could review detainees' status under international treaties and that the military commissions were subject to congressional regulations through statute and the Uniform Code of Military Justice. The majority said Guantanamo tribunals' processes violated the Uniform Code of Military Justice and the Geneva Conventions. Justice Stephen Breyer's brief concurrence, joined by Justices Anthony Kennedy, David Souter, and Ruth Bader Ginsburg, said that the ball was in Congress's court: "Congress has not issued the Executive a 'blank check.' Indeed, Congress has denied the President the legislative authority to create military commissions of the kind at issue here. Nothing prevents the President from returning to Congress to seek the authority he believes necessary. . . . The Constitution places its faith in those democratic means. Our Court today simply does the same."[67]

In response to the *Hamdan* decision's criticism of the DTA, Congress passed the Military Commission Act (MCA) in 2006. The law authorized an extended list of alleged crimes eligible for trial by military commissions, forbade the invocation of the Geneva Convention by detainees via habeas corpus petitions, took the process completely out of federal court jurisdiction, and applied these provisions to current judicial proceedings. As Richard Pious argues, "The provisions of the law came close to what the administration favored because of the president's influence in Congress, not because of his interpretation of [inherent] constitutional powers."[68] In effect, Republicans holding the majority in Congress assisted the administration in meeting the *Youngstown* standard with more explicit authority: "a High Court decision can act as a catalyst, but it is unlikely to have transformative impact if congressional majorities remain protective of presidential prerogative and act to legitimize rather than curtail it."[69]

But could Congress revoke jurisdiction from the Guantanamo habeas corpus cases? *Boumediene v. Bush* raised the question, combining the *Hamdan* decision, DTA, and MCA issues, including whether the suspension clause was appropriately invoked (Article I, section 9, clause 2 of the Constitution says "The Privilege of the Writ of Habeas Corpus shall not be suspended, unless when in Cases of Rebellion or Invasion the public Safety may require it."). Lakhdar Boumediene was an Algerian detainee at Guantanamo previously seized in Bosnia under the allegation he and others were plotting an attack on the U.S. embassy in 2002. A three-judge panel dismissed the detainees' cases (consolidated under this name) 2–1, saying the MCA precluded continuation of the cases and there was no inherent constitutional habeas right for aliens to warrant reversal of the jurisdiction-stripping provisions. The original understanding of habeas in 1789 would not include Boumediene or Guantanamo. The Supreme Court ruled in a 5–4 decision that the MCA operated as an unconstitutional interpretation (effective suspension) of the habeas corpus writ under the procedures laid out in the DTA.[70]

Looking at the entirety of post-9/11 cases, some scholars view this history through the lens of partisanship, with robust checks and balances from Congress and the federal court more likely under divided government than unified.[71] Others see the judiciary as bolstering separation of powers theory and practice under difficult political and policy circumstances,[72] as well as maintaining the fundamental protection of constitutional habeas rights. As Kim Scheppele concludes, "the separation of powers system must continue to pursue the ideal of protecting constitutional habeas rights, requiring consent of both executive and legislative branches to emergency measures, and providing guarantees of procedural fair-

ness that are maintained even in the face of threat are policies that constitutionalists can live with over the long term."[73]

Recognition Power: *Zivotovsky I* and *II*

In 2002, the U.S. Congress passed the Foreign Relations Authorization Act, which,
among other things, moved the recognized capital of Israel from Tel Aviv to
Jerusalem. The United States had tried to avoid excessive provocation on the sensitive matter of Jerusalem's status since recognizing Israel in 1948. However, all
three branches of the Israeli government are located in Jerusalem. This fact was
one of a few reasons Congress had urged the president to relocate the U.S. embassy to the center of government business for decades, including a law passed
by the House and Senate in 1995 that did not receive President Clinton's signature.[74] In December 2017, President Trump decided to recognize Jerusalem as
the capital as part of his "fresh thinking" on the Israel-Palestinian conflict. He
noted that the 1995 law had received bipartisan majorities, yet the Jerusalem
provision had been waived by three presidents. Saying he saw no positive result
from his predecessors' decisions on the issue, Trump broke with them.[75]

Fifteen years earlier, the 2002 law had directed the U.S. Department of State
to allow the birthplace "Jerusalem, Israel" to appear on U.S. passports for American citizens born in Jerusalem, if requested by the passport holder. But the Department of State under both Presidents Bush and Obama ordered "Jerusalem"
alone to be listed on the passport, without a country.[76] In his signing statement,
Bush argued he would take this part of the law as "advisory," not mandatory. Congress's mandate "would impermissibly interfere with the President's constitutional authority to formulate the position of the United States, speak for the Nation in international affairs, and determine the terms on which recognition is
given to foreign states. U.S. policy regarding Jerusalem has not changed."[77]

The private litigation stemmed from an American couple whose child, Men-
achem Binyamin Zivotofsky, was born in Jerusalem after the 2002 law was in effect, but whose passport birthplace did not include "Israel." The Supreme Court
heard the case twice, first to reverse and remand to the appellate court, which
agreed with the district court that it was a political question but disagreed with it
on standing.[78] On remand the court of appeals held the Foreign Relations Authorization Act unconstitutional, saying, "The President exclusively holds the power
to determine whether to recognize a foreign sovereign," and that "section 214(d)
directly contradicts a carefully considered exercise of the Executive branch's recognition power."[79] The second time, the Supreme Court upheld the district and
appeals court rulings that section 214(d) was unconstitutional. Conceiving the

case as an infringement on presidential recognition, which is stated in Article II of the Constitution, the majority of Supreme Court said "because the President's refusal to implement Sec. 214(d) falls into Justice Jackson's third category, his claim must be 'scrutinized with caution,' and he may rely solely on powers the Constitution grants to him alone."[80]

The opinions tackled two different questions. First, can Congress direct presidential recognition power in the area of passports? The 6–3 majority said no. Second, can Congress control presidential recognition power as it relates to consular reports on births abroad? On this question, a 5–4 majority said no (Justice Clarence Thomas argued that passports are an executive function, but Congress can direct consular reports under its naturalization power). Justice Kennedy wrote the majority opinion. "The text and structure of the Constitution grant the President the power to recognize foreign nations and governments. The question then becomes whether that power is exclusive. The various ways in which the President may unilaterally effect recognition—and the lack of any similar power vested in Congress—suggest that it is."[81]

Writing for the dissent, Chief Justice John Roberts (joined by Justice Samuel Alito) said neither the Constitution nor foreign policy history shows definitively that the president has unilateral power over recognition. "Today's decision is a first: Never before has this Court accepted a President's direct defiance of an Act of Congress in the field of foreign affairs. We have instead stressed that the President's power reaches 'its lowest ebb' when he contravenes the express will of Congress, "for what is at stake is the equilibrium established by our constitutional system."[82] Interestingly, both sides of the decision agreed to reduce the precedent weight of *United States v. Curtiss-Wright*, a 1936 case about congressional delegation of foreign policy power that the Supreme Court twisted into a novel constitutional argument that the president is the "sole organ" of foreign affairs.[83] Although the Court tried to soften the legacy of its past deference to presidential power, the *Zivotofsky* case is still a reminder that federal judges are far more likely to support executive branch expansion than not. The promise of the *Youngstown* landmark has atrophied considerably.

Both parties revel in presidential power when they are the side wielding it. When a Democrat is in the White House, Republicans in Congress cry foul, and vice versa. Members of Congress are not consistent in their own institutional protection, but presidents are. Modern presidents routinely push the constitutional limits of their powers, often melding domestic matters into foreign policy contexts. One example is Franklin Roosevelt's plea to Congress to pass a seven-point economic plan in 1942 on prices, wages, and rents, two points of which he acknowl-edged required legislative action first. "However, we are carrying out, by execu-tive action, the other parts. . . . Inaction on your part [within roughly three weeks] will leave me with an inescapable responsibility to the people of this country to see to it that the war effort is no longer imperiled by threat of economic chaos. In the event that the Congress should fail to act, and act adequately, I shall accept the responsibility, and I will act. . . . When the war is won, the powers under which I act automatically revert to the people—to whom they belong."[84]

Of course, even if a particular series of executive actions expires, the cultural norm of presidential-led governance continues. The courts are often placed by private litigants in the unenviable position of sorting out executive authority when Congress members do nothing, or show ambivalent and conflicting signals about their intent. Justice Jackson's useful typology of three kinds of executive action (authorized, denied, or neither) still does not cover all contingencies, nor does it make the job any easier for federal judges. Although he said the framers did not want a king nor any version of unchecked executive power, Jackson mused, "what our forefathers did envision, or would have envisioned had they fore-seen modern conditions, must be divined from materials almost as enigmatic as the dreams Joseph was called upon to interpret for Pharaoh. A century and a half of partisan debate and scholarly speculation yields no net result, but only supplies more or less apt quotations from respected sources on each side of any question. They largely cancel each other. And court decisions are inde-cisive because of the judicial practice of dealing with the largest questions in the most narrow way."[85]

During Donald Trump's presidency, Democrats succeeded in capturing the majority of the House of Representatives in the midterm elections of 2018. In the first months of the 116th Congress, Democrats have led the way on pushing back against Trump's executive actions, most notably on their votes in the House and Senate to disapprove his 2019 emergency declaration to build a southern border wall.[86] Without the needed supermajorities in Congress to override his veto, or to change the Emergency Act that Trump invoked, the President and the presidency will prevail.[87]

Private and member litigation opened another front in this saga. As in other recent administrations, states, private groups, and citizens will go to court to try to undo executive branch actions, motivated by policy and partisan goals.[88] If suc-cessful, these suits will show the continuing relevance of the judicial branch to separation of powers despite the continuing patterns of expansion from the ex-ecutive and accommodation from Congress, regardless of party. Yet even when the courthouse doors are open in theory, federal judges at all levels do not relish taking up such fights until Congress acts decisively and repeatedly to change the laws that built the modern presidency. The 2019 emergency declaration story inspired many to revisit the *Youngstown* decision, as the President was trying to do something by unilateral action (funding the construction of a border wall) after Congress considered and rejected the same action through the regular appropriation process, leading to a partial government shutdown.

SO SUE HIM

Since President Donald Trump took office, dozens of public and private litigants have challenged him on the legality of his family's business dealings, separate from various public policy actions. One legal dispute concerns whether foreign governments' payments to his companies, including his hotels in Washington, DC, and elsewhere, are "emoluments" forbidden by the Constitution. Article I, Section 9 does not define the term but says that Congress must give its consent to such payments (among other gifts), if a president chooses to accept them. President Trump gave his adult sons control over the family's business empire; they and their attorneys say that hotel bills and like payments by foreign governments are not emoluments.[1] Democrats might try to prevent such payments through the legislative process if they could override a sure veto. In the meantime, around 200 Democratic members of the House and Senate have decided to sue. The members argued that they were denied the opportunity to vote on this question, as implied by the Constitution. In fall 2018, a federal judge ruled that the group of lawmakers demonstrated sufficient injury for standing. Federal district judge Emmet Sullivan said, "The central question for standing purposes is how to characterize the injury that occurs when the President fails to seek the consent of Congress, as required by the Clause."[2]

The emoluments question may seem trivial next to other controversies about presidential power that have been challenged by members of the House and Senate over the past five decades. Yet, as Judge Sullivan hewed closely to precedent, it is worth noting what was different about this case than so many others that failed to clear the justiciability hurdle. The little-known Nixon-era pocket veto case, *Kennedy v. Sampson*, defined an individual-level member injury to be when one or more members' votes are nullified. Sullivan relied on this case to say that individual members had not had a chance to vote on authorizing Trump's alleged accepted emoluments before he accepted them, and that absence possibly constitutes nullification.

Another avenue for member litigation success can come from "institutional injury." As defined in the 1997 line-item veto case *Raines v. Byrd*, the Supreme Court said chamber consent to a lawsuit could convey the extent of institutional injury to confer standing. A more recent case arose at the end of the Obama administration, as the Republican-dominated House of Representatives voted to sue the Department of Health and Human Services to block implementation of certain provisions of the 2010 Patient Protection and Affordable Care Act ("Affordable Care Act"). Although the parties to this case settled in late 2017, is important to note that a different federal judge from the emoluments case said the courts were appropriate to bring into the ACA interinstitutional conflict.[3] This chapter examines these cases, and four more between President Richard Nixon's administration and Trump's, to argue that even though these two narrow paths may allow member lawsuits to succeed, such suits are more symptomatic of separation of powers dysfunction than long-term cures. "Injuries" rooted in member vote nullification and chamber-sanctioned litigation are ultimately based upon partisan differences on public policy. Neither type of case would likely get filed by members against a president of their own party. If courts are being dragged into separation of powers questions just to expand the arena of partisan combat, there is no deep reset of systemic balance of power in the constitutional order. Congressional power should mean more than defending one's own party when in the minority or in the majority under conditions of divided government.

Presidents of both parties are more consistent. They have asserted controversial unilateral powers outside of war powers covered in part 1, from executive orders to treaty abrogation, without explicit prior authorization from the House and/or Senate (depending on the issue). Even if members score a temporary litigation win, there are two downsides of their pursuing judicial resolution for these bigger issues. First, if a court refuses to hear a member suit on the merits, the challenged executive action is constitutional, in effect, by default. Second, the court can take the case and rule explicitly for the president. Either way, going to court repeatedly can build precedent that relegates Congress to an after-the-fact "disapproval" body, rather than an authorizing one. Litigation can inadvertently achieve the opposite of its intention and help to flip the Constitution's order of operations, in addition to the many other reasons for presidential eclipse of Congress over the last century. Although there may be times when certain separation of powers conflicts require judicial resolution, routine member challenges to presidential power are better expressed through regular politics, regardless of party in power.

Member Cases on Executive Unilateralism

Kennedy v. Sampson shows that members can win in litigation when an allegation is narrowly tailored and there is no reasonable way for the court to punt the issue back to the conventional legislative process. In subsequent cases related to treaty terminations and an executive order, all but one were dismissed nearly unanimously on standing grounds. An important exception to this trend is the fascinating 1979 case *Goldwater v. Carter*, which divided the federal court deeply. The question was whether a group of senators' claim that President Jimmy Carter did not seek or receive permission before breaking a treaty with Taiwan was justiciable. Over three decades later, in *House v. Burwell*, a federal district judge held for the members on standing and merits regarding executive branch unilateralism, in part because a (Republican) majority of the House voted to sanction the suit. But after the changed partisan landscape in 2017, the litigants settled. The pocket veto, health care, and emoluments cases therefore demonstrate small-scale, partisan victories rather than lasting institutional rebalance.

Kennedy v. Sampson (1973)

The pocket veto is an enumerated executive power described in Article I, Section 7, of the Constitution, which also details the president's regular veto power. If the House and Senate pass an identical bill and the president does not want it to become law, he or she has two methods of response. One is to return the bill within ten days (excluding Sundays) to the originating chamber, with a message of disapproval. The pocket veto occurs when the president fails to sign a bill and the House and Senate have adjourned during that required ten-day period, preventing the receipt of a veto message. "If any Bill shall not be returned by the President within ten Days (Sundays excepted) after it shall have been presented to him, the Same shall be a Law, in like Manner as if he had signed it, unless the Congress by their Adjournment prevent its Return, in which Case it shall not be a Law."

The pocket veto is more controversial because it is, in effect, an absolute veto, whereas the "regular" veto can be overridden with two-thirds vote. If the House and Senate want to take up a bill that had been pocket-vetoed, they must redo the floor votes and have the appropriate time and supermajorities to override, if needed. In the twentieth century, numerous interbranch flare-ups have centered on the timing considerations inherent to a pocket veto, with several receiving attention in the federal court system. As *Kennedy v. Sampson* was resolved prior to getting to the Supreme Court, the precise dynamics of intra- and intersession pocket vetoes remain open to interpretation between Congress and the presidents, including its use in combination with a regular veto.[4] However, for our purposes, this story illustrates the narrow nature of judicial standing precedents because, while successful, this early example of a member lawsuit came from a precise set of circumstances that is unique in interbranch conflicts.

On December 14, 1970, a $225 million authorization bill for three years of appropriations for family medicine-related hospital and medical school grants (S. 3418) was presented to President Nixon, after a 64–1 favorable vote in the Senate and 346–2 in the House of Representatives. These lopsided approvals are significant because they imply that a regular veto by Nixon would be overruled easily by two-thirds vote. On December 22, both chambers of Congress adjourned for an intrasession Christmas break, with the Senate set to return on the 28th and the House on the 29th. Not counting Sunday, per Article I, Section 7, the House was absent for four days and the Senate for five days. During this recess, both chambers designated the process to receive presidential messages and sign enrolled bills. On December 24, Nixon signed a memorandum of disapproval for S. 3418. Neither the president nor the chief of White House Records transmitted the bill to the administrator of the General Services Administration and it was not published in slip form or in the official Statutes at Large record of U.S. laws. The following year, in December 1971, the Congress passed a token appropriations of $100,000 for fiscal year 1972 per S. 3418 to set up the legal fight.[5]

The lawsuit was filed by Senator Ted Kennedy (D-MA) and nineteen other senators alleging an unconstitutional pocket veto by President Nixon. DC district judge Joseph Waddy heard the case and considered whether S. 3418 was valid law (which can occur without the signature of the president) or properly vetoed. Building upon *Coleman v. Miller*'s individual-level legislator "injury" test, Judge Waddy held for the senators: "It becomes clear that this plaintiff has the requisite standing to sue. The precise injury of which he claims is that the President's exercise of the Pocket Veto to disapprove S. 3418 was an unconstitutional act that rendered plaintiff's vote in the Senate for the bill ineffective and deprived him of his constitutional right to vote to override the Presidential Veto in an effort to have the bill passed without the President's signature."[6]

Turning to the merits of the case, Judge Waddy walked through each timed step of the legislative process, concluding that the president was not prevented from returning the bill via the normal veto afforded to him in Article I, Section 7: "The Senate returned from the recess on December 28, 1970. It did not adjourn *sine die* until January 2, 1971. There was ample opportunity to consider the President's objections to the bill and on such consideration to pass it over the veto provided there were the requisite votes. . . . The short recess of the Senate in this case, extending only two days beyond the ten day period the President had to sign or disapprove the bill, did not *prevent* the return of the bill to the Senate in which it originated."[7]

In 1974, on appeal, Circuit Judge Tamm wrote for the majority and affirmed the district court's holding. He noted that "intrasession" pocket vetoes are a relatively new phenomenon, with thirty of thirty-eight (up to 1973) occurring since 1932. "The present case arises from the shortest intrasession recess ever relied upon by any President as having prevented the return of a disapproved bill. It is also significant that, in the single case which presented the issue of whether an intrasession adjournment precluded a return veto, the Supreme Court ruled that it had not. In our view, therefore, the question raised in this case is still very much an open one, prior executive practice notwithstanding."[8] Judge Charles Fahy wrote a concurrence for himself and Judge Bazelon. He was skeptical of the senators' standing in this case compared to the *Coleman* precedent, which granted standing to state legislators who challenged a 1937 U.S. constitutional amendment ratification vote in Kansas. "In the present case, Senator Kennedy's vote did not control passage of S. 3418. Nevertheless, his interest is substantial. As a United States Senator he represents a sovereign State whose people have a deep interest in the Act and look to their Senators to protect that interest; and he, as Senator, it seems to me, has a legal right not only to seek judicial protection of those interests, believed by him to be threatened by an invalid veto, but also, in the circumstances, to protect his own interest as a national legislator in the bill for which he voted."[9]

The Nixon Department of Justice did not appeal their loss at the appellate level to the Supreme Court. The bill was printed as a public law and backdated to Christmas Day 1970, which was the end of the ten-day period for presidential review, per Article I, section 7. As *Kennedy v. Sampson* wended its way through the court, the House and Senate held several hearings on bills to clarify the process, with none becoming law. In 1976, another federal case on the pocket veto arose, also with Senator Kennedy as plaintiff, and the federal district court reiterated the ruling of *Kennedy*, which said that the pocket veto was only appropriate after a sine die adjournment, as long as the chambers did not designate someone to receive the president's regular veto messages.[10]

Edwards v. Carter (1978)

In this case, sixty members of the House of Representatives (mostly Republicans, including lead plaintiff Mickey Edwards, R-OK) tried to utilize the *Kennedy* case when they filed suit to protest the exclusion of the House from property disposition related to the transfer of the Panama Canal Zone to its home country. In September 1977, President Carter submitted two treaties related to this action to the Senate per Article II of the Constitution for ratification. The two treaties, under negotiation for over a decade, would have abrogated prior agreements so that Panama would have sovereignty over the area and property in the Canal Zone. Opposition to the treaty was stronger in the House than in the Senate and concerned changes in national security and prestige from the transfer. In the agreements, the United States would operate the canal until 2000 and canal neutrality would be the responsibility of both countries afterward.[11] The House plaintiffs argued for a separate legislative opportunity to approve the real property transfers per Article IV, Section 3, Clause 2, which says, "Congress shall have Power to dispose of . . . the Territory or other Property belonging to the United States." The members challenged the constitutionality of the Senate's exclusive role in property-related issues stemming from the treaty ratification.

The case was dismissed at the district level by Judge Barrington D. Parker on standing grounds in February 1978. Taking the second point first, Judge Parker rejected the plaintiffs' attempt to attach their institutional injury to the successful *Kennedy* case by noting that proposed legislation toward the same end was stuck in the House. He noted that the *Kennedy* case centered on Nixon's nullification of the senator's actual vote, not the "specificity of the legislation upon which a legislator hoped to vote. . . . President Carter has not frustrated or prevented [these member-plaintiffs] from voting. If the relevant bills and resolutions are snared in the legislative process, they have only their colleagues and themselves to blame."[12] Parker did acknowledge that the pending bills in the House to approve or disapprove of the property transfers could be undermined by the Senate's first voting on the treaties and that once the Senate has voted, the members had a stronger claim to injury if the House voted differently. But he also said it would be "improper" for the court to schedule the legislative process and "monitor" the interchamber relationship in any way, especially as the Senate was not party to the suit.

On the standing question, Judge Parker rejected the injury claim. In effect, he blamed the House opposition for not acting quickly enough to undermine the Senate's ratification votes. "In essence, the House Members are asking the Court to interpret Article IV to mean that the House is entitled to vote on the same provisions concerning property disposition at the same time as the Senate. Such an interpretation would contradict the *Kennedy* standing requirement that a legislator must demonstrate interference with his official influence on the legislative process. . . . The fact that legislators have been hampered in their legislative functions is not sufficient to show a nonspeculative concrete injury in fact."[13]

An appeal to the DC circuit was dismissed in early April 1978 by Judges Fahy and Carl McGowan, with a dissent filed by Judge George MacKinnon. The majority confirmed standing and political question concerns and rejected the plaintiffs' claims on the merits as well. "Thus it appears from the very language used in the property clause that this provision was not intended to preclude the availability of self-executing treaties as a means for disposing of United States property. The history of the drafting and ratification of that clause confirms this conclusion. . . . In view of the lack of ambiguity as to the intended effects of the treaty and property clauses, it may be surprising that judicial pronouncements over the past two centuries relating to these constitutional provisions are somewhat vague and conflicting. However, none of the actual holdings in these cases addressed the precise issue before us whether the property clause prohibits the transfer of United States property to foreign nations through self-executing treaties."[14]

MacKinnon, however, dissented on both standing and political question points, as well as the merits. He argued that the standing requirements of *Kennedy* were satisfied. He then went through an exhaustive discussion of constitutional convention notes, treaty making related to Panama going back to the early 1900s, additional legislative debate on the issue in the 1940s, and President Dwight D. Eisenhower's apparent assumption that both chambers of Congress were necessary to obtain authority before the transfer of a depot of the Panama Railroad to Panama in 1955. The point was that the Panama property transfers at issue went against prior norms: "[The opinion] does not satisfactorily explain why this enormous disposition of property to the Republic of Panama should not recognize the proper role of Congress in such transfer as was followed in all prior transfers where the value of the property was infinitesimal compared to what is involved here. . . . The House is, in fact, being denied its right to participate, and the existence of this circumstance is enough to confer standing on this court to declare the law. . . . Moreover, there is no suggestion here that a judicial ruling on the merits will circumvent the legislative process in any way. Rather, the judicial ruling sought here would protect and implement the constitutional legislative process."[15]

The legislative process did continue parallel to this litigation and the basic treaty was approved by the Senate on April 17, 1978. Soon after, the House (but not the Senate) added language to the Department of State authorization bill that prohibited funds authorized by the bill from being used directly or indirectly to effect implementation of the treaties unless separately authorized by Congress. The conference committee ultimately said (ambiguously) that funds could be used if authorized either by Congress or the Constitution.[16] A plaintiff in the case said in an interview that he did not turn to the federal courts frivolously. Although there was a legislative push to get the House more involved, the treaties had already been negotiated and were difficult to unravel at that point. "As a general rule . . . I don't like an activist court. . . . But in a case like this, my view is that this a violation of the federal Constitution."[17]

Goldwater v. Carter (1979)

Edwards v. Carter was not a conflict on treaty termination at all, but rather concerned House inclusion in the U.S. government's property transfers that resulted from a treaty replacement with Panama. The next case is focused on the termination process itself, which is another facet of separation of powers not fully laid out in the Constitution. As we saw in the previous case, the text is clear about treaty ratification, but two subsequent lawsuits centered on the text's silence regarding how to withdraw from one. Like the removal controversies discussed in chapter 5, lawsuits exposed the lack of explicit guidance on a major institutional matter. Regarding treaties, "the two-thirds vote means that successful treaties must gain support that overcomes partisan division. The two-thirds requirement adds to the burdens of the Senate leadership, and may also encourage opponents of a treaty to engage in a variety of dilatory tactics in hopes of obtaining sufficient votes to ensure its defeat."[18] Political and policy concerns on treaty dissolution have a long history in the United States. The only example of congressional termination relates to a mutual defense treaty with France in 1798, which exacerbated tensions, leading to the "Quasi War" that was authorized only two days after the vote on the joint resolution.[19] As early as 1857, the Senate Committee on Foreign Relations took the position that "the President and Senate, acting together, [were competent] to terminate a treaty," and that in certain circumstances termination was appropriate by joint action of the president and Congress.[20]

The story behind the Taiwan accord begins after the Chinese Revolution in 1949 and the Korean War. The United States and Taiwan entered into a mutual defense treaty in 1954, which was ratified by the Senate by the needed two-thirds in 1955. A termination provision said either country could give one year's notice to the other. In December 1978, President Carter announced that on January 1, 1979, the United States would recognize the government of the Peoples Republic of China (PRC) as the only government of China (the so-called One China policy), and agreed to exchange ambassadors and set up embassies a few months later. Later that month, the Department of State formally terminated unilaterally the 1954 Mutual Defense Treaty with Taiwan as of January 1, 1980. This announcement reflected a decade of increasing international diplomatic recognition that the PRC was the legitimate government, reflecting the thaw between the United States and the PRC begun by the Nixon administration.

The main controversy was not the United States' right to terminate according to the treaty's provisions, but how President Carter did so. Anticipating the shift, in 1978 Congress passed the International Security Assistance Act, which had a section on the Taiwan treaty. Section 26(b) states, "It is the sense of the Congress that there should be prior consultation between the Congress and the executive branch on any proposed policy changes affecting the continuation in force of the Mutual Defense Treaty of 1954."[21] While severing all official ties with Taiwan, the United States has sought to preserve "extensive, close, and friendly commercial, cultural, and other relations between the people of the United States and the people on Taiwan." The Taiwan Relations Act, signed into law on April 10, 1979, established the statutory framework for future relations through a nonprofit corporation, the American Institute in Taiwan, and provided for defense material and services.[22]

As the litigation began in 1978, the Carter administration took the position that this act showed Senate agreement with administration policy. But in hearings, the Senate Committee on Foreign Relations saw broader patterns in these episodes of interbranch relations: "The constitutional role of the Congress has too often been short-circuited because it was viewed in the executive branch and even by some Members of Congress as an impediment to the expeditious adoption of substantive policies commanding the support of a majority. . . . The lesson was learned the hard way: procedural requirements prescribed by the Constitution must not be disregarded in the name of efficiency, and the substance of a policy, however, attractive, can never justify circumventing the procedure required by the Constitution for its adoption. . . . The issue of treaty termination, in the judgment of the Committee, must be viewed pursuant to this principle."[23]

This report was part of an unfinished legislative response to Carter's actions to abrogate the treaty. In early 1979, Senator Harry Byrd (D-VA) introduced a resolution concerning the Taiwan treaty to the Senate Foreign Relations Committee, which passed it unanimously with an amendment after hearings that included Senator Barry Goldwater (R-AZ), various executive officials, and Professor Louis Henkin (whose disagreement with the political question doctrine in foreign affairs was discussed in the introduction to this book). The original "sense of the Senate" assertion was short and to the point: that "approval of the U.S. Senate is required to terminate any mutual defense treaty between the United States and another nation."[24] The resolution that emerged from the committee was more nuanced, spelling out certain circumstances where Congress would not be required, such as when treaty provisions have already been superseded by law, another treaty, or if the other parties breach the treaty, among other factors.[25]

After four days of floor consideration in June 1979, the measure died without a formal vote.[26]

Meanwhile, during this yearlong series of interbranch actions, congressional plaintiffs filed a lawsuit in December 1978. Judge Oliver Gasch ruled on June 6, 1979, that the eight current senators, one former senator, and sixteen members of the House of Representatives lacked standing to prevent the treaty termination without approval by the Senate or both houses of Congress. He also pointed out that two litigants, Strom Thurmond (R-NC) and former senator Carl Curtis (R-NE), had originally voted for the 1955 ratification of the treaty. He dismissed the suit without ruling on the merits, saying that the current members of Congress had not acted on legislation to show their institutional position regarding the treaty abrogation and their contention that Carter violated section 26 of the International Security Assistance Act of 1978.[27] After reviewing fifty instances of treaty termination by the president alone, or with one or both chambers of Congress, he concluded, "The Court believes the power to terminate treaties is a power shared by the political branches of this government, namely, the President and the Congress. In this instance, however, since the Congress has not yet acted on the question of treaty termination, a serious question arises concerning the standing of these congressional plaintiffs to seek a judicial injunction or declaration respecting the power of the executive."[28]

While hinting at his agreement with the plaintiffs on the merits, Judge Gasch noted at least three Senate resolutions pending, as mentioned above. So, he concluded, unlike in *Kennedy v. Sampson*, the plaintiffs had not shown an injury through completion of the legislative process. "Although the Court is inclined to agree with plaintiffs' assertion that the power to terminate the 1954 Mutual Defense Treaty is a shared power to be exercised by the action of both political branches, at the present time there is no indication that the Congress as a whole intends to assert its prerogative to act. Under these circumstances, the President's notice of termination does not constitute injury. In the absence of any injury to the institution as a whole, the individual legislators here cannot claim a derivative injury."[29] If Congress approved the actions by President Carter, the challenge would be moot. But if either chamber explicitly rejects the president's actions, Judge Gasch said the conflict would be "ripe."

Later on the same day that the district order was issued, the Senate brought Senate Resolution 15 to the floor, which laid out fourteen types of situations that allowed for unilateral presidential termination. But the floor passed an amendment in the form of a substitute resolution by Senator Harry Byrd Jr.: "That it is the sense of the Senate that approval of the United States Senate is required to terminate any mutual defense treaty between the United States and another nation." However, subsequent amendment attempts, including by Senator

Goldwater, showed that the senators disagreed on whether the amendment was prospective or retrospective, among other things, and no final vote was taken on an amended version of the Byrd resolution.[30] Although no floor vote happened, the plaintiffs filed for reconsideration since there was now a "justiciable controversy."[31]

On October 17, 1979, Judge Gasch granted the motion for an alteration or amendment of the original order, and the case could now be decided on the merits.[32] The substance of the case was also in the plaintiffs' favor: "Any decision of the United States to terminate [the Taiwan treaty] must be made with the advice and consent of the Senate or the approval of both houses of Congress. That decision cannot be made by the President alone."[33] Gasch acknowledged that the action in the Senate was not "decisive," since at least two subsequent amendments had not come up for a vote, and so the Byrd resolution was returned to the Senate calendar without further action. Nevertheless, it "stands as the last expression of Senate position on its constitutional role in the treaty termination process. By that vote, the Senate rejected a Committee substitute that would have expressly approved of the action taken by the President in terminating this treaty."[34] Gasch added, "Termination of a treaty also involves a repeal of the 'law of the land' established by the agreement. It is in this area that congressional participation is required under the present circumstances."[35] This favorable decision was reversed by the court of appeals, which held in a *per curium* opinion that "the President did not exceed his authority when he took action to withdraw from the . . . treaty, without the consent of the Senate or other legislative concurrences."[36]

Then the Second Circuit sitting en banc heard the case and decided it within two weeks, in November 1979. The appellate panel took a pragmatic view of what the plaintiffs were asking the court to do—force the president to submit the abrogation to the Senate alone or to both houses for an up-or-down vote. Of course, as unlikely as this scenario was to the panel, the prognosis for after-the-fact disapproval was even more remote as the Congress would have to overcome a near-certain presidential veto with two sets of two-thirds votes. It was not clear to the judges how the Senate might vote if given the opportunity. However, standing was upheld since "there is no conceivable senatorial action that could likely prevent termination of the Treaty. . . . The President's action has deprived them of this opportunity completely, in the sense that they have no legislative power to exercise an equivalent voting opportunity. Therefore, appellee Senators have standing."[37]

Around two weeks after the appellate decision, the Supreme Court vacated it and dismissed the members' complaint without a majority opinion. Justices William Rehnquist, Warren Burger, Potter Stewart, and John Paul Stevens agreed the litigation was a political question. Justice Lewis Powell concurred but said the problem was ripeness, not political questions. Justices Harry Blackmun and Byron White dissented, briefly, to explain their preference that the case to go to full oral argument. Justice Thurgood Marshall concurred without a separate opinion. The only dissent was Justice William Brennan, who argued that the appellate decision should be affirmed with a new precedent for presidential withdrawal authority as part of his foreign policy portfolio. The outcome of this case left the president's self-proclaimed authority intact by default. Another no-decision was indeed one in effect. As Roy E. Brownell II argues, "These judicial non-decisions have essentially added a further gloss to historical practice."[38]

Justice Powell concurred with the outcome, which remanded the case to the district court for dismissal, but argued that the writ of certiorari should not have been granted by the Supreme Court. He went through each element of *Baker v. Carr*'s political question doctrine (PQD) standard from 1962 and determined the issue did not qualify for that precedent's application. "Prudential considerations persuade me that a dispute between Congress and the President is not ready for judicial review unless and until each branch has taken action asserting its constitutional authority. . . . If the Congress chooses not to confront the President, it is not our task to do so."[39] He said that the court should not inadvertently encourage groups of members to seek resolution in the courts before the political process finishes. "If the Congress, by appropriate formal action, had challenged the President's authority to terminate the treaty with Taiwan, the resulting uncertainty could have serious consequences for our country. In that situation, it would be the duty of this Court to resolve the issue."[40]

Justice Rehnquist, joined by Chief Justice Burger and Justices Stewart and Stevens, had raised more alarm in their view of the institutional consequences of any federal court's taking this case. To them, it was indeed a standard political question. They came within one vote of imposing this position. "I am of the view that the basic question presented by the petitioners in this case is 'political,' and therefore nonjusticiable because it involves the authority of the President in the conduct of our country's foreign relations and the extent to which the Senate or the Congress is authorized to negate the action of the President. . . . An Art. III court's resolution of a question that is "'political' in character can create far more disruption among the three coequal branches of Government than the resolution of a question presented in a moot controversy."[41]

Justices Blackmun and White dissented in part by saying the issue deserves more time and study. "If the President does not have the power to terminate the treaty (a substantial issue that we should address only after briefing and oral argument), the notice of intention to terminate surely has no legal effect. It is also indefensible, without further study, to pass on the issue of justiciability or on the issues of standing or ripeness. While I therefore join in the grant of the petition for certiorari, I would set the case for oral argument and give it the plenary consideration it so obviously deserves."[42] Justice Brennan also dissented, but separately, squarely rejecting the political question doctrine's relevance. He said the law comes down clearly in the president's favor. This type of opinion is a cautionary tale when championing member suits. Federal judges can rule against them on merits. "The issue of decisionmaking authority must be resolved as a matter of constitutional law, not political discretion; accordingly, it falls within the competence of the courts. The constitutional question raised here is prudently answered in narrow terms. Abrogation of the defense treaty with Taiwan was a necessary incident to Executive recognition of the Peking Government. . . . Our cases firmly establish that the Constitution commits to the President alone the power to recognize, and withdraw recognition from, foreign regimes."[43]

Goldwater v. Carter received more attention in scholarship than the average member suit, especially among law professors. Some argued that the case showed the challenges facing federal courts in applying standing doctrine to members of Congress. Judge McGowan explained his preferred doctrine of equitable discretion in a law review article in 1981, arguing *Goldwater* belied the application of traditional standing or even political question doctrine rationales to member-plaintiffs, of whom he was still wary.[44] But others defended this type of litigation. Jonathan Wagner, for example, argues that "even outside the treaty context, requiring exhaustion of legislative remedies is unduly burdensome and may effectively shield improper executive action from either congressional or judicial review. A President who takes an allegedly illegal action and cannot be challenged in court by an individual legislator consequently gains an important advantage by shifting the burden of obtaining the supportive legislative action onto the complaining lawmaker."[45]

Regardless of differing opinions of (and within) the *Goldwater* case, it was treated as a clear precedent by the next member challenge to treaty abrogation, which came in in 2002. In the meantime, under a different set of political and policy circumstances, member litigants failed again to gain traction in court, this time on an environmental regulation put into place by executive order.

Chenoweth v. Clinton (1999)

President Bill Clinton announced his plan to create the American Heritage Rivers Initiative (AHRI) in the State of Union Address delivered on February 4, 1997. After describing other successes in environmental safety and restoration, he said, "Now we must be as vigilant with our rivers as we are with our lands. Tonight, I announce that this year I will designate 10 American Heritage Rivers, to help communities alongside them revitalize their waterfronts and clean up pollution in the rivers, proving once again that we can grow the economy as we protect the environment."[46] The next step was a published notice in the *Federal Register* by the Council on Environmental Quality, which said federal agencies would support various local efforts to preserve "certain historically significant rivers and riverside communities." The president would designate the AHRI communities following an examination of local nominations. Qualifications and nominating procedures were included.[47]

One month later, in June 1997, Representatives Helen Chenoweth (R-ID), Bob Schaffer (R-CO), and Richard Pombo (R-CA) introduced a bill "to terminate further development and implementation" of the AHRI. The bill never came to a vote on the House floor, although the House Committee on Natural Resources voted 15–8 in favor of floor consideration. In the meantime, the same committee also organized two sets of oversight hearings regarding the published guidelines by the Council on Environmental Quality in July and September 1997.[48] The House majority on the committee argued that President Clinton's planned initiative was excluding Congress and creating a new level of environmental bureaucracy that intruded upon local and private land rights.

The president formally established the AHRI by two executive orders in September 1997 and April 1998. He created the American Heritage Rivers Advisory Council (in effect for up to two years) to recommend up to twenty rivers for the special designation. He cited authority under the National Environmental Policy Act (signed into law by President Nixon in 1970) as the legal basis for the executive orders.[49] On July 30, 1998, Clinton then announced fourteen "American Heritage Rivers" recommended by the council, which included a website announcement: "Communities along these rivers—from New York's Hudson, to the mighty Mississippi, to Hawaii's Hanalei—will receive help over the next five years tapping federal resources to carry out their plans for revitalizing their rivers and riverfronts. This initiative reflects the Administration's strong commitment to building partnerships that promote prosperity while protecting our environment."[50]

Conservative critics of the president argued that this executive order was part of a larger agenda, spanning over thirty executive orders over both terms, to confiscate and/or regulate private property and harm local commercial enterprises.[51] The House Committee on Natural Resources' report arrived in October 1998 and detailed several policy and constitutional objections to the initiative's origination and intent. "Many believe that AHRI clearly violates the doctrine of separation of powers as intended by our Founding Fathers by completely bypassing the Congress."[52]

A year later, on October 27, 1999, the House Rules Committee (still under a Republican majority) convened a hearing to discuss executive orders and interbranch and constitutional relations.[53] In the same week, a subcommittee of the Republican-dominated House Judiciary Committee held hearings on three legislative proposals to rein in executive orders generally. Subcommittee chair George Gekas (R-PA), who placed the blame on both parties in the White House, said that executive orders are most often useful public statements that provide appropriate guidance to the administration. While admitting that the legislative process frustrates presidents of both parties, he stated that executive orders are not an appropriate method to circumvent the "intransigent" legislators. "I believe and hope that we, as Members of Congress, can protect the institution in which we serve without wasting too much time and effort on who did what to whom in the past. . . . When Executive orders become a way of doing an end-run around the Congress, or a form of administration without administrative law, I will vigorously dissent."[54]

The ranking member of the subcommittee, Jerrold Nadler (D-NY), opened with general agreement with Representative Gekas, although he named offending presidents and policies that he thought demonstrated disregard for the constitutional role of Congress, including Nixon's bombing of Cambodia and the Iran-Contra scandal under Ronald Reagan. Nadler continued, "I would just caution my colleagues on both sides of the aisle not to attempt to politicize this question. The White House does, much as it pains me, change hands from time to time. While it may be natural for members of one party to attack the actions of the President of another party, I think it might just prove helpful for us to get a non-partisan view of this important constitutional issue."[55]

One of the witnesses, Jack Metcalf (R-WA), explained his success in challenging the AHRI through informal means. "The President's executive order required States to give up certain rivers to Federal control, and it was a threat to citizens' private property rights. [It] also gave the President the power to reprogram government funds and spend taxpayer money on projects without congressional approval. In my district, I vigorously objected to this, and I was able to have the Snohomish River removed from Federal control under the Heritage River. I don't know how we did that, and I don't know what authority I had, but I just yelled loud enough, and we got it taken off."[56]

During this time, parallel to the symbolic and substantive attention to the AHRI in Congress, and the broader question of executive orders, four Republican members of the House (Representatives Chenoweth, Pombo, Schaffer, as well as House Committee on Natural Resources chairman Don Young, R-AK), filed suit against President Clinton. They claimed his action violated the "doctrine of separation of powers," as well as the Commerce Clause (Art. I, Sec. 8, Cl. 3), Property Clause (Art. IV, Sec. 3, Cl. 2), Spending Clause (Art. I, Sec. 9, Cl. 7), and the Tenth Amendment of the Constitution, as well as the Anti-Deficiency Act, the Federal Land Management and Policy Act, and the aforementioned National Environmental Policy Act. Federal district judge Henry Kennedy (appointed by Clinton) presided over the first round of the case, and dismissed on standing grounds. Judge Kennedy relied on *Raines v. Byrd* (discussed in part 2) to examine the nature of the institutional injury and concluded the plaintiff's complaints were too abstract and nonspecific.[57]

The plaintiffs appealed to the DC circuit, where the case was heard by Judges Harry T. Edwards, Douglas Ginsburg, and David Tatel, all of whom had previous experience with member-plaintiff litigation. Ginsburg wrote the opinion for himself and Edwards. They acknowledged the messy precedents. In *Kennedy v. Sampson*, the suit had standing because it demonstrated "a diminution of congressional influence in the legislative process." Afterward, he explained how federal courts became worried about judicial interference in separation of powers after *Goldwater v. Carter*, as seen in the development of the doctrine of equitable discretion, as well as continuation of strict standing requirements. "Against the backdrop of *Raines* and our own decisions after *Goldwater*, the futility of the present Representatives' claim is apparent."[58]

Judge Tatel concurred in the dismissal of the case, but argued that that the member-plaintiffs could not point to any "defect" in the legislative process to this point that arguably denied them voting rights as members. "I think the court should have deferred addressing the implications of *Raines* until presented with a case in which legislators assert injury involving a discrete aspect of the process by which a specific bill has become (or failed to become) law."[59] Funding battles continued on AHRI and, in 2001, one local news outlet reported that the incoming Bush administration had not prioritized the program. It appears that the initiative was defunded by Congress or discontinued by President Bush. The opponents of Clinton's executive actions won through politics.[60]

Another Treaty—*Kucinich v. Bush* (2002)

Kucinich v. Bush reflected the reverse political situation from *Goldwater v. Carter*: Goldwater was a conservative Republican senator suing a Democratic president; Kucinich was a liberal House member suing a Republican president. The institutional and constitutional questions were still the same. Could a president unilaterally terminate a treaty that requires a two-thirds vote in the Senate to ratify? In theory, the Constitution's silence on the issue could have allowed the case to go any number of ways. The fragmented *Goldwater* decision was a controversial precedent, since there was no single holding. But in light of the then-recent *Chenoweth* case, as well as *Raines v. Byrd* in 1997 (discussed in part 2) and *Campbell v. Clinton* in 2000 (discussed in part 1), the district court did not see any disapproval from Congress and, therefore, was not inclined to get involved.

The Antiballistic Missile (ABM) Treaty was signed in 1972 as part of a series of talks with the Soviet Union to control the arms race while maintaining a strategy of nuclear deterrence. The Senate approved ratification of the treaty by the requisite two-thirds vote on August 3, 1972; President Nixon ratified it two months later. While perceived at the time as a victory for national security, subsequent presidents were critical of its terms and tried to reinterpret the treaty in ways that would permit the development of missile defense systems. President Reagan, for example, explored loopholes for a national missile defense system, also known as "Star Wars."

President George W. Bush took a more direct course and simply canceled the agreement unilaterally.[61] However, the timing of the cancelation, three months after the 9/11 attacks, may have suppressed some legislative action. Bush's December 13, 2001, announcement of the United States' withdrawal from the ABM Treaty was explained in the context of the terrorist attacks, the end of the Cold War, and the existence of "rogue states" with access to long-range missiles that may threaten U.S. forces and territory in the future. Bush pledged cooperation with Russia going forward on numerous international fronts. "Under the terms of the ABM Treaty, the United States is prohibited from defending its homeland against ballistic missile attack. We are also prohibited from cooperating in developing missile defenses against long-range threats with our friends and allies. Given the emergence of these new threats to our national security and the imperative of defending against them, the United States is today providing formal notification of its withdrawal from the ABM Treaty. As provided in Article XV of that Treaty, the effective date of withdrawal will be six months from today."[62] According to news reports, Russian president Vladimir Putin was neither supportive of the U.S. withdrawal nor alarmed by it, saying it did not impact Russia's national security.[63]

Within a few weeks of the announcement, Representative Dennis Kucinich and thirty-one fellow House members (all Democrats, plus Independent Bernie Sanders) filed suit against President Bush, while simultaneously filing bills and resolutions against the unilateral withdrawal. For example, on June 6, 2002, Representative Kucinich offered a resolution saying, "The President should respect the Constitutional role of Congress and seek the approval of Congress for the withdrawal of the United States of America from the Anti-Ballistic Missile Treaty."[64] In reply, Judiciary Committee Chair Henry Hyde (R-IL) made a point of order against the resolution, saying the substance of the treaties violated House rules on member floor privileges (specifically rule IX, sec. 702, of the House manual) because it was not appropriate. He cited the provisions of the treaty concerning withdrawal and explained the House's exclusion from the process: "As we all know, the Constitution gives the House of Representatives no role in the approval of treaties. . . . The sponsor of this resolution argues that even though the House of Representatives had no role in bringing the ABM treaty into force, we somehow have an indispensable constitutional role in deciding whether to approve the termination of the treaty. I could understand someone in the Senate making such an argument about the prerogative of the Senate in such matters, but I am mystified how anyone could read such a prerogative into the Constitution for the House of Representatives."[65]

Hyde added that the *Goldwater* case in 1979 proved that even the Senate would have a difficult time making Kucinich's argument. He said that he understood Senator Goldwater's opposition at the time, but "disagreeing with the substance of the action is very different from claiming that the action itself was unconstitutional. . . . I would urge the sponsor of this resolution to take that lesson to heart."[66] Hyde said Kucinich should withdraw the resolution or risk embarrassing himself and the House by accusing Bush of violating the Constitution. Kucinich responded that the issue at hand was more symbolic than substantive: "This is not about the ABM treaty. This is really about the role that this institution has in a democracy. . . . How many injuries and usurpations must this Congress endure before it fights back?"[67] After a lively debate including at least two other coplaintiffs in the suit, Hyde proposed a motion to table the appeal of the point of order—it passed 254–168 on a party-line vote.[68] All thirty-two congressmen who were plaintiffs voted against the motion to table Kucinich's resolution.

Two other legislative actions on the treaty died without much attention. The same month as the House debate (June 2002), Senator Russ Feingold (D-WI) introduced a resolution that died in committee, saying it was the sense of the Senate that it was required to get approval from the chamber to terminate a treaty, and the Senate would determine the manner of its approval process. Specifically, the proposed resolution said the Senate did not approve of the ABM Treaty withdrawal.[69] And on June 12, 2002, Representative Barbara Lee (D-CA), Kucinich, and six others who were also coplaintiffs on the suit, filed a new bill in the House to keep the United States within the obligations of the ABM Treaty. The bill died in the House International Relations Committee.[70]

While these legislative conflicts continued, in December 2002 a federal district court dismissed the case as a political question, without reviewing the merits of the lawsuit. The court relied heavily on *Raines v. Byrd* for standing and ripeness grounds, and *Goldwater v. Carter* for political questions, even though only four of the nine justices had emphasized PQD in their 1979 opinion.[71] Federal judge John D. Bates wrote the opinion. Judge Bates drew a tight parallel between this case and the line-item veto litigation, saying, "*Raines* teaches that generalized injuries that affect all members of Congress in the same broad and undifferentiated manner are not sufficiently 'personal' or 'particularized,' but rather are *institutional*, and too widely dispersed to confer standing."[72] He also pointed to the fact that the Kucinich and Feingold resolutions did not win the attention and votes of either chamber. In effect, he was calling the member-litigants in each case sore losers, a term that echoed the item veto case. "Like the congressmen in *Raines*, *Goldwater*, and *Campbell*, plaintiffs here had extensive 'self-help' remedies available to pressure President Bush on terminating the ABM Treaty without Congressional consent."[73] Self-help included direct legislation on the ABM Treaty (and preparing to override a veto) as well as using the budget and nomination processes, and even impeachment threats, to get heard.

Judge Bates next argued that the chambers have not sanctioned the lawsuit "implicitly or explicitly" on behalf of the House or both chambers. He cited *United States v. Ballin* (1892), which said "the two houses of Congress are legislative bodies representing larger constituencies. Power is not vested in any one individual, but in the aggregate of the members who compose the body, and its action is not the action of any separate number of members, but the action of the body as a whole." For this reason, he discouraged members from running "to federal court any time they are on the losing end of some vote or issue . . . and risk substituting judicial considerations and assessments for legislative ones."[74] Bates further explained that even if Congress had standing, the courts would not touch the case under the political question doctrine. While acknowledging there was no controlling opinion in *Goldwater* (again, six justices voted for dismissal on jurisdictional grounds, but only four of them on PQD), he nonetheless found Justice Rehnquist's opinion "instructive and compelling" here because there was no textual basis to find a constitutional answer to the question and even private litigation on a separate treaty case under Reagan found the PQD relevant.[75] Quoting Justice Powell in *Goldwater*, Bates added that the ABM Treaty dispute was not ripe and represented the interests of a small group of members.[76] Bates also borrowed from Powell on noting the "disrespect" shown to the elected branches when federal courts intrude into these types of political disputes.[77]

After several Republican senators filed an amicus brief in the case defending President Bush, Kucinich lodged opposition, noting the "turnaround" of two amici. "Senators Strom Thurmond and Jesse Helms, were parties to *Goldwater v. Carter*, in which they espoused Plaintiffs' position in this case—the need for congressional authorization for treaty termination. This facile turnaround casts doubt on *amici*'s argument."[78] This point shows how some members of Congress, on both sides of the partisan aisle, viewed the treaty abrogation power through partisan lenses while invoking broader constitutional questions. Members do not challenge their own party's president as readily. In February, 2019, President Trump announced the US was pulling out of the Intermediate Range Nuclear Forces Treaty, which was negotiated between President Reagan and President

Mikhail Gorbachev in 1987. The treaty resulted in the mutual destruction of almost 2,700 nuclear missiles.[79] Trump had already pulled out of the Iranian nuclear agreement, which was negotiated by President Obama and not submitted to the Senate, but in this instance Trump invoked agreement with the Obama administration's negative assessment of Russia's compliance.[80] Neither recent action is likely to be challenged in Congress or federal court by Republicans, but Trump's announcement of the treaty withdrawal spurred at least one Democrat in both the House and Senate to file protest bills within weeks of the President's decision.[81]

House of Representatives v. Burwell (2016)

In the hyperpartisan divided government that marked Obama's second term as president, the GOP majority in the House of Representatives formally authorized an interbranch lawsuit through regular legislative processes on a party-line vote. This action was designed to answer one of the judicial arguments posed in *Raines* and subsequent cases, such as *Kucinich v. Bush*, about articulating a perceived institutional injury via formal chamber action rather than individual members purporting to speak for the whole body. The House lawsuit was one of many different legal methods utilized by Republicans to attack the Affordable Care Act after its passage in 2010, which had survived a series of state and private plaintiff legal tests culminating in 2012 in the Supreme Court.[82] The act also survived over sixty repeal attempts in the Republican-controlled House after the majority switched in the off-year election in November 2010.[83]

The House suit challenged a type of spending administered by then health and human services secretary Sylvia Matthews Burwell and Secretary of the Treasury Jack Lew. The court case highlighted two types of health insurance subsidies related to the law. Section 1401 enumerated "premium tax credit" administered by the Internal Revenue Service to help households buy insurance under the law if they met an income range. Section 1402, meanwhile, related to a "cost-sharing" provision with insurance companies who offer health plans through the Affordable Care Act with reduced out-of-pocket costs to customers. The federal government would offset these losses through reimbursements to the insurance companies. The House argued in the case that the first type of subsidy was funded by a permanent appropriation but the second type required an annual appropriations approval. The complaint said that "Congress has not, and never has, appropriated any funds (whether through temporary appropriations or permanent appropriations) to make any Section 1402 Offset Program payments to Insurers." Therefore, the main legal challenge was whether president violated Article I, Section 9, Clause 7 of the Constitution: "No Money shall be drawn from the Treasury, but in Consequence of Appropriations made by Law."[84]

After a protracted and inconclusive budget process spanning late 2014 and early 2014, President Obama signed into law two continuing resolutions to keep the government operating. Despite a funding proposal for cost-sharing by the president's budget plan, neither resolution ultimately included an appropriation for section 1402.[85] In protest that July, the House passed a resolution to authorize the Speaker to file suit in federal court against an executive agency head administering the health care act for "failure . . . to act in a manner consistent with that official's duties under the Constitution and laws of the United States with respect to implementation of any provision of the Patient Protection and Affordable Care Act." The bill passed along strict party lines, by a vote of 225–201.[86] When the 113th Congress expired, the next Congress approved an updated resolution replacing the new Congress as the plaintiff.[87]

During that first round of legislative action to authorize the lawsuit, the House Rules Committee issued a report that laid out an ironic position of pushing for full Affordable Care Act enforcement. The broader point was, as we have seen repeatedly, a selective pushback against opposition party presidents. "The President has failed on numerous occasions to fulfill his duty under Article II, section 3 of the Constitution of the United States to faithfully execute the laws passed by Congress. He has ignored certain statutes completely, selectively enforced others, and bypassed the legislative process to create his own laws by executive fiat. These unilateral actions have led to a shift in the balance of power in favor of the presidency, challenging Congress' ability to effectively represent the American people." In response to the criticism of such lawsuits generally that say Congress must use its legislative processes to stop unauthorized executive actions already in progress, the report added that "the Founders never intended that Congress legislate twice just to ensure its laws have meaning.[88] In the report's dissenting views, Democrats on the House Rules Committee argued that the exercise was a "a partisan, one-House political gimmick. This Republican-led House, which refuses to do its own job, is instead suing the President for doing his."[89]

In the first round of the case, district judge Rosemary Collyer observed that the two alleged violations had different legal origins and potential: "Distilled to their essences, the Non-Appropriation Theory alleges that the Executive was unfaithful to the Constitution, while the Employer-Mandate Theory alleges that the Executive was unfaithful to a statute, the [Affordable Care Act]." Judge Collyer found the House had standing to assert the first claim but not the second. "Properly understood, however, the Non-Appropriation Theory is not about the implementation, interpretation, or execution of any federal statute. It is a complaint that the Executive has drawn funds from the Treasury without a congressional appropriation—not in violation of any statute, but in violation of Article I, § 9, cl. 7 of the Constitution."[90] Collyer said the House had standing to sue because it "has suffered a concrete, particularized injury. . . . The Congress . . . is the only body empowered by the Constitution to adopt laws directing monies to be spent from the U.S. Treasury. . . . Yet this constitutional structure would collapse, and the role of the House would be meaningless, if the Executive could circumvent the appropriations process and spend funds however it pleases."[91]

Judge Collyer went further to say that "prudential considerations do not counsel avoidance of this dispute. . . . Despite its potential political ramifications, this suit remains a plain dispute over a constitutional command, of which the Judiciary has long been the ultimate interpreter."[92] Her main point was that the existence of the House members as plaintiffs did not automatically trigger PQD concerns, nor would (in the judge's view) her decision suddenly "open floodgates," as it was limited to the unique facts under consideration. She added that "the rarity of these circumstances itself militates against dismissing the case as nonjusticiable."[93] Yet Collyer acknowledged that there was no straight line between *Raines*, other precedents, and the House suit.[94]

In the second round of the case, getting to the merits, Judge Collyer forged a new path to think about the origins and significance of this type of congressional action. After allowing the standing claim, the merits of the case centered on whether Congress appropriated the billions spent on section 1402 reimbursements to insurance companies, which were implemented by the executive branch. On this question, Collyer's decision was, again, in the House's favor. "Paying out Section 1402 reimbursements without an appropriation thus violates the Constitution. Congress authorized reduced cost sharing but did not appropriate monies for it, in the FY 2014 budget or since. Congress is the only source for such an appropriation, and no public money can be spent without one. The Secretaries' textual and contextual arguments fail. . . . The House's injury depends on the Constitution and not on the U.S. Code."[95]

But Judge Collyer stayed the injunction pending appeal. The next year, President Trump and the House plaintiffs settled the case, although the Trump administration had already continued the Obama administration's legal argument, more for the institutional posture than a policy defense of any feature of the Affordable Care Act. The result of the settlement was that Collyer's rulings remain in place, but the court's order to the Trump administration to stop making the payments was vacated.[96] As noted by one law blogger, this settlement shows the remaining institutional differences between the Congress and the executive branch, even when both are held by the same party. Presidents act to defend their prerogatives as presidents, regardless of party. Congress does not act consistently and is much more likely to defend its constitutional place against an opposition president. Congress's cause was further deflated in the settlement, which said decisions by Collyer do not stand as precedent. Future congressional plaintiffs (of either party) may not benefit from those rare victories.[97]

This question became relevant soon after the settlement regarding Trump's emergency declaration in February 2019. As noted in chapter 5, the House and Senate disapproved of the President's action that month, in a first since the National Emergencies Act was passed in 1976. The president responded with a veto of the disapproval.[98] Although Congress did not have the two-thirds majority to override, it is possible that this legislative process, along with the earlier appropriations conflicts that lead to Trump's decision to fund the border wall through the emergency measure, may "count" for private or public litigation as showing clear and repeated legislative intent. As always, the first legal battle is over who is "injured" by these actions to bring standing, which may disadvantage state-based plaintiffs in the ongoing litigation filed by at least 17 states' Democratic attorneys general.[99] In April 2019, the Democratic leadership of the House of Representatives also filed a lawsuit challenging Trump's emergency declaration. Despite the clear record of legislative intent, a half century of precedent created a formidable obstacle course for this avenue to resolve both longstanding imbalances of institutional power and specific policy and partisan disagreements.

For most of the twentieth century, Democratic and Republican presidents were enthusiastic defenders (and expanders) of their office's constitutional authority, while members and leaders in Congress routinely struggled to speak and act consistently on institutional prerogatives. From the perspective of members, finger-wagging after presidential "overreach" is much easier than getting their preferences organized through the challenging legislative processes in the House and Senate. Neither party in Congress has shown sustained interest in holding their own presidents to the constitutional fire. What is clear from this chapter, and the previous ones, is that federal courts are hesitant to jump into separation of powers disputes unless members prove injuries at the narrow, member level or broad chamber level. Federal courts use standing and other justiciability doctrines to force private and public plaintiffs to demonstrate why courts are the appropriate venue to correct a problem. The difference between private and public plaintiffs in executive powers cases is that private plaintiffs do not have as many avenues to express and resolve their grievances as members of Congress. Members have had some success in getting court attention to their conflicts, but the outcomes do not, and cannot, revamp the larger imbalances of power that drive the legal strategy. Legal routes may only be easier than legislative processes in the short term.

LAWFUL BUT AWFUL

After Democrats lost their House majority in the 2010 midterm election, President Barack Obama announced his intention to act unilaterally whenever possible, while still pressuring the newly divided Congress to pass his legislative program. Obama said that he had an obligation to fulfill campaign promises and his vision of the national interest. His communications director started a White House blog in 2011 listing the administration's economic and regulatory efforts, called "We Can't Wait."[1] In 2014, after repeated Republican criticism of these and other executive orders, proclamations, and memoranda spanning a variety of domestic and foreign policies, Obama made headlines by responding to these partisan attacks with an institutional shrug: "so sue me."[2] As Chapter 6 discussed, House Republicans did so and achieved rare success on standing and merits related to the implementation of the Affordable Care Act.

Also in 2014, members of the House of Representatives considered the Executive Needs to Faithfully Observe and Respect Congressional Enactments (ENFORCE) Act. This bill was designed to convey members' standing more consistently in future lawsuits against the executive branch. As noted throughout the previous chapters, some federal judges over the past fifty years of member lawsuits ruled favorably on these suits' justiciability, but their rulings were almost always overturned on appeal or expressed in dissenting opinions. The bill was sponsored by Trey Gowdy (R-SC), a prominent critic of President Barack Obama and his administration, and passed the House in a party-line vote.[3] Although he stated the problem of interbranch imbalances clearly, debates over this bill served to illuminate partisan inconsistency on pursuing congressional power.

Gowdy was requesting more judicial intervention to stop executive branch over-reach, but targeted President Obama specifically. "If a President does not faith-fully execute the law, Mr. Chairman, what are our remedies? Do we just sit and wait on another election? Do we use the power of the purse, the power of im-peachment? Those are punishments; those are not remedies. The remedy is to do exactly what Barack Obama said to do: to go to court, to go to the Supreme Court and have the Supreme Court say once and for all. We don't pass suggestions in this body, Mr. Chairman, we don't pass ideas; we pass laws, and we expect them to be faithfully executed."[4]

Ranking member of the House Judiciary Committee, John Conyers (D-MI), responded by dismissing the entire exercise as a gimmick. He said the executive branch has the constitutional right, and even duty, to interpret the laws of Con-gress and the Constitution through executive action, such as the Emancipation Proclamation under President Abraham Lincoln and the desegregation of the armed forces under Harry Truman. "The ENFORCE Act would essentially allow Federal courts to second-guess decisions by the executive branch in a potentially vast range of areas that are committed under the Constitution to the discretion of the political branches like the conduct of foreign affairs."[5] But Democrats have also sued to stop Republican presidents on both foreign and domestic policy. In 2014, however, the ENFORCE Act was dead-on-arrival in the then-Democratic-dominated Senate. President Obama issued a veto threat, but did not need to fol-low through.[6]

During the debate, Gowdy also quoted extensively from Obama's scathing crit-icism of executive branch overreach when George W. Bush was in office. Gowdy contrasted Senator Obama's rhetoric with President Obama's own embrace of ex-pansive executive authority, at home and abroad. Other journalists and scholars have noted this type of candidate turnaround in Obama and many others.[7] But there are few punishments meted out by Congress for this institutional pattern seen time and again, unless fueled by partisan opposition in Congress. It has be-come part of our national political culture to expect presidents to expand the institutional waistline of their office and hand the expanded presidential pants to their successor, who will utilize and stretch them even farther, regardless of party. Each modern president thus helps all future presidents make their institutional arguments for, and legal defenses of, unilateralism, but Congress does not help future Congresses with a similar consistency. In the decades after the bipartisan rebuke of President Richard Nixon, members and leaders of Congress defend their branch against executive encroachment with transparent sensitivity to the parti-san landscape.

Can federal courts stop this systemic dysfunction in the separation of powers by policing every allegedly egregious instance of presidential overreach and/or force members of the House and Senate to revive institutional ambition? This book answers no, while also acknowledging the deep and broad existential crisis that has led hundreds of members to seek relief outside of the chambers' vast arsenal of existing constitutional weapons.

The twelve interviews conducted for this book explored the "awful" side of congressional delegation of power and executive expansion, which are more than theoretical constitutional arguments. The human consequences of executive branch unilateralism can be tragic, with ripple effects that last decades. These points were especially prominent among members and attorneys on specific foreign policies that have destabilized governments around the world and inflicted lasting harm to innocent civilians and, some argue, long-term U.S. national security. Member-litigants and attorneys explained that they went to court because they could not muster the supermajorities to stop presidents from doing what Congress never authorized in the first place through simple majorities. They also expressed deep frustration that otherwise "activist" judges became restrained on separation of powers questions.

The "lawful" perspective of these conflicts is not necessarily a defense of these policies, nor a muscular executive branch in general.[8] Rather, federal judges cannot take on the presidency in sustained and meaningful ways without Congress's support for its own prerogatives and powers—regardless of which party is in power and where. Congress seems to turn against the presidency—and to the federal courts—for short-term partisan policy objectives. The vast majority of plaintiffs in challenges to executive branch authority come from the opposition party in Congress. The legal arguments are consistent on each side—presidents defend themselves like their predecessors, and members echo previous litigants' claims as well. But when the lineups are partisan, this route of action can be dismissed as political theater. Aside from the issues at stake in each lawsuit, together these cases reflect deep inconsistencies within Congress about its role in forging a vision of the national interest when political pressures do not align with consistent institutional ambition.

In previous work, I examined patterns of ambivalence in congressional behavior on core enumerated institutional powers spanning budgets, war, trade, and base closures.[9] I found that members and leaders of Congress (in both parties) sometimes eagerly delegated power to automatic processes and even opposition party presidents, then expressed regret when policy outcomes did not go as planned or potentially harmed their own states and districts. But when the next opportunity to take back power came to Congress, the branches often renewed and even expanded the delegation, or otherwise punted an opportunity to put those previous regrets into new law. Federal courts cannot possibly direct the House and Senate's struggle to reconcile difficult political puzzles surrounding how, when, and why to use their powers on national public policies that will have profound consequences for local, state, and regional interests. In fact, as the book shows in each part, judicial decisions can exacerbate Congress's difficulties.

An example of these complex layers came in the institutional and policy conflicts surrounding President Trump's emergency declaration in 2019. Trump invoked the 1976 National Emergencies Act (NEA), which was designed at a time of a resurgent Congress to end existing emergencies stretching back to Harry Truman's administration. It also created a process by which the House and Senate could stop future declarations, if it wished, by simple majorities. The contours of what constituted an emergency were not defined by the statute. But if the House and Senate wanted to disapprove, for any reason, it could do so by a concurrent resolution that required a simple majority vote in both chambers and would not be presented to the President. On an unrelated issue in 1983, the Supreme Court's landmark *INS v. Chadha* declared all legislative vetoes unconstitutional. The House and Senate amended the NEA in 1985 to say that Congress would now have to pass a joint resolution to disapprove, which the President could veto.[10] Although Congress could have attempted to revisit the entire statute, the 1985 procedural update came in a "Miscellaneous Provisions" title of an authorization bill that funded the Department of State and other foreign relations projects.[11]

As anticipated in 2019, Trump did veto the congressional disapproval of his emergency declaration, and the House and Senate did not have the votes to override by two-thirds. With twenty-five Republicans across both chambers as exceptions, the entire episode was predictably partisan. The Republican members of the House and Senate who went against their party's President explained their action on one or more of three types of arguments: partisan pragmatism (this weapon will be used by Democratic presidents to get around Republican opposition in the future), textual constitutional prohibitions (Congress has appropriations power, per Article I, sections 8 and 9), and a constituency representation argument (the money Trump is trying to redirect will come from Department of Defense projects that are vital to the economic interests in the districts). Put together, these arguments have the pretense of institutional ambition, but it is hard to take this lesson from such a divisive partisan moment. Senator Lamar Alexander (R-TN) invoked all three categories of argument in his floor statement before voting for the disapproval.[12] Alexander is not seeking reelection in 2020. Of the eleven other Republicans who voted against Trump, only one will face voters in that year—Senator Susan Collins of Maine.[13] Private litigation on the issue of the emergency declaration is more likely to succeed than public litigation by states or members of Congress. Private litigants can claim an injury related to economic harm if eminent domain conflicts come from government seizure for new wall construction.[14] Courts are far more inclined to accept and hear these types of cases than those claiming vaguer injuries related to shifting budget priorities or institutional policy preferences. As we saw in each part of the book, federal courts have on occasion delivered institutional power back to Congress via private litigation. But the refusal of the House and Senate to protect their own prerogatives through regular legislative processes dilutes these victories or makes them hollow in the longer story of interbranch balance. As Justice Robert Jackson said in his landmark concurrence in *Youngstown Sheet & Tube v. Sawyer*, "But I have no illusion that any decision by this Court can keep power in the hands of Congress if it is not wise and timely in meeting its problems. A crisis that challenges the President equally, or perhaps primarily, challenges Congress. . . . We may say that power to legislate for emergencies belongs in the hands of Congress, but only Congress itself can prevent power from slipping through its fingers."[15]

Federal courts are still necessary to protect private citizens and groups, and the courts can unwittingly still be caught up in partisan fights along the way. The American Civil Liberties Union has filed 170 private plaintiff lawsuits since 2017 against the Trump administration,[16] and partisan state attorneys general targeted Obama and are targeting Trump, with some success.[17] These kinds of lawsuits have different origins and consequences than member suits, but together show the breadth and depth of both parties' methods of detouring around the Congress to make, or unmake, public policy.

Constitutional questions should be part of everyday politics and policy in Congress. Shunting these issues to the courts as legal disputes may backfire whether or not judges decide cases on the merits. Each part of this book explains how even nondecisions by courts turn into lasting precedent. When members tried to sue on war powers and other types of executive unilateralism and were rebuffed on justiciability, a flipped constitutional order was built and cemented inadvertently. Members were told to come back to court to be heard on the merits only after they had exhausted other remedies, which implied the controversial presidential action at issue was constitutional until members of the House and Senate passed two rounds of legislation—the second in the unlikely form of a veto override. On various legislative processes, members asked federal courts to undo procedural "reforms" that purposefully disadvantaged Congress. When the members "won" directly in a member suit (Gramm-Rudman-Hollings) or indirectly through a private suit (Line Item Veto Act), the chambers reacted by attempting to get around the decision and re-delegate power in a new way.

Recent attention to congressional gridlock and partisan polarization is only part of the story of what is wrong with the separation of powers in recent decades.[18] Scholars and the media should also explore the rhythms of constitutional dysfunction that remain stubbornly consistent between the three branches under different partisan and policy landscapes. Partisanship and electoral dynamics may always dominate daily headlines, but both parties bear some responsibility for expanded presidential power, congressional ambivalence, and judicial discomfort about getting involved. Member lawsuits are a diagnostic tool to expose and dissect each of these points. Even if a court cure for these challenges is misguided, member suits shed needed light on deep institutional pathologies.

Member suits can bring needed attention to the constitutional obstacle course that Congress must clear to assert its enumerated Article I powers. But the unintended outcomes of these cases also illuminate the many reasons to keep courts out of certain intra- and interbranch conflicts. Federal judges may not welcome new fronts of partisan and policy division. Formal actions by members of Congress, in committees and on the floors, create a public record of accountability. Many in the media took note about one week in March 2019, when President Trump sustained three blows on the floors of the House and Senate. First, the House and Senate passed a measure invoking the War Powers Resolution to reduce the U.S.'s support of a Saudi Arabian–led coalition to defeat the Houthi rebels in Yemen, who are backed by Saudi and U.S. rival Iran.[19] Second, the House and Senate passed the emergency declaration disapproval bill, as mentioned. Third, the House passed 420-0 a nonbinding concurrent resolution to release the special counsel report investigating the President.[20] The President could prevail in the end on all of these fronts, but members' decisions and reasons are now part of the institutional record, which may be more significant in the long-run than a day in court.

Acknowledgments

This book began as a vague, but persistent, question over twenty years ago. Jeffrey K. Tulis assigned parts of Jesse H. Choper's 1980 book, *Judicial Review and the National Political Process: A Functional Reconsideration of the Role of the Supreme Court* in a graduate seminar at the University of Texas at Austin. Choper's preference that the Supreme Court stay out of separation of powers conflicts remained in the back of my mind as I wrote two books on congressional delegation of power (and resulting legal conflicts) related to budget process reform, base closure commissions, presidential trade promotion authority, and various domestic and foreign policies after 9/11, including the Patriot Act and second Iraq war. These events made me wonder if Choper was wrong. Perhaps federal courts could help reset systemic pathologies in separation of powers. Then I found a little-explored corner of jurisprudence to focus the question: around two dozen lawsuits filed by members of Congress beginning in the early 1970s.

Three conferences in particular assisted the book's early focus and development. In 2014, I had an opportunity to organize panels for the Southern Political Science Association conference and decided to use this opportunity to engage Jesse Choper in person. I organized a roundtable to celebrate the early thirty-fifth anniversary of his 1980 book. To my delight, he accepted the invitation. I put myself on the panel and confronted him with the member lawsuits on war powers that I thought showed the federal court's missed opportunities to help Congress fight executive unilateralism. He listened politely and offered new insights but did not budge on his core points. The entire project began to turn in a different direction after this exchange. In 2015, I gave two papers on parts 1 and 2 of this book at the American Political Science Association's annual meeting. I started to see the subtle ways that the lawsuits were backfiring on the plaintiffs. In a panel organized by J. Mitchell Pickerill, I argued that judicial activism in legislative process cases had not curtailed congressional compulsions to delegate. In a panel organized by James P. Pfiffner, I explored how judicial restraint had unintentionally helped to flip constitutional war powers (and won the presidency section's conference paper award, thanks to his nomination).

As I embarked on the book's final phase, I was grateful to be invited by Benjamin A. Kleinerman to give a paper in 2018 at the 2nd Annual Lincoln Symposium on American Political Thought at the Jack Miller Center in Philadelphia.

He and other conference attendees (especially Sotirios A. Barber, Jeffrey Tulis, and Mariah Zeisberg) offered nuanced, compelling suggestions that guided me through one more round of revisions. The project also benefitted immensely from a polite-yet-thorough examination by my paper's assigned discussant at the conference, Keith E. Whittington.

I have also been fortunate to connect with another group of scholars and practitioners who take separation of powers questions seriously. I am grateful for Louis Fisher's mentorship and his including me in the "Lou-niverse." With special attention from Jim Pfiffner, Nancy Kassop, and Robert Spitzer, portions of chapter 2 first appeared in the June 2016 issue of *Presidential Studies Quarterly*. Words cannot capture fully my appreciation to the three precise and generous readers of the full manuscript at various stages: Roy E. Brownell II, Chris Edelson, and Richard M. Pious. Twelve extensive in-person or phone interviews with members and attorneys involved firsthand in one or more congressional lawsuits deepened my understanding of the legal, policy, and political contours of the cases. Of course, I am responsible for all remaining errors and omissions.

For financial and institutional assistance at the University of Louisville, I thank former department chair Rodger Payne for supporting my applications for a sabbatical and an internal grant, which allowed me to travel to archives at the Library of Congress and conduct in-person interviews. In the Department of Political Science, I am grateful for intellectual energy and inspiration from current and former colleagues, as well as students. For their friendship and astute advice during this project, in and out of the office, I am especially thankful to Anne Caldwell, David Imbroscio, Amanda LeDuke, and Laura Moyer.

At Cornell University Press, I thank senior editor Michael J. McGandy for his patience as the book took shape over several years, as well as his bracing honesty about how to make it more accessible and engaging to potential readers. For final production and marketing, I thank Susan Specter, Martyn Beeny, and Kristen Bettcher, as well as Kate Mertes for preparing the index.

I could not be at this moment without decades of love, encouragement, and keenly observant political banter from all my family circles: Frockt-Steinfeld-Alters, Haydens, Shusters, and my college friends from UW–Madison. I must also express profound gratitude to the special circle from graduate school for our magical years in Austin together: Kelly Bond, Suzanne Globetti, Marc Hetherington, Nicole Mellow, John Nugent, Bruce Peabody, and Joe Smith.

For their affection, encouragement, and flexibility as the book's gestation permeated the entire family's life, I thank my husband Dan and our daughters, Tovah and Talia, to whom the book is lovingly dedicated. Finally, I must recognize my parents, Bonnie Farrier, Alan Beck, and Arthur Farrier, for long conveying an incisive combination of ideals and realpolitik.

Notes

INTRODUCTION

1. See Jerry M. Lewis and Thomas R. Hensley, "The May 4 Shootings at Kent State University: The Search for Historical Accuracy," Kent State University, accessed February 11, 2019, https://www.kent.edu/may-4-historical-accuracy.

2. "Cambodia Bombing Ban: Aug. 15 Cutoff Date Set," *CQ Almanac*, 29th ed. (Washington, DC: Congressional Quarterly, 1974), 861–862.

3. See Fisher 2000; Farrier 2004, 2010; Tulis, 2017.

4. "Federalist 78," *The Federalist Papers*, Congress.gov, accessed February 11, 2019, https://www.congress.gov/resources/display/content/The+Federalist+Papers#TheFederalistPapers-78.

5. See Perry 1991.

6. See Orren and Walker 2013.

7. See *Skaggs v. Carle*, 110 F. 3d 831; 324 U.S. App. D.C. 87 (1997).

8. See Gunther 1964; Nichol 1986; Dessem 1986; Wagner 1982.

9. See Shampansky 2001; Dolan 2016; Cole 2014.

10. "Federalist 51," *The Federalist Papers*, Congress.gov, accessed February 11, 2019, https://www.congress.gov/resources/display/content/The+Federalist+Papers#TheFederalistPapers-51.

11. Bickel 1962, 184, 200.

12. *Baker v. Carr*, 369 U.S. 186, 217 (1962).

13. See Scharpf 1962.

14. Henkin 1976.

15. Choper 1980; see also Mulhern 1988.

16. McGowan 1981, 265.

17. See Abel 1985; Goodman 1990.

18. Christenson and Kriner 2017.

19. See, for example, Rosenberg 1991; Burgess 1992; Tushnet 1999; Pickerill 2004; Whittington 2007; Silverstein 2009; Devins and Fisher 2015.

20. Redish 1985, 1059.

21. Wechsler 1959, 19; see also Thayer 1893, 136–137.

22. Epstein and Posner 2016; Alford 2017; Fisher 2017b.

23. Fisher 2011.

24. See Rubin and Rubin 2012; Seidman 2013; Mosely 2013.

25. See Farrier 2004; 2010.

26. See Kiewiet and McCubbins 1991; Epstein and O'Halloran 1999.

27. See Silverstein 1997 and 2009.

28. *Youngstown Sheet & Tube v. Sawyer*, 343 U.S. 655 (1952).

1. WAR IS JUSTICIABLE, UNTIL IT ISN'T

1. See Bessette and Schmitt 2009; Frisch 2007; Schmitt 2009.

2. See James Madison's convention notes, August 17, 1787, Avalon Project, accessed February 11, 2019, http://avalon.law.yale.edu/18th_century/debates_817.asp; see also Adler 2000, 105–106.

3. "Memorandum from John C. Yoo, Deputy Assistant Attorney General, U.S. Department of Justice, to the Deputy Counsel to the President, "The President's Constitutional Authority to Conduct Military Operations against Terrorists and Nations Supporting Them," September 25, 2001, https://lawfare.s3-us-west-2.amazonaws.com/staging/s3fs-public/uploads/2013/10/Memorandum-from-John-C-Yoo-Sept-25-2001.pdf; see also Prakash and Ramsey 2001.

4. Caroline D. Krass, Office of Legal Counsel, Department of Justice, Memorandum Opinion for the Attorney General, "Authorization to Use Military Force in Libya," April 1, 2011, https://www.justice.gov/sites/default/files/olc/opinions/2011/04/31/authority-military-use-in-libya.pdf.

5. "The Federalist No. 69 [14 March 1788]," *Founders Online*, National Archives, accessed February 11, 2019, http://founders.archives.gov/documents/Hamilton/01-04-02-0220; emphasis in the original.

6. "The Federalist No. 78 [28 May 1788]," *Founders Online*, National Archives, accessed February 11, 2019, http://founders.archives.gov/documents/Hamilton/01-04-02-0241.

7. Rudalevige 2006.

8. Yoo 2010; Posner and Vermeule 2011.

9. Fisher 2013.

10. Howell and Pevehouse 2007; Kriner 2010.

11. Fisher 2000a; Farrier 2010.

12. See Kleinerman 2009; Zeisberg 2013.

13. Yoo 2003; Fisher 2005.

14. Tigar 1970, 1148–1149; Glennon 1990.

15. Ely 1993, 54.

16. Tigar 1970, 1148–1149; see also Franck 1992; Keynes 1982; Redish 1985.

17. *Baker v. Carr*, 369 U.S. 186, 211–212 (1962).

18. Bickel 1971, 145.

19. Choper 1980, 314.

20. Choper 2005, 1497.

21. Devins and Fisher 2004, 103, 126.

22. Fisher 2007.

23. Brownell 2000, 29.

24. *Deciding to Use Force Abroad: War Powers in a System of Checks and Balances*, Constitution Project, 2005, 21, http://www.constitutionproject.org/pdf/War_Powers_Deciding_To_Use_Force_Abroad1.pdf.

25. Adler 2000, 159.

26. Fisher 2005, 469.

27. *Bas v. Tingy*, 4 U.S. (4 Dall.), 37, 40–41 (1800).

28. *Talbot v. Seeman*, 5 U.S. (1 Cranch), 1, 28–29 (1801).

29. *Little v. Barreme*, 6 U.S. (2 Cranch), 170, 179 (1804). Michael Glennon (1990, 110–111) notes the in-depth analysis of this case in 1971 congressional hearings on the initial legislative drafts of the WPR.

30. Keynes 1982, 95.

31. Glennon 1990, 7; Keynes 1982, 95; Ely 1993, 55; Silverstein 1997, 27.

32. *United States v. Smith*, 27 Fed. Case 1192, 1230 (C.C. N.Y. 1806).

33. *Ex parte Bollman*, 8 U.S. (4 Cr.) 75, 94 (1807), cited in Fisher 2005, 471.

34. *United States v. Brown*, 12 U.S. (8 Cr.) 110, 128 (1814), cited in Fisher 2005, 471.

35. *Martin v. Mott*, 25 U.S. (12 Wheat.) 19 (1827), and *Luther v. Borden*, 48 U.S. (7 How.) 1 (1849), both cited in Fisher 2005, 472.

36. *Fleming v. Page*, 50 U.S. (9 How.) 603 (1850), *Mitchell v. Harmony*, 54 U.S. (13 How.) 115 (1851), and *Jecken v. Montgomery*, 54 U.S. (13 How.) 498 (1852), all cited in Fisher 2005, 473–474.

37. Abraham Lincoln, "July 4, 1861: July 4th Message to Congress," Miller Center, accessed February 11, 2019, https://millercenter.org/the-presidency/presidential-speeches /july-4-1861-july-4th-message-congress.

38. See Dueholm 2008.

39. See Bruce A. Ragsdale, "*Ex parte Merryman* and Debates on Civil Liberties during the Civil War," Federal Judicial Center, 2007, p. 7, https://www.fjc.gov/sites/default/files /trials/merryman.pdf.

40. See additional cases in Fisher 2005, 475–479, and Ragsdale 2007, 16–20.

41. *Prize Cases*, 67 U.S. (2 Black), 635, 668 (1862).

42. Ibid., 698–699.

43. *United States v. Anderson*, 76 U.S. (9 Wall.) 56, 70 (1870); *United States v. Runell*, 13 Wall. 623 (1871); and *The Protector*, 12 Wall. 700 (1872), all cited in Fisher 2005, 479.

44. See *The Chinese Exclusion Case*, 130 U.S. 581, 591 (1889); *Dooley v. United States*, 182 U.S. 222, 234 (1901), *Hijo v. United States*, 194 U.S. 315, 323 (1904); *Hamilton v. McClaughry*, 136 Fed. 445, 449 (C.C. Kan. 1905); *Ex parte Orozco*, 201 F. 106, 112 (W.D. Tex. 1012), dismissed, 229 U.S. 633 (1913); *Hamilton v. Kentucky Distilleries Co.*, 251 U.S. 146, 156 (1919); *Ruppert v. Caffey*, 251 U.S. 264 (1920); *United States v. Standard Brewery*, 251 U.S. 210 (1920); *United States v. Cohen Grocery Co.*, 255 U.S. 81 (1921); *Commercial Trust Co. v. Miffer*, 262 U.S. 51 (1923); *U.S. Trust Co. v. Miffer*, 262 U.S. 58 (1923); *Ahrenfeldt v. Miller*, 262 U.S. 60 (1923); *Chastleton Corp. v. Sinclair*, 264 U.S. 543, 547–548 (1924), all cited in Fisher 2005, 479–481; see also Silverstein 1997, 35–36. For more on the "Insular Cases" stemming from the United States' acquisition of territories Cuba, Puerto Rico, the Philippines, and Guam, see Sparrow 2006.

45. *Durand v. Hollins*, 8 Fed. Cas. 111 (S.D. N.Y. 1860) (No. 4,186), cited in Silverstein 1997, 32.

46. *Oetjen v. Central Leather Co.*, 246 U.S. 297, 302 (1917), cited in Silverstein 1997, 37.

47. *United States v. Curtiss-Wright Export Corp.*, 299 U.S. 304 (1936).

48. *Korematsu v. United States*, 323 U.S. 214 (1944).

49. Fisher 2016.

50. *Zivotofsky v. Kerry*, 576 U.S. 1059 (2015).

51. See *Trump v. Hawaii* 585 U.S. ___ (2018).

52. Wildavsky 1966; see also Clark, Egeland, and Sanford 1985, 4.

53. Wormuth and Firmage 1989, 28.

54. "Notes regarding Meeting with Congressional Leaders," June 27, 1950, Harry S. Truman Library and Museum, accessed February 11, 2019, http://www.trumanlibrary.org /whistlestop/study_collections/korea/large/documents/pdfs/ki-2-40.pdf#zoom=100; "Memo of Conversation," June 27, 1950, Harry S. Truman Library and Museum, accessed February 11, 2019, http://www.trumanlibrary.org/whistlestop/study_collections/koreanwar /documents/index.php?pagenumber=2&documentdate=1950-06-27&documentid=ki -12-4.

55. Fisher2013.

56. Keynes 1982, 111.

57. See R. F. Turner 1996.

58. *Weissman v. Metropolitan Life Ins. Co.*, 112 F. Supp. 420, 425 (D. Cal. 1953); *Gaglionnella v. Metropolitan Life Ins. Co.*, 122 F. Supp. 246, 250 (D. Mass. 1954); *Carius v.*

New York Life Insurance Co., 124 F. Supp. 388, 390 (D. Ill. 1954), all cited in Fisher 2005, 484; see also *United States v. Bolton*, 192 F. 2d 805 (2d Cir. 1951), cited in Kelman 1971, 71.

59. *Luftig v. McNamara*, 252 E. Supp. 819, 821 (D.D.C. 1966), aff'd, 373 E. 2d 664 (D.C. Cir. 1967), cert. denied, 387 U.S. 945 (967); *Berk v. Laird*, 317 F. Supp. 715, 721–727 (E.D. N.Y. 1970); *Orlando v. Laird,* 317 F. Supp. 1013, 1016 (E.D. N.Y. 1970); *Orlando v. Laird*, 443 F. 2d 1039, 1042 (2d Cir. 1970), cert. denied, 404 U.S. 869 (971); *Mottola v. Nixon*, 318 E. Supp. 538 (N.D. Cal. 1970), rev'd, 464 E. 2d 178 (9th Cir. 1972); *DaCosta v. Laird*, 448 E. 2d 1368, 1369 (2d Cir. 1971), cert. denied, 405 U.S. 979 (1972); *DaCosta v. Laird*, 471 F. 2d; 1146, 1147 (2d Cir. 1973); *Mora v. McNamara*, 387 E. 2d 862 (D.C. Cir. 1967), cert. denied, 389 U.S. 934 (1967); *Velvel v. Johnson*, 287 F. Supp. 846 (D.D.C. 1968), aff'd, 415 F. 2d 236 10th Cir. 1969), cert. denied, 396 U.S. 1042 (1970); *McArthur v. Clifford*, 402 E. 2d 58 (4th Cir. 1968), cert. denied, 393 U.S. 1002 (1968); *Massachusetts v. Laird*, 400 U.S. 886 (1970); *Massachusetts v. Laird*, 327 E. Supp. 378, 381 (D. Mass. 1971); *Massachusetts v. Laird*, 451 F. 2d 26, 34 (1971); *Campen v. Nixon*, 56 F.R.D. 404 (N.D. Cal. 1972); *Atlee v. Laird*, 347 F. Supp. 689 (E.D. Pa 1972) (three-judge court), aff'd, 411 U.S. 911 (1973); *Gravel v. Laird*, 347 F. Supp. 7 (D.D.C. 1972); *Sarnoff v. Connally*, 457 E. 2d 809 (9th Cir. 1972); *Head v. Nixon*, 342 E. Supp. 521 (E.D. La. 1972), aff'd, 468 F. 2d 951 (5th Cir. 1972); *Atlee v. Laird*, 347 F. Supp. 689, 694 (E.D. Pa.1972), aff'd summarily, 411 U.S. 911 (1973); *Drinan v. Nixon*, 364 E. Supp. 854, 856 (D. Mass. 1973); *Pietsch v. President of the United States*, 434 E. 2d 861, 863 (2d Cir. 1970); *Davi v. Laird*, 318 F. Supp. 478 (W.D. Va. 1970); all cited in Fisher 2005, 485–488.

60. In 1974, the House Judiciary Committee debated an additional article of impeachment against President Nixon concerned the secret bombing of Cambodia, but it was rejected. https://www.nytimes.com/1974/07/28/archives/a-historic-charge-two-more-articles.html.

61. See Ely 1993, 15–26; Fisher 2013, 128–132; Keynes 1982, 110–115; among others.

62. "Tonkin Gulf Resolution," Public Law 88–408, 88th Congress, August 7, 1964, General Records of the United States Government, Record Group 11, National Archives, accessed February 11, 2019, http://www.ourdocuments.gov/doc.php?flash=true&doc=98 and http://www.ourdocuments.gov/doc.php?flash=true&doc=98&page=transcript; repealed by Public Law 91–672, January 11, 1971, as part of an update of the Foreign Military Sales Act. 91st Cong., 2nd sess.

63. See "Gulf of Tonkin Resolution Is Repealed without Furor," *New York Times*, January 14, 1971, https://www.nytimes.com/1971/01/14/archives/gulf-of-tonkin-resolution-is-repealed-without-furor.html.

64. William Beecher, "Raids in Cambodia by U.S. Unprotested," *New York Times*, May 9, 1969, http://nsarchive.gwu.edu/IMG/Beecherstory.pdf; see also "Operation Menu—Breakfast," March 16, 1969, Richard Nixon Foundation, accessed February 11, 2019, https://www.nixonfoundation.org/artifact/operation-menu-breakfast for additional documents.

65. The proviso said "nothing [herein] shall be construed as authorizing the use of any such funds to support Vietnamese or other free world forces in actions designed to provide military support and assistance to the Government of Cambodia or Laos. . . . *Provided further,* That nothing contained in this section shall be construed to prohibit support of actions required to insure the safe and orderly withdrawal or disengagement of U.S. Forces from Southeast Asia, or to aid in the release of Americans held as prisoners of war" (cited in *Holtzman v. Schlesinger*, 361 F. Supp. 553 [1973]).

66. *The Honorable Parren J. Mitchell et al., Appellants, v. Melvin R. Laird et al.*, 488 F. 2d 611; 159 U.S. App. D.C. 344 (1973).

67. *Commonwealth of Massachusetts v. Laird*, 400 U.S. 886, 896 (1970).

68. *The Honorable Parren J. Mitchell et al., Appellants, v. Melvin R. Laird et al.*, 488 F. 2d 611; 159 U.S. App. D.C. 344 (1973).

69. Ibid.

70. Ibid., 611, 613.

71. Ibid., 614.

72. Ibid., 611, 616. Petition for rehearing en banc was denied, as was the petition for writ of certiorari to the Supreme Court.

73. Phone interview, December 13, 2013.

74. "Cambodia Bombing Ban: Aug. 15 Cutoff Date Set," *CQ Almanac*, 29th ed. (Washington, DC: Congressional Quarterly, 1974), 861–862,

75. *Holtzman v. Richardson*, 361 F. Supp. 544 (E.D. N.Y. 1973).

76. See Richard L. Madden, "Nixon Agrees to Stop Bombing by U.S. in Cambodia by Aug. 15, with New Raids Up To Congress," *New York Times*, June 30, 1973, https://www .nytimes.com/1973/06/30/archives/nixon-a-grees-to-stop-bombing-by-us-in-cambodia -byaug-15with-new.html.

77. *Holtzman v. Richardson*, 549, 554. See *Berk v. Laird*, 429 F. 2d 302 (2d Cir. 1970) and *Orlando v. Laird*, 443 F. 2d 1039 (2d Cir. 1971). Both cases concluded that from 1970 onward, Congress had authorized hostilities in Vietnam to that date through a series of appropriation acts.

78. *Holtzman v. Richardson*, 550. See *Trombetta v. State of Florida*, 353 F. Supp. 575 (M.D. Fla. 1973); *Coleman v. Miller*, 307 U.S. 433, 59 S. Ct. 972, 83 L. Ed. 1385 (1939).

79. *Holtzman v. Richardson*, 549.

80. Ibid., 552–553.

81. *Holtzman v. Schlesinger*, 361 F. Supp. 553.

82. Richard Nixon, "Statement on Signing the Second Supplemental and Continuing Appropriations Bills," July 1, 1973, American Presidency Project, accessed February 11, 2019,https://www.presidency.ucsb.edu/node/255613. See also "Cambodia Bombing Ban."

83. *Holtzman v. Schlesinger*, 361 F. Supp. 553, 565.

84. *Holtzman v. Schlesinger*, 414 U.S. 1304, 1312–1313 (1973).

85. Ibid., 1319–1320. According to news accounts, Holtzman's attorney personally took the appeal from Justice Marshall to Justice Douglas, in Goose Prairie, Washington State. "The attorney flew to Seattle . . . drove five hours towards Goose Prairie, and walked the last mile through the woods to deliver the appeal to Douglas' cabin. Douglas agreed to hear arguments in the matter on Aug. 3; he ruled early in the morning of Aug. 4" ("Cambodia Bombing Ban"), 861.

86. In *Da Costa v. Laird*, 448 F. 2d 1368 (2d Cir. 1971), cert. denied, 405 U.S. 979, 92 S. Ct. 1193, 31 L. Ed. 2d 255 (1972), the Court rejected the contention that the repeal by Congress of the Tonkin Gulf Resolution removed the congressional authorization that was previously sustained in *Orlando v. Laird*, 443 F. 2d 1039 (2d Cir.), cert. denied, 404 U.S. 869, 92 S. Ct. 94, 30 L. Ed. 2d 113 (1971). In *Orlando*, the Court held that the question of whether or not Congress was required to take some action to authorize the Indo-China War not justiciable under *Baker v. Carr*, because the complaint lacked a "judicially discoverable and manageable issue."

87. *Holtzman et al. v. Schlesinger*, 484 F. 2d 1307, 1308–1309 (2d Cir. 1973).

88. Ibid., 1309–1310.

89. The *Joint Resolution Continuing Appropriations for Fiscal 1974*, Public Law 93–52, 93rd Cong., 1st sess., enacted into law July 1, 1973, contains the following provision: "Sec. 108. Notwithstanding any other provision of law, on or after August 15, 1973, no funds herein or heretofore appropriated may be obligated or expended to finance directly or indirectly combat activities by United States military forces in or over or from off the shores of North Vietnam, South Vietnam, Laos or Cambodia." See also *Congressional*

Record 119, 93rd Cong., 1st sess. (June 29, 1973): S12562. Both are cited in *Holtzman et al. v. Schlesinger*, 1313–1314.

90. *Holtzman v. Schlesinger*, 414 US. 1304, 1315–1316.

91. See *Hamdi v. Rumsfeld*, 542 U.S. 507 (2004); *Rasul v. Bush*, 542 U.S. 466 (2004); *Hamdan v. Rumsfeld*, 548 U.S. 557 (2006); *Boumediene v. Bush*, 553 U.S. 723 (2008).

92. Mark Landler, "Asking Congress to Back ISIS Strikes in Syria Is Tricky for Obama," *New York Times*, August 29, 2014, http://www.nytimes.com/2014/08/29/world/middleeast /obama-isis-syria-iraq.html.

93. Representatives Walter Jones (R-NC), James McGovern (D-MA), and Barbara Lee (D-CA) wrote to Speaker Boehner requesting a congressional authorization vote on ISIS bombings on August 27, 2014. See "Lawmakers Ask Boehner for Vote on Iraq," *New York Times*, August 27, 2014, http://www.nytimes.com/interactive/2014/08/27/us /politics/Letter-to-Boehner.html?action=click&contentCollection=Politics&module =RelatedCoverage&region=Marginalia&pgtype=article. Lawmakers are still concerned almost five years later; see Austin Wright, "Lawmakers to Trump: End Unchecked War Powers," *Politico*, February 21, 2017, http://www.politico.com/story/2017/02/lawmakers -trump-end-unchecked-war-powers-235194.

2. SUING TO SAVE THE WAR POWERS RESOLUTION

1. "The President's News Conference," *Weekly Compilation of Presidential Documents* 35, no. 12 (March 19, 1999): 471–484, https://www.govinfo.gov/content/pkg/WCPD-1999 -03-29/pdf/WCPD-1999-03-29-Pg471.pdf.

2. "Letter to Congressional Leaders Reporting on Airstrikes against Serbian Targets in the Federal Republic of Yugoslavia (Serbia and Montenegro)," *Weekly Compilation of Presidential Documents* 35, no. 14 (April 7, 1999): 603, https://www.govinfo.gov/content/pkg /WCPD-1999-04-12/pdf/WCPD-1999-04-12-Pg602.pdf.

3. Adler 2000, 163.

4. A close version of this section of the chapter was published in Jasmine Farrier, "Judicial Restraint and the New War Powers," *Presidential Studies Quarterly* 46 (2016): 387–410. See Richard Nixon, "Veto Message," October 24, 1973, in *Public Papers of the Presidents, Richard M. Nixon* (Washington, DC: Government Printing Office, 1973), 893–895. For the legislative process and additional history of the WPR, see "War Powers," Library of Congress, November 27, 2017, http://www.loc.gov/law/help/war-powers.php.

5. Weed 2019, app. A.

6. *Joint Resolution concerning the War Powers of Congress and the President*, Public Law 93–148, 93rd Cong., 1st sess., 1973. For full text, see "War Powers Resolution," Avalon Project, accessed February 11, 2019, http://avalon.law.yale.edu/20th_century/warpower.asp.

7. Bypassing section 2(c), presidents have often reported military deployments to Congress after the action began, saying the communication is "consistent with" the WPR requirement without acknowledging any sixty–ninety-day "clock" triggered by the report. Only one president, Gerald R. Ford, explicitly cited section 4(a) of the WPR. And Congress has waived the sixty-day period to allow the military action to continue in just four instances (see Weed 2019).

8. For more information on the Supreme Court's invalidation of the legislative veto in *INS v. Chadha*, 462 U.S. 919 (1983), and its effects on the WPR, see Glennon 1990, 43–50, 98–104; Fisher 2013, 299–302.

9. Harris and Espinosa 1981, 297.

10. LeoGrande 1981.

11. Phone interview, October 23, 2013. The "nullification" standard comes from *Coleman v. Miller*, 307 U.S. 433 (1939).

12. *Crockett v. Reagan*, 558 F. Supp. 893, 897–898 (D.D.C. 1982).

13. *Crockett v. Reagan*, 720 F. 2d 1355, 1357 (D.C. Cir. 1983), Bork, J. concurring.

14. *Defense Appropriations Act for FY 1983*, Public Law 97–377 (1982) 97th Cong., 2nd sess. For a summary of Contra funding before and after the Iran-Contra scandal, see "Executive Summary," FAS.org, accessed February 11, 2019, https://fas.org/irp/offdocs /walsh/execsum.htm.

15. Michaels 1987.

16. *Sanchez-Espinoza v. Reagan*, 568 F. Supp. 596, 599–600 (D.D.C. 1983).

17. Ibid., 599.

18. *Sanchez-Espinoza v. Reagan*, 770 F. 2d 202, 210 (D.C. Cir. 1985).

19. Ibid., 211.

20. Rubner 1985, 629.

21. See *Congressional Record* 129, 98th Cong., 1st sess. (October 26, 1983): S14610 and Roll Call 321; *Congressional Record* 129, 98th Cong., 1st sess. (October 28, 1983): S14876– 14877.

22. *Conyers v. Reagan*, 578 F. Supp. 327 (D.D.C. 1984); see McGowan 1981.

23. Rubner 1985, 628.

24. Ciarrocchi 1987, 7.

25. House of Representatives, Subcommittee on Arms Control, International Security, and Science, Hearing, "War Powers: Origins, Purposes, and Applications," 100th Cong., 2nd sess., August 4 and September 22, 1988, 278.

26. Grimmett 2012, 16–17.

27. Democratic Study Group Records, 1912–1995, Library of Congress, box 170, folder 12, memos November–December 1987.

28. *Lowry v. Reagan*, 676 F. Supp. 333, 337–339, 341 (D.D.C. 1987).

29. In a December 15, 2014, phone interview, an attorney involved in this case expressed disappointment in the three-judge panel, two of whom were appointed by Democrats.

30. Grimmett 2012, 21.

31. Selected documents related to the Persian Gulf Conflict are available online at the George H. W. Bush Presidential Library and Museum, accessed February 11, 2019, https:// bush41library.tamu.edu/archives/persian-gulf.

32. *Dellums v. Bush*, 752 F. Supp. 1141, 1145 (1990).

33. Ibid., 1150–1051. Federal district judge Rosemary M. Collyer upheld member-litigant standing in part because the House of Representatives sanctioned the current lawsuit on Affordable Care Act enforcement (*House v. Burwell* 2015, 41). The memorandum opinion can be cited as Civil Action No. 14-1967.

34. Signing Statement, January 14, 1991, Public Law 102–1. George Bush, Statement on Signing the Resolution Authorizing the Use of Military Force Against Iraq Online by Gerhard Peters and John T. Woolley, The American Presidency Project, https://www .presidency.ucsb.edu/node/265739.

35. Grimmett 2012, 24.

36. Adler 2000.

37. "Letter to Congressional Leaders," 603.

38. *1999 Emergency Supplemental Appropriations Act*, Public Law 106–31, 106th Cong., 1st sess. For full background, see also the House Committee on Appropriations' conference report (H. Rept. 106–143), Congress.gov, accessed February 11, 2019, https://www .congress.gov/congressional-report/106th-congress/house-report/143.

39. *Campbell v. Clinton* 203 F. 3d 19 (D.C. Cir. 2000).

40. *Campbell v. Clinton* 52 F. Supp. 2d 44 (D.D.C.1999).

41. *Campbell v. Clinton* 203 F. 3d, 16–37.

42. Phone interviews with a former member-plaintiff (July 13, 2013) and a current member's staffer (August 13, 2013).

43. See "October 11, 2000 Debate Transcript," Commission on Presidential Debates, accessed February 11, 2019, https://www.debates.org/voter-education/debate-transcripts/october-11-2000-debate-transcript.

44. *Joint Resolution to Authorize the Use of United States Armed Forces against Iraq*, Public Law 107–243, 107th Cong., 2nd sess., October 16, 2002. For full legislative history, see "H. J.Res. 114," Congress.gov, accessed February 11, 2019, https://www.congress.gov/bill/107th-congress/house-joint-resolution/114.

45. *Doe v. Bush*, 323 F.3d 440 (1st Cir. 2003).

46. Ibid., 138.

47. Thirty-two members of the House challenged Bush's unilateral abrogation of an Antiballistic Missile Treaty with Russia in December 2001; the case was dismissed on the *Goldwater v. Carter*, 444 U.S. 996 (1979) precedent. See *Kucinich v. Bush*, 236 F. Supp. 2d 1 (2002).

48. See Edelson and Starr-Deelen 2015.

49. See "Precursor to Operation Unified Protector," *NATO and Libya (Archived)*, accessed February 11, 2019, http://www.nato.int/cps/en/natolive/topics_71652.htm.

50. "Remarks by the President on the Situation in Libya," March 18, 2011, Office of the Press Secretary, White House, http://www.whitehouse.gov/the-press-office/2011/03/18/remarks-president-situation-libya.

51. "Letter from the President regarding the Commencement of Operations in Libya," March 21, 2011, Office of the Press Secretary, White House, http://www.whitehouse.gov/the-press-office/2011/03/21/letter-president-regarding-commencement-operations-libya.

52. Fisher 2013, 240.

53. Caroline D. Krass, Office of Legal Counsel, Department of Justice, Memorandum Opinion for the Attorney General, "Authorization to Use Military Force in Libya," April 1, 2011, p. 8, https://www.justice.gov/sites/default/files/olc/opinions/2011/04/31/authority-military-use-in-libya.pdf.

54. For more information on legal position and debates within the administration on this issue, see Edelson and Starr-Deelen 2015; Savage 2011; and Savage and Lander 2011.

55. See "Final Vote Results for Roll Call 412," Office of the Clerk, http://clerk.house.gov/evs/2011/roll412.xml; "Final Vote Results for Roll Call 411," Office of the Clerk, http://clerk.house.gov/evs/2011/roll411.xml; http://www.speaker.gov/press-release/speaker-boehner-challenges-president-obama-legal-justification-continued-operations; "Final Vote Results for Roll Call 483," Office of the Clerk, http://clerk.house.gov/evs/2011/roll493.xml; "Final Vote Results for Roll Call 494," Office of the Clerk, http://clerk.house.gov/evs/2011/roll494.xml (all 112th Cong., 1st sess.; all accessed February 11, 2019).

56. Bennett 2011.

57. *Kucinich v. Obama* 2011, 113.

58. Ibid.

59. *Smith v. Obama*, Civil Action No. 16–843 (D.D.C. 2016); see also Fisher 2017.

60. Mark Landler and Helene Cooper, "In Latest Shift, Trump Agrees to Leave 400 Troops in Syria," *New York Times*, February 22, 2019, https://www.nytimes.com/2019/02/22/world/middleeast/trump-troops-syria-.html.

61. See "Operation Inherent Resolve," U.S. Department of Defense, accessed February 11, 2019, https://dod.defense.gov/OIR.

62. Conor Friedersdorf, "Congress May Declare the Forever War," *Atlantic*, June 12, 2018, https://www.theatlantic.com/ideas/archive/2018/06/congress-may-declare-the-forever-war/562175.

63. See Weed 2019, 52054, and Andrew Rudalevige, "When did Congress Authorize Fighting in Niger? That's an Excellent Question," *Washington Post* ("Monkey Cage" feature), November 17, 2018, https://www.washingtonpost.com/news/monkey-cage/wp/2017/11/11/when-did-congress-authorize-fighting-in-niger-thats-an-excellent-question/?utm_term=.0de075ee8410.

64. S.J. Res. 7, 116th Cong., 1st sess., https://www.congress.gov/bill/116th-congress/senate-joint-resolution/7/text. See also White House, Presidential Veto Message, April 16, 2019, https://www.whitehouse.gov/presidential-actions/presidential-veto-message-senate-accompany-s-j-res-7/.

65. "Report on the Legal and Policy Frameworks Guiding the United States' Use of Military Force and Related National Security Operations," 3–4, report accessed from Matthew Kahn, "Document: White House Legal and Policy Frameworks for Use of Military Force," *Lawfare*, March 14, 2018, https://www.lawfareblog.com/document-white-house-legal-and-policy-frameworks-use-military-force.

3. LEGISLATIVE PROCESSES ARE CONSTITUTIONAL QUESTIONS

1. See Shesol 2010; William E. Leuchtenburg, "When Franklin Roosevelt Clashed with the Supreme Court—and Lost," *Smithsonian.com*, May 2005, https://www.smithsonianmag.com/history/when-franklin-roosevelt-clashed-with-the-supreme-court-and-lost-78497994.

2. See, for example, Barber 1975.

3. *Baker v. Carr*, 369 U.S. 186 (1962) offers the landmark definition of "political questions"; see also Choper 1980.

4. Choper 1980; Campbell 2004.

5. Kiewiet and McCubbins 1991; Epstein and O'Halloran 1999.

6. Tulis 2017; Fisher 2000a.

7. *J. W. Hampton, Jr. & Co. v. United States*, 276 U.S. 394 (1928).

8. *Panama Refining Co. v. Ryan*, 293 U.S. 388 (1935).

9. *Schechter Poultry Corp. v. United States*, 295 U.S. 495 (1935). *Carter v. Carter Coal Company*, 298 U.S. 238 (1936) is sometimes referred to as a third instance of the nondelegation delegation striking down New Deal legislation.

10. *Synar et. al. v. United States*, 626 F. Supp. 1374, 1384 (D.D.C. 1986), discussed in chapter 4.

11. See Vikram David Amar, "*Chevron* Deference and the Proposed 'Separation of Powers Restoration Act of 2016': A Sign of the Times," *Verdict*, July 26, 2016, https://verdict.justia.com/2016/07/26/chevron-deference-proposed-separation-powers-restoration-act-2016-sign-times.

12. See *Wayman v. Southard*, 23 U.S. 1 (1825), concerning state judicial processes that implement parts of the Judiciary Act of 1789.

13. *Field v. Clark*, 143 U.S. 649, 692 (1892).

14. Ibid., 693.

15. Ibid., 697.

16. "Section 315(a), Title III, of the Tariff Act of Sept. 21, 1922, empowers and directs the President to increase or decrease duties imposed by the Act so as to equalize the differences which, upon investigation, he finds and ascertains between the costs of producing at home and in competing foreign countries the kinds of articles to which such duties apply. The Act lays down certain criteria to be taken into consideration in ascertaining the differences, fixes certain limits of change, and makes an investigation by the Tariff Commission, in aid of the President, a necessary preliminary to any proclamation changing the duties" (*J. W. Hampton, Jr. & Co. v. United States*) 276 U.S. 395.

17. Ibid., 409–410.

18. Ibid., 412.

19. For more on "fast track" legislative processes related to trade, see Farrier 2010, 80–113. For more information on the origins and use of presidential tariff power from The Trade Expansion Act of 1962 (P.L. 87–794, 76 Stat. 872.,1962), see U.S. Department of Commerce, "Section 232 Investigations: The Effect of Imports on the National Security," at https://www.bis.doc.gov/232.

20. See Cushman 2008.

21. Public Law 73–67, 48 Stat. 195. (1933). 73rd Cong., 1st sess.

22. Franklin D. Roosevelt, "Executive Order 6204 regarding Interstate Commerce of Petroleum," July 14, 1933, American Presidency Project, accessed February 11, 2019, http://www.presidency.ucsb.edu/ws/?pid=14480.

23. *Panama Refining Co. v. Ryan*, 293 U.S. 388, 415 (1935).

24. Ibid., 420 (1935).

25. Ibid., 434.

26. See Alex McBride, "*Schechter v. U.S.* (1935)," *The Supreme Court*, accessed February 11, 2019, http://www.pbs.org/wnet/supremecourt/capitalism/landmark_schechter.html for a summary of the case.

27. *Schechter Poultry Co. v. United States*, 295 U.S. 495, 528–529 (1935).

28. Ibid., 542.

29. *Yakus v. United States*, 321 U.S. 414, 424 (1944).

30. See *National Labor Relations Board v. Jones and Laughlin Steel Corporation*, 301 U.S. 1 (1937).

31. Ibid., 460.

32. Sunstein 1999, 13.

33. See Moe 2002.

34. Devins and Fisher 2015, 124–125.

35. Korn 1996, 121.

36. See Campbell 2004, 188–189.

37. Korn 1996.

38. Devins and Fisher 2015, 124.

39. The resolution was passed without debate or vote. H.R. 926, 94th Cong., 2nd sess., Congress.gov, accessed February 11, 2019, https://www.congress.gov/bill/94th-congress/house-resolution/926?resultIndex=91.

40. See *INS v. Chadha*, 462 U.S. 919, 929–931 (1983).

41. Ibid., 956–959.

42. Ibid., 959–960.

43. Ibid., 967–968.

44. Ibid., 974.

45. Devins and Fisher 2015, 126; Campbell 2004, 189–190.

46. See Beth 2001.

47. Devins and Fisher 2015, 127.

48. Koh 1990, 141–142.

49. Ibid., 144.

50. *Morrison v. Olson*, 487 U.S. 654, 676 (1988).

51. Ibid., 682.

52. Ibid., 695.

53. Ibid., 699.

54. Ibid., 709–710.

55. See Maskell 2013; "Appointment of Special Counsel," Department of Justice, May 17, 2017, https://www.justice.gov/opa/pr/appointment-special-counsel.

56. *Mistretta v. United States*, 468 U.S., 361, 365 (1989).

57. For current Sentencing Commission guidelines and reports, see https://www.ussc .gov.

58. *Mistretta v. United States*, 367–368.

59. Ibid., 372.

60. Ibid., 374.

61. Ibid., 381.

62. Ibid., 382.

63. Ibid., 388.

64. Ibid., 408.

65. Ibid., 413.

66. Ibid., 422.

67. Ibid., 427.

68. *INS v. Chadha*, 919, 942.

4. COURTS CANNOT UNKNOT CONGRESS

1. "Historical Debt—Outstanding Annual 1950–1999," TreasuryDirect, accessed February 11, 2019, https://www.treasurydirect.gov/govt/reports/pd/histdebt/histdebt _histo4.htm, and Eric Reed, "What is the National Debt by Year from 1790 to 2019?" *The Street,* February 26, 2019, https://www.thestreet.com/politics/national-debt-year-by -year-14876008; see also https://www.cbo.gov/system/files?file=2019-01/54918-Outlook .pdf, and Farrier 2004 and 2011.

2. For a summary of the 1974 Budget Act and a bibliography, see "1974 Congressional Budget and Impoundment Control Act," Slaying the Dragon of Debt, accessed February 11, 2019, http://bancroft.berkeley.edu/ROHO/projects/debt/budgetcontrolact .html.

3. *Balanced Budget and Emergency Deficit Control Act of 1985*, Public Law 99–177, secs. 241, 251–253, 99th Cong., 1st sess., 1985.

4. See 31 U.S. Code 703(e)(1); "About GAO: Comptroller General," U.S. Government Accountability Office, accessed February 11, 2019, https://www.gao.gov/about/workforce /ocg.html.

5. Phone interview with attorney in *Synar v. United States*, 626 F. Supp. 1374 (D.D.C. 1986), and *Bowsher v. Synar*, 478 U.S. 714 (1986).

6. *Balanced Budget and Emergency Deficit Control Act of 1985*, sec. 274(a)(b)(c) and 275 (f).

7. See Farrier 2016.

8. *Synar v. United States*, 1381–1382.

9. Ibid., 1388–1389.

10. Ibid., 1403–1404.

11. *Bowsher v. Synar*, 726.

12. See *INS v. Chadha*, 462 U.S. 919 (1983); Fisher 1987.

13. *INS v. Chadha*, 736–737.

14. Ibid., 759, 760.

15. Ibid., 777–778, 787.

16. Farrier 2004, 117–118.

17. See Epstein and O'Halloran 1999.

18. Farrier 2010, 45–81.

19. *National Defense Authorization Act for Fiscal Year 1991*, Public Law 101–510, Title XXIX—Defense Base Closures and Realignment, 101st Cong., 2nd sess., October 26, 1990. Senator Spector voted "yea" on the conference report. See "Roll Call Vote

101st Congress—2nd Session," Senate.gov, accessed February 11, 2019, http://www.senate
.gov/legislative/LIS/roll_call_lists/roll_call_vote_cfm.cfm?congress=101&session=2&vote
=00320.

20. *Disapproving the Recommendations of the Defense Base Closure and Realignment Commission*, H.J. Res. 308, 102nd Congress, 1st sess., July 30, 1991; see "Final Vote Results for Roll Call 232," Office of the Clerk, accessed February 11, 2019, http://clerk.house
.gov/evs/1991/roll232.xml.

21. H.R. Conf. Rep. 101–923, 101st Cong., 2nd sess., 706, cited in *Specter v. Garrett*, 777 F. Supp. 1226, 1228 (E.D. Penn 1991).

22. *Specter v. Garrett*, 1229.

23. *Specter v. Garrett*, 971 F. 2d 936, 946 (3d Cir. 1992).

24. Ibid., 947.

25. Ibid., 953–954.

26. Ibid., 961.

27. *Franklin v. Massachusetts*, 505 U.S. 788 (1992), which applied the Administrative Procedure Act on the question of what constituted "final agency action." Only final agency action is reviewable by the federal court. The Franklin case involved in a suit against the "President, the Secretary of Commerce, and various public officials, challenging the manner in which seats in the House of Representatives had been apportioned among the States," and challenged the method by which the Secretary of Commerce prepared the census report. The president could revise the Secretary's report before submitting to Congress so the action was not "final."

28. Reargued, *Specter v. Garrett*, 995 F. 2d 404 (3d Cir. 1993).

29. *Dalton v. Specter*, 511 U.S. 462, 463 (1994).

30. Aaron Mehta and Joe Gould, "Pentagon to Congress: We Need Base Closures," *DefenseNews*, April 15, 2016, http://www.defensenews.com/story/defense/2016/04/15/pentagon
-requests-brac/83082038.

31. Rubenfeld 1996.

32. The text of the contract can be found here: https://global.oup.com/us/companion
.websites/9780195385168/resources/chapter6/contract/america.pdf.

33. H.R. Res. 6, 104th Cong., sec. 106(a) (1995), reprinted in H.R. Doc. No. 103–342, at 658 (1995).

34. Rubenfeld 1996, 73.

35. See Ackerman 1995; McGinnis and Rappaport 1995.

36. A transcript of the Constitution can be found at https://www.archives.gov/founding
-docs/constitution-transcript.

37. *David E. Skaggs et al. v. Robin H. Carle*, 898 F. Supp. 1, 2 (D.D.C. 1995).

38. *Michel v. Anderson*, 817 F. Supp. 126, 141 (D.D.C. 1993).

39. *David E. Skaggs et al. v. Robin H. Carle*, 110 F. 3d 831, 834–835 (D.C. Cir. 1997).

40. The case cited H. Res. 238, 104th Cong., 1st sess., 141 Cong. Rec. 10314, 10327–28 (1995) (suspending application of Rules XXI(5)(c) and (d) in connection with Medicare Preservation Act); H. Res. 245, 104th Cong., 1st Sess., 141 Cong. Rec. 10853, 10867–68 (1995) (same in connection with Seven Year Balanced Budget Reconciliation Act); H. Res. 392, 104th Cong., 2nd Sess., 142 Cong. Rec. 3029, 3045 (1996) (same in connection with Health Coverage Availability and Affordability Act); and H. Res. 440, 104th Cong., 2nd Sess., 142 Cong. Rec. 5432, 5444–45 (1996) (same in connection with Small Business Job Protection Act).

41. *Skaggs v. Carle*, 110 F. 3d 831, 836–837 (D.C. Cir. 1997).

42. Ibid., 838–839.

43. *Riegel v. Federal Open Market Committee*, 656 F. 2d 873 (1981); *Vander Jagt v. O'Neill*, 699 F. 2d 1166 (D.C. Cir. 1983); *Michel v. Anderson*, 817 F. Supp. 126 (1993).

44. *Skaggs v. Carle*, 847.

45. Phone interviews July 12, 2013, and October 3, 2013.

46. See Saturno and Lynch 2019, 1, https://fas.org/sgp/crs/misc/R45552.pdf.

47. See Farrier 2004, 165–214; *Line Item Veto Act*, Public Law 104–130, 104th Cong., 2nd sess., sec. 3.

48. The United States Senate and House of Representatives' Bipartisan Legal Advisory Group jointly appeared as amici curiae to defend the act. Defendants were OMB director Raines and Secretary of the Treasury Robert Rubin.

49. "In each case the D.C. Circuit found no separation-of-powers impediments to adjudication of the merits because, as in the present case, Members' alleged injuries arose from interference with the exercise of identifiable constitutional powers. . . . Although the Supreme Court has never endorsed the Circuit's analysis of standing in such cases, for this Court's purposes these precedents are controlling" (*Raines v. Byrd*, 956 F. Supp. 25, 30–31 [D.D.C., 1997]).

50. Ibid.

51. Ibid., 37.

52. *Raines v. Byrd*, 521 U.S. 811, 859 (1997).

53. Ibid., 824.

54. Ibid., 834.

55. Ibid., 835–836.

56. Ibid., 837.

57. Ibid., 840.

58. Ibid., 841–842. See also *Coleman v. Miller*, 307 U.S. 433 (1939). The Supreme Court split on whether it had jurisdiction over an intrastate suit filed by Kansas state legislators to reverse a constitutional amendment ratification.

59. For a news item about Clinton's first use of the item veto, see Allen R. Myerson, "Billionaire Feels Sting of Line Item Veto," *New York Times*, August 12, 1997, http://www.nytimes.com/1997/08/12/us/billionaire-feels-sting-of-line-item-veto.html.

60. *William J. Clinton, President of the United States, et al. v. City of New York et al.*, 524 U.S. 417 (1998); *Snake River Potato Growers, Inc., et al., v. Robert E. Rubin et al.* 985 F. Supp. 168, 171 (D.D.C., 1998).

61. *Clinton v. City of New York*, 447–449.

62. Ibid., 466.

63. Ibid., 496–497.

64. See Fisher 2000a, 149–150; Stewart M. Powell, "In Another Defeat, Congress Overrides Line-Item Veto," *Sun-Sentinel*, February 26, 1998, https://www.sun-sentinel.com/news/fl-xpm-1998-02-26-9802250657-story.html.

65. For more information on post-*Clinton* line-item veto bills in 2006 and 2012, see H.R. 4890, 109th Cong., 2nd sess., Congress.gov, accessed February 11, 2019, https://www.congress.gov/bill/109th-congress/house-bill/4890/actions; Molly K. Hooper, "Line-Item Veto Bill Hits Senate Wall," *The Hill*, May 21, 2012, http://thehill.com/homenews/house/228483-popular-line-item-veto-bill-hits-brick-wall-in-senate.

66. See *Updated Rescission Statistics, Fiscal Years 1974–2017* U.S. Government Accountability Office, September 27, 2018 (https://www.gao.gov/products/B-330019).

67. See Farrier 2004, 2009, and 2011.

68. See "Cloture Motions," Senate.gov, accessed February 11, 2019, http://www.senate.gov/pagelayout/reference/cloture_motions/clotureCounts.htm. See also Binder and Smith 1997; Wawro and Schickler 2006; Koger 2010.

69. See https://www.rules.senate.gov/rules-of-the-senate.

70. *United States v. Ballin*, 144 U.S. 1 (1892). This case upheld the procedures of the House and Senate of counting members present for a quorum to do business. In 1890, the

House eliminated the "disappearing quorum," which allowed members in the chamber to not acknowledge being present for the purpose of preventing business.

71. *Removal Clarification Act*, H.R. 5281, 111th Cong., 2nd sess., December 18, 2010. See also "Senate Vote 278—Fails to Advance Dream Act," Pro Publica, accessed February 11, 2019, https://projects.propublica.org/represent/votes/111/senate/2/278/?nyt=true.

72. On the cloture motion, see DISCLOSE Act, S. 3628, 111th Cong., 2nd sess., July 27, 2010, Senate.gov, accessed February 11, 2019, http://www.senate.gov/legislative/LIS/roll _call_lists/roll_call_vote_cfm.cfm?congress=111&session=2&vote=00220 (technically the vote was fifty-nine in favor, with a vote switch by Harry Reid for procedural reasons and an absent vote by a committed "yea"; Dan Eggen, "Bill on Political Ad Disclosures Falls a Little Short in Senate," *Washington Post*, July 28, 2010, http://www.washingtonpost.com /wp-dyn/content/article/2010/07/27/AR2010072704656.html.

73. *Judicial Watch, Inc. v. United States Senate*, 340 F. Supp. 2d 26 (D.D.C.), aff'd, 432 F.3d 359 (D.C. Cir. 2005); *Page v. Shelby*, 995 F. Supp. 23, 29 (D.D.C.), aff'd, 172 F.3d 920 (D.C. Cir. 1998); *Page v. Dole*, No. 93-1546 (D.D.C. August 18, 1994), vacated as moot, all cited in *Common Cause v. Biden*, 909 F. Supp. 2d 9, 17–27, 27, footnote 2 (D.D.C. 2012).

74. *Common Cause v. Biden*, 909 F. Supp. 2d 9, 17–27, 18 (D.D.C. 2012).

75. *Common Cause v. Biden*, 748 F. 3d 1280 (D.C. Cir. 2014).

76. Phone interview, October 16, 2013.

77. For more examples of filibustered legislation in the Senate, see Dylan Matthews, "17 Bills That Likely Would Have Passed the Senate If It Didn't Have the Filibuster," *Washington Post*, December 5, 2012, https://www.washingtonpost.com/news/wonk/wp/2012 /12/05/17-bills-that-likely-would-have-passed-the-senate-if-it-didnt-have-the-filibuster; Adam Liptak and Michael D. Shear, "Supreme Court to Hear Challenge to Obama Immigration Actions," *New York Times*, January 19, 2016, http://www.nytimes.com/2016/01 /20/us/politics/supreme-court-to-hear-challenge-to-obama-immigration-actions.html and an updated summary of legal actions spanning the Obama and Trump presidencies from the National Immigration Law Center, February 7, 2019, https://www.nilc.org/issues/daca /status-current-daca-litigation/.

78. See Ted Barrett, "Here's Why Senators Don't Want to Change Senate Filibuster Rules," *CNN.com*, May 2, 2017, http://www.cnn.com/2017/05/02/politics/senate-filibuster -rule-change-donald-trump.

79. *U.S. House of Representatives v. Burwell*, 130 F. Supp. 3d 53, 81 (D.D.C. 2015); Opinion [on Motion for Summary Judgment], *U.S. House of Representatives v. Burwell*, No. 14-cv-01967 (D.D.C. May 12, 2016). See also Dolan, 2016, 5.

5. SILENCE IS CONSENT FOR THE MODERN PRESIDENCY

1. *Trump v. Hawaii*, U.S. Supreme Court No. 17-965 (slip opinion, 2018).

2. "President Barack Obama's State of the Union Address," Office of Press Secretary, White House, January 28, 2014, https://www.whitehouse.gov/the-press-office/2014/01/28 /president-barack-obamas-state-union-address.

3. Bessette and Tulis 2009, 12.

4. Fisher 2014, 415.

5. Marshall 2008, 509.

6. See the special volume of *Presidential Studies Quarterly* on inherent power (vol. 47, no. 1, March 2007).

7. Ellis 2009, 3.

8. "Federalist 77," *The Federalist Papers*, Congress.gov, accessed February 11, 2019, https://www.congress.gov/resources/display/content/The+Federalist+Papers#TheFederal istPapers-76.

9. Ellis 2009, 3–4.

10. Fisher 2014, 85.

11. Ellis 2009, 4; Fisher 2014, 85–86.

12. Ellis 2009, 4.

13. See Entin 2015.

14. *Myers v. United States*, 272 U.S. 52, 122 (1926).

15. Ibid., 177.

16. Ibid., 293.

17. Entin 2015, 1081.

18. Ellis 2009, 17.

19. Ibid., 19.

20. *Humphrey's Executor v. United States*, 295 U.S. 602, 626 (1935).

21. Ibid., 627.

22. Ibid., 632. Two such cases arose in *Wiener v. United States*, 357 U.S. 349 (1958), concerning Eisenhower's attempted removal of a member of the post–World War II War Crimes Commission, and *Morrison v. Olson*, 487 U.S. 654 (1988), concerning the creation of the Office of Independent Counsel, discussed in part 2 of this book. The Supreme Court said the commission exercised quasi-judicial functions and therefore ruled unanimously against the president in *Wiener*. In *Morrison*, again, the question concerned whether the appointee, who was selected by a panel of federal judges, could be fired. The Reagan administration argued that the office was a purely executive function, under the *Myers* umbrella and the "for cause" stipulation in the law was an unconstitutional restraint on his power. The Supreme Court disagreed. But, as the law was unpopular with both parties over time, Congress allowed it to expire over a decade later. Although the ball is in Congress's court to include or revisit specific instructions in laws regarding executive branch appointments, litigation can be successful. In 2014, a private company argued that a National Labor Relations Board ruling was void because two board members were improperly installed by President Obama, who claimed he could act unilaterally during a Senate recess. The Court disagreed with the president's definition of "recess" and sided against him. *National Labor Relations Board v. Noel Canning*, 573 U.S. ___ (2014).

23. See Jess Bravin and Brent Kendall, "The Case That Shaped Brett Kavanaugh's Feelings on Executive Power," *Wall Street Journal*, August 31, 2018, https://www.wsj.com/articles /the-case-that-shaped-brett-kavanaughs-thinking-on-presidential-power-1535744028.

24. See Mayer 2001; 2009; Howell 2003.

25. See Fisher 2014, 102; "Immigration Action," Department of Homeland Security, accessed February 11, 2019, https://www.dhs.gov/immigration-action.

26. "Executive Orders Disposition Tables," *Federal Register*, National Archives, accessed February 11, 2019, http://www.archives.gov/federal-register/executive-orders/1952.html; Harry S. Truman, "Executive Order 10340—Directing the Secretary of Commerce to Take Possession of and Operate the Plants and Facilities of Certain Steel Companies," American Presidency Project, accessed February 11, 2019, https://www.presidency.ucsb.edu/node /278590.

27. *Congressional Record* 98, 82nd Cong., 2nd sess. (April 9, 1952): H3916, cited in Fisher 2014, 335.

28. Ibid., April 10, 1952: S3964, 4033–4034.

29. *The Steel Seizure Case*, H. Doc. 534 (Part 1), 82nd Cong., 2nd sess. (1952), 255–266, cited in Fisher 2014, 335–334.

30. *The Steel Seizure Case*, 386 and 426–427, cited in Fisher 2014, 336.

31. *Youngstown Sheet & Tube v. Sawyer*, 103 F. Supp. 569, 573 (D.D.C. 1952).

32. Additional details on the relevant sections of Taft-Hartley that the executive branch could have used is detailed in Justice Burton's concurrence, *Youngstown Sheet &*

Tube v. Sawyer, 343 U.S. 579, 656–660 (1952). Justice Clark's concurrence elaborates on this point and adds two other statutes that Truman could have engaged: the Defense Production Act of 1950 and Selective Service Act of 1948 (ibid., 663).

33. *Youngstown Sheet & Tube v. Sawyer*, 343 U.S. 589.

34. Ibid., 609.

35. Ibid., 614.

36. Ibid., 629.

37. Ibid., 633–634.

38. Ibid., 635.

39. Ibid., 635–638.

40. Ibid., 647.

41. Ibid., 700, 701.

42. See also "Senate's Role in Treaties," Senate.gov, accessed February 11, 2019, http://www.senate.gov/artandhistory/history/common/briefing/Treaties.htm; Fisher 2014, 290.

43. *United States v. Belmont*, 301 U.S. 324, 330 (1937).

44. *United States v. Pink*, 315 U.S. 203, 229 (1942).

45. *Reid v. Covert*, 354 U.S. 1, 16 (1957), Justice Black, J., cited in Fisher 2014, 292.

46. *Dames & Moore v. Regan* 453 U.S. 654, 669 (1981) cited in M. J. Turner 2009.

47. Carter signed Executive Order 12170—Blocking Iranian Government Property on November 14, 1979; see updates available at "1979 Executive Orders Disposition Table," *Federal Register*, National Archives, accessed February 11, 2019, http://www.archives.gov/federal-register/executive-orders/1979.html. He signed Executive Order 12277—Direction to Transfer Iranian Assets on January 19, 1981. Reagan's Executive Order 12294—Suspension of Litigation against Iran, which was signed on February 24, 1981, upheld Carter's orders and detailed the tribunal.

48. Some reports/law reviews describe the decision as unanimous based on a short partial dissent by Justice Powell.

49. *Dames & Moore v. Regan*, 453 U.S. 654, 659 and 661 (1981).

50. Marks and Grabow 1982.

51. See ibid., 69; M. J. Turner 2009, 677–678.

52. Ibid., 656 (case syllabus). For more information on the history of the Hostage Act of 1868 and its connection to the Iranian case, see Mikva and Neuman 1982.

53. *Dames and Moore v. Regan*, 686–688.

54. *United States v. Midwest Oil*, 236 U.S. 459 (1915); Justice Frankfurter's dictum in *Youngstown* (1952), and *Haig v. Agee*, 453 U.S. 280 (1981), which upheld the secretary of state's power to revoke a U.S. citizen's passport under certain circumstances.

55. Koh 1990, 139.

56. D'Arcy 2003, 293.

57. Ibid., 293–294.

58. Koh 1990, 139–140.

59. Memorandum from John C. Yoo, Deputy Assistant Attorney General, U.S. Department of Justice, to the Deputy Counsel to the President, "The President's Constitutional Authority to Conduct Military Operations against Terrorist s and Nations Supporting Them," September 25, 2001, https://lawfare.s3-us-west-2.amazonaws.com/staging/s3fs-public/uploads/2013/10/Memorandum-from-John-C-Yoo-Sept-25-2001.pdf; and "Military Order of November 13, 2001—Detention, Treatment, and Trial of Certain Non-Citizens in the War against Terrorism," *Federal Register* 66, no. 222 (November 16, 2001), Fas.org, https://fas.org/irp/offdocs/eo/mo-111301.htm.

60. Public Law 107–40, emphasis added. See S. J.Res. 23, Congress.gov, accessed February 11, 2019, https://www.congress.gov/bill/107th-congress/senate-joint-resolution/23. See also Kassop 2003.

61. "Executive Order 13425 of February 14, 2007—Trial of Alien Unlawful Enemy Combatants by Military Commission," *Federal Register*, National Archives, accessed February 11, 2019, https://www.federalregister.gov/articles/2007/02/20/07–780/trial-of-alien -unlawful-enemy-combatants-by-military-commission.

62. *Rasul v. Bush*, 542 U.S. 466, 466–467 (2004).

63. See Kathleen T. Rhem, "Status Review Tribunals Under Way at Guantanamo," *DoD News*, August 13, 2004, http://archive.defense.gov/news/newsarticle.aspx?id=25522.

64. *Hamdi v. Rumsfeld*, 542 U.S. 507 (2004).

65. The Detainee Treatment Act was passed as Title X of Division, *Defense Appropriations Act of Fiscal Year 2006*, P. L.109-148 (119 STAT. 2739), 109th Congress, 1st sess., 2005.

66. *Padilla v. Rumsfeld*, 352 F. 3d 695, 712–713 (2d Cir. 2003). *Hamdan v. Rumsfeld*, 548 U.S. 557, 636 (2006), Justice Breyer, S., concurring.

67. *Hamdan v. Rumsfeld*, 636.

68. Pious 2009, 142.

69. Ibid. 148. Hamdan's military commission was reinstated after the MCA of 2006; he was acquitted of the more serious charge of conspiracy to commit acts of terrorism and convicted on the charge of supporting terrorism.

70. *Boumediene v. Bush*, 553 U.S. 723 (2008).

71. Pious 2009.

72. Ryan 2015.

73. Scheppele 2012, 167.

74. Elsea 2015, 2.

75. "Statement by President Trump on Jerusalem," White House, December 6, 2017, https://www.whitehouse.gov/briefings-statements/statement-president-trump -jerusalem.

76. Public Law 107–228, sec. 214(d), 107th Cong., 2nd sess.

77. George W. Bush, "Statement on Signing the Foreign Relations Authorization Act, Fiscal Year 2003," September 30, 2002, American Presidency Project, accessed February 11, 2019, https://www.presidency.ucsb.edu/node/213776. Fisher (2016, 200) argued the Department of Justice's brief in this case failed to note the controversial nature of this signing statement nor the "take care" clause that implies executive adherence to legislation in administration.

78. The Court of Appeals for the DC Circuit reversed on the standing issue, *Zivotofsky v. Secretary of State*, 444 F. 3d 614, 617–619 (2006), but later affirmed the district court's political question determination. See *Zivotofsky v. Secretary of State*, 571 F. 3d 1227, 1228 (2009).

79. *Zivotofsky v. Clinton*, 725 F. 3d, 214, 217 (2011/2012).

80. *Youngstown Sheet and Tube v. Sawyer*, 638.

81. *Zivotofsky v. Kerry*, 576 U.S. 1059(2015).

82. Ibid., Chief Justice Roberts, J., concurring.

83. But both majorities also rejected the executive branch's legal argument that embraced the long-controversial "sole organ" *Curtiss-Wright* dicta. See Fisher 2014, pref., for information on his brief.

84. Franklin D. Roosevelt, "Message to Congress on Stabilizing the Economy," September 7, 1942, American Presidency Project, accessed February 11, 2019, https://www .presidency.ucsb.edu/node/210858.

85. *Youngstown Sheet and Tube v. Sawyer*, 343 U.S. 635, Justice Jackson, R., concurring.

86. Erica Werner, Seung Min Kim, and John Wagner, "Senate Votes to Reject Trump's Emergency Declaration, Setting up President's First Veto," *Washington Post*, March 14, 2019, https://www.washingtonpost.com/politics/trump-renews-veto-threat-as-senate

-prepares-to-rebuke-him-on-national-emergency/2019/03/14/2efbea36-4647-11e9-aaf8
-4512a6fe3439_story.html?noredirect=on&utm_term=.7473c8fcf5da.

87. The National Emergencies Act (NEA), P.L. 94–412, 90 Stat. 1255 (1976), 94th Cong., 2nd sess.

88. See Alan Neuhauser, "State Attorneys General Lead the Charge against President Donald Trump," *U.S. News and World Report*, October 27, 2017, https://www.usnews.com /news/best-states/articles/2017-10-27/state-attorneys-general-lead-the-charge-against -president-donald-trump.

6. SO SUE HIM

1. See Autumn Callan, "Nearly 200 Democratic Lawmakers Sue Trump for Accepting Foreign Payments," *Jurist*, June 14, 2017, https://www.jurist.org/news/2017/06/nearly-200 -democratic-lawmakers-sue-trump-for-accepting-foreign-payments.

2. See *Blumenthal et al. v. Trump*, No. 1:17-cv-01154 (D.D.C. 2017), available online at https://ecf.dcd.uscourts.gov/cgi-bin/show_public_doc?2017cv1154-59.

3. Joint Status Report, *United States House of Representatives v. Eric Hargan, Acting Secretary of Health and Human Services*, No. 16-5202 (D.D.C. 2017), https://images.law.com /contrib/content/uploads/documents/398/6808/16-5202_Documents.pdf.

4. See Fisher 2001, 3–5; Spitzer 2001.

5. *Kennedy v. Sampson*, 364 F. Supp. 1075 (D.D.C. 1973).

6. Ibid. 1075, 1079.

7. Ibid., 1086.

8. *Kennedy v. Sampson*, 511 F. 2d 430 (D.C. Cir. 1974), citing *Wright v. United States*, 302 U.S. 583 (1938).

9. Ibid., page 446.

10. See *Kennedy v. Jones*, 412 F. Supp. 353 (D.D.C. 1976), and Fisher 2001, 5–8.

11. Summary in *Edwards v. Carter*, 445 F. Supp. 1279, 1281 (1978).

12. Ibid., 1283.

13. Ibid., 1284.

14. *Edwards v. Carter*, 580 F.2d 1055, 1061 (D.C. Cir. 1978).

15. Ibid., 1065.

16. For more details on the legislative process and issue background, see "Panama Canal Treaties: Major Victory for President Carter," *CQ Almanac*, 34th ed. (Washington, DC: Congressional Quarterly, 1978), 379–397.

17. Phone interview, December 2, 2016.

18. "The Senate's Role in Treaties," Senate.gov, accessed February 11, 2019, http://www .senate.gov/artandhistory/history/common/briefing/Treaties.htm. This site also explains that the senators vote on a resolution of ratification while the countries that are parties to the agreement are technically the ratifying bodies.

19. Ibid.

20. S. Rept. 97, 34th Cong., 1st sess. (1857), 3, cited in *Treaties and Other International Agreements: The Role of The U.S. Senate: A Study Prepared for the Committee on Foreign Relations, United States Senate*, Congressional Research Service, January 2001, 198, fn. 135, Government Publishing Office, https://www.gpo.gov/fdsys/pkg/CPRT-106SPRT66922/pdf /CPRT-106SPRT66922.pdf.

21. Public Law 95–384, sec. 26, 95th Cong., 2nd sess., 1978, Government Publishing Office, https://www.gpo.gov/fdsys/pkg/STATUTE-92/pdf/STATUTE-92-Pg730.pdf.

22. Public Law 96–8, 96th Cong., 1st. sess., 1979, Congress.gov, accessed February 11, 2019, https://www.congress.gov/bill/96th-congress/house-bill/2479.

23. S. Rept. 96–119, 96th Cong., 1st sess. (1979), 5–6., cited in *Treaties and Other International Agreements*, 198, fn. 135.

24. *Congressional Record* 125 (Part 2), 96th Cong., 1st sess. (June 6, 1979): S13673.

25. Ibid.

26. Additional Senate actions included Resolution 10, introduced by Senator Dole on January 15, 1979, that said "the Senate disapproves of the action of the President of the United States in sending notice of termination of the Mutual Defense Treaty with the Republic of China" (*Congressional Record* 125, 96th Cong., 1st sess. [January 15, 1979]: S2099). Senate Concurrent Resolution 2, "To uphold the separation of powers between the executive and legislative branches of Government in the termination of treaties," by Senator Goldwater, in *Congressional Record* 125 (January 18, 1979): S474.

27. *Goldwater v. Carter,* Civil Action No. 78-2412 (D.D.C. 1979), 3–4.

28. Ibid., 6–7.

29. Ibid., 14.

30. *Congressional Record* 125, 96th Cong., 1st sess. (June 6, 1979): S7015, S7038–S7039 (daily edition).

31. According to Judge Gasch's overview of the subsequent actions: the Senate Foreign Relations Committee on May 1 reported Resolution 15 with an amendment to strike all after the resolving clause and insert substitute language providing several grounds for unilateral presidential terminations of treaties. It was this substitute committee amendment that was displaced by the Byrd amendment on June 6. *Congressional Record* 125: S5018.

32. *Goldwater v. Carter,* 481 F. Supp. 949, 950 (D.D.C. 1979).

33. Ibid., 965.

34. "The Church amendment would add the following language: The provisions of this Resolution shall not apply with respect to any treaty the notice of termination of which was transmitted prior to the date of adoption of this Resolution. 125 Cong. Rec. S7061 (June 6, 1979). The Goldwater amendment would add the following language: (1) The provisions of this resolution shall not be construed to approve or disapprove of the proposed termination of the Mutual Defense Treaty with the Republic of China, such proposed termination not having been submitted to the Senate or the Congress for approval prior to the date of adoption of this resolution. (2) Nor shall anything in this resolution reduce or prejudice any of the Constitutional powers of the Senate. 125 Cong. Rec. S7861–62 (June 18, 1979)" (ibid., 954, fn. 15).

35. Ibid., 962.

36. *Goldwater v. Carter,* 617 F. 2d 697, 709 (D.C. Cir. 1979).

37. Ibid., 703.

38. Brownell 2008, 366–367.

39. *Goldwater v. Carter,* 444 U.S. 996, 997, 1001 (1979), J. Powell, concurring.

40. Ibid., 997–998 and 1001–1002.

41. Ibid., 1003 and 1005–1006.

42. Ibid., 1006.

43. Ibid., 1006–1007.

44. McGowan 1981.

45. Wagner 1982, 536–537.

46. Bill Clinton, "Address Before a Joint Session of the Congress on the State of the Union," *Weekly Compilation of Presidential Documents* 136, February 4, 1997, 136–144, https://www.govinfo.gov/content/pkg/WCPD-1997-02-10/pdf/WCPD-1997-02-10-Pg136.pdf.

47. *Federal Register* 62: 27253 (May 19, 1997), Government Publishing Office, https://www.gpo.gov/fdsys/pkg/FR-1997-05-19/pdf/97-13210.pdf.

48. H. Rept. 105–781 to accompany H.R. 1842, "Terminate Further Development and Implementation of the American Rivers Heritage Initiative," House Committee on

Resources, 105th Cong., 2nd sess., October 6, 1998, Congress.gov, accessed February 11, 2019, https://www.congress.gov/congressional-report/105th-congress/house-report/781.

49. "Executive Order 13080, April 7, 1998," *Federal Register* 63, no. 69 (April 10, 1998): 17667–17668, Government Publishing Office, https://www.gpo.gov/fdsys/pkg/FR-1998-04 -10/pdf/98-9709.pdf. See also "Executive Order 13061—Federal Support of Community Efforts along American Heritage Rivers, September 11, 1997," *Federal Register* 62, no. 178 (September 15, 1997): 48445–48448, Government Publishing Office, https://www.gpo.gov /fdsys/pkg/FR-1997-09-15/pdf/97-24591.pdf. For more on the National Environmental Policy Act, see https://ceq.doe.gov.

50. Cited in Zinn and Cody 1998, 1.

51. See, for example, Conservative Action website's list of executive orders on the environment, 1993–2001, at http://www.conservativeaction.org/resources.php3?nameid =worsteo.

52. U.S. House of Representatives, Committee on Natural Resources, "American Heritage Rivers," H. Rep. 105–771, 105th Cong. 2nd sess. 1998, 2.

53. Hearing, "Impact of Executive Orders on the Legislative Process: Executive Lawmaking?," Subcommittee on Legislative and Budget Process, House Committee on Rules, 106th Cong., 1st sess., October 27, 1999, Government Publishing Office, https://www.gpo .gov/fdsys/pkg/CHRG-106hhrg62209/html/CHRG-106hhrg62209.htm.

54. H.R. 3131, H. Con. Res. 30, and H.R. 2655, all covered in "Congressional Limitation of Executive Orders," Hearing, House Subcommittee on Commercial and Administrative Law, Committee on the Judiciary, 106th Cong., 1st sess., October 28, 1999, prepared remarks, 12–13, http://commdocs.house.gov/committees/judiciary/hju63865.000 /hju63865_0.HTM. None of the bills progressed beyond the committee hearing stage.

55. Ibid., 16.

56. Ibid., 34.

57. *Chenoweth v. Clinton*, 997 F. Supp. 36, 37–39 (D.D.C. 1999).

58. *Chenoweth v. Clinton*, 181 F. 3d 112, 114–115 (D.C. Cir. 1999).

59. Ibid., 117–118.

60. Bruce I. Friedland, "Future of American Heritage Rivers Plan Still up in the Air," *Florida Times-Union*, February 28, 2001.

61. "The Secret History of the ABM Treaty, 1969–1972," National Security Archive, accessed February 11, 2019, http://nsarchive.gwu.edu/NSAEBB/NSAEBB60.

62. "ABM Treaty Factsheet/Statement of Withdrawal," Office of the Press Secretary, White House, December 13, 2001, https://georgewbush-whitehouse.archives.gov/news /releases/2001/12/20011213-2.html.

63. Terence Neilan, "Bush Pulls Out of ABM Treaty; Putin Calls Move a Mistake," *New York Times*, December 13, 2001, http://www.nytimes.com/2001/12/13/international/bush -pulls-out-of-abm-treaty-putin-calls-move-a-mistake.html?_r=0.

64. *Congressional Record* 148, 107th Cong., 2nd sess. (June 6, 2002): H3232.

65. Ibid.

66. Ibid., H3233.

67. Ibid., H3233–H3234.

68. Ibid., H3237. See also "Final Vote Results for Roll Call 214," Office of the Clerk, accessed February 11, 2019, http://clerk.house.gov/evs/2018/roll214.xml.

69. S. Res. 282, 107th Cong., 2nd sess., Congress.gov, accessed February 11, 2019, https://www.congress.gov/bill/107th-congress/senate-resolution/282/text.

70. H.R. 4920, "To Provide for the Continued Applicability of the Requirements of the ABM Treaty to the United States," 107th Cong., 2nd sess., Congress.gov, accessed February 11, 2019, https://www.congress.gov/bill/107th-congress/house-bill/4920/cosponsors.

71. 236 F. Supp. 2d 1 (D.D.C. 2002).

72. Ibid., 6.

73. Ibid., 9–10.

74. Ibid., 11. *United States v. Ballin*, 144 U.S. 1, 7 (1892).

75. *Beacon Products Corp. v. Reagan*, 633 F. Supp. 1191, 1198–99 (D. Mass. 1986), 814 F. 2d 1 (1st Cir. 1987) (affirmed on other grounds). The case concerned President Reagan's unilateral termination of the Treaty of Friendship, Commerce, and Navigation with Nicaragua, also without congressional consent.

76. *Kucinich v. Bush*, 17.

77. This point in particular was criticized by Adler (2007, 236) for this "respect test" to shut down congressional lawsuits.

78. "Opposition to Motion of *Amici Curiae* for Leave to File a Memorandum in Support of Defendants' Motion to Dismiss and Memorandum in Support of Plaintiffs' Motion to Strike" Civ. No. 02-1137, 1.

79. Tal Axelrod, "Trump Confirms US Will Withdraw from Key Arms Control Treaty," *The Hill*, October 20, 2018, https://thehill.com/homenews/administration/412401-trump-confirms-us-will-withdraw-from-key-arms-control-treaty.

80. See David E. Sanger and William J. Broad, "U.S. Suspends Nuclear Arms Treaty with Russia, *New York Times,* February 1, 2019, https://www.nytimes.com/2019/02/01/us/politics/trump-inf-nuclear-treaty.html.

81. See S.705, filed by Chris Van Hollen (D-MD), "A bill to prohibit the use of funds to take any action that would constitute a violation of the Intermediate-Range Nuclear Forces Treaty for the duration of the six-month withdrawal period from the INF Treaty, and for other purposes," and H.R.1249, filed by Tulsi Gabbard (D-HI), "INF Treaty Compliance Act of 2019," both 116th Cong., 1st sess., 2019.

82. For more information on the state and private-sponsored federal cases surrounding the ACA, see "Legal Challenges to Obamacare: Court Cases on ObamaCare," NYU Libraries, https://guides.nyu.edu/c.php?g=277087&p=1847008.

83. In early 2016, the Senate and House finally both passed a repeal bill, which the president vetoed. See Jennifer Steinhauer, "House Votes to Send Bill to Repeal Health Law to Obama's Desk," *New York Times*, January 6, 2016, http://www.nytimes.com/2016/01/07/us/politics/house-votes-to-send-bill-to-repeal-health-law-to-obamas-desk.html?_r=0; Peter Sullivan, "House Fails to Override ObamaCare Veto," *The Hill*, February 2, 2016, http://thehill.com/policy/healthcare/267963-house-fails-to-override-veto-of-obamacare-repeal.

84. *House of Representatives v. Burwell*, 130 F. Supp. 3d 53, 60 (D.D.C. 2015).

85. See *Continuing Appropriations Act for 2014*, Public Law 113–46 (2013); *Joint Resolution*, Public Law 113–73 (2014), 113th Cong., 1st sess.

86. H. Res. 676, July 30, 2014, 113th Cong., 2nd sess. See "Final Vote results for Roll Call 468," Office of the Clerk, accessed February 11, 2019,http://clerk.house.gov/evs/2014/roll468.xml.

87. H.R. 676, sec. 3(a), 113th Cong., 2nd sess. See also H.R. 5, sec. 3(f), 114th Cong., 1st sess.

88. H. Rept. 113–561 (Part 1), 2–3, Congress.gov, accessed February 11, 2019, https://www.congress.gov/113/crpt/hrpt561/CRPT-113hrpt561-pt1.pdf.

89. Ibid., 27.

90. *House of Representatives v. Burwell*, 70.

91. Ibid., 76.

92. Ibid., 80.

93. Ibid., 80–81.

94. Before the ACA suit, there were four institutionally sanctioned law suits: three were committee-generated regarding executive officials' lack of response to subpoenas, and one was an institutional suit on the issue of sampling in the 2000 Census; see Dolan 2016, 1.

95. *House of Representatives v. Burwell*, second round, Civil Action 14–1967 (D.D.C. 2016), 19–20, 38.

96. Ibid., Exhibit A, https://images.law.com/contrib/content/uploads/documents/398 /6808/16-5202_Documents.pdf.

97. Josh Blackman, "Settlement Reached in House of Representatives Cost-Sharing Re-duction (CSR) Subsidies Suit," *Josh Blackman's Blog*, December 15, 2017, http:// joshblackman.com/blog/2017/12/15/settlement-reached-in-house-of-representatives -cost-sharing-reduction-csr-subsidies-suit.

98. White House, Veto Message to the House of Representatives for H.J. Res. 46, March 15, 2019, https://www.whitehouse.gov/briefings-statements/veto-message-house -representatives-h-j-res-46/.

99. Emily Cochrane and Charlie Savage, "House Adds Lawsuit to Challenges Against Trump's Emergency Declaration," *New York Times*, April 9, 2019, https://www.nytimes .com/2019/04/04/us/politics/national-emergency-act-lawsuit.html.

CONCLUSION

1. See Dan Pfeiffer, "We Can't Wait," White House Blog, October 24, 2011, https:// obamawhitehouse.archives.gov/blog/2011/10/24/we-cant-wait.

2. Keith Laing, "Obama Dares GOP: 'Sue Me,'" *The Hill*, July 1, 2014, https://thehill .com/policy/transportation/211100-obama-to-executive-action-critics-sue-me.

3. H.R. 4138, 113th Cong., 2nd sess. For full bill history and institutional actions, see "H.R.4138—ENFORCE the Law Act of 2014," Congress.gov, https://www.congress.gov/bill /113th-congress/house-bill/4138/all-actions; "Final Vote Results for Roll Call 124," http:// clerk.house.gov/evs/2014/roll124.xml.

4. *Congressional Record* 160, 113th Cong., 2nd sess. (March 12, 2014): H2321, https:// www.congress.gov/crec/2014/03/12/CREC-2014-03-12.pdf.

5. Ibid., H2320–H2321.

6. Ed O'Keefe, "House Passes Bill Making It Easier for Congress to Sue the President," *Washington Post*, March 12, 2014, https://www.washingtonpost.com/news/post-politics/wp /2014/03/12/house-passes-bill-making-it-easier-for-congress-to-sue-the-president/?utm _term=.0bc46c2bee93.

7. Charlie Savage, "Shift on Executive Power Lets Obama Bypass Rivals," *New York Times*, April 22, 2012, https://www.nytimes.com/2012/04/23/us/politics/shift-on-executive -powers-let-obama-bypass-congress.html; Melvyn P. Leffler, "Think Again: Bush's For-eign Policy," *Foreign Policy*, October 23, 2009, https://foreignpolicy.com/2009/10/23/think -again-bushs-foreign-policy.

8. The phrase "lawful but awful" has no clear origin when referring to a variety of legal questions, but in this conclusion, I am borrowing it from Bobby Chesney and Steven Vladek, "Episode 111: This National Emergency Podcast Requires the Use of the Armed Forces," *National Security Law Podcast*, February 19, 2019.

9. See Farrier 2004 and 2010.

10. Halchin 2019, 7, 11.

11. To Authorize Appropriations for Fiscal Years 1986–1987 for the Department of State, the United States Information Agency, the Board for International Broadcasting, and Other Purposes, P.L. 99-93, 99 Stat. 405 (1985), Title VIII, sec. 801, 99th Cong., 1st sess.

12. *Congressional Record* 165 (47): S1858, March 14, 2019, 116th Cong, 1st sess., https:// www.congress.gov/116/crec/2019/03/14/CREC-2019-03-14-pt1-PgS1857-3.pdf.

13. U.S. Senate, Roll Call Vote 49 Summary, On the Joint Resolution (H.J. Res. 46), March 14, 2019, 116th Cong., 1st sess., https://www.senate.gov/legislative/LIS/roll_call_lists /roll_call_vote_cfm.cfm?congress=116&session=1&vote=00049#position.

14. Rachel Adams-Heard, "Trump's Border Wall Faces Texas-Sized Backlash from Land Owners," *Houston Chronicle/Bloomberg*, February 18, 2019.

15. *Youngstown Sheet & Tube v. Sawyer*, 343 U.S. 589, 654 (1952), Jackson, J., concurring.

16. Joel Lovell, "Can the A.C.L.U. Become the N.R.A. for the Left?," *New York Times*, July 2, 2018, https://nyti.ms/2lOCs2m.

17. Lisa Friedman and John Schwartz, "Borrowing G.O.P. Playbook, Democratic States Sue the Government and Rack up Wins," *New York Times*, March 21, 2018, https://nyti.ms/2FSDOWe. See also the current emoluments case *District of Columbia et al. v. Trump*, U.S. District Court, District of Maryland, No. 17–01596.

18. Thomas E. Mann and Norman J. Ornstein, "How the Republicans Broke Congress," *New York Times*, December 2, 2017, https://www.nytimes.com/2017/12/02/opinion/sunday/republicans-broke-congress-politics.html?_r=0. See also Mann and Ornstein 2012.

19. Sheryl Gay Stolberg and Michael Shear, "Congress Has a Breaking Point. This Week Trump Might Have Found It," *New York Times,* March 14, 2019, https://www.nytimes.com/2019/03/14/us/politics/trump-congress-rebuke.html.

20. H. Con. Res. 24, Expressing the sense of Congress that the report of Special Counsel Mueller should be made available to the public and to Congress, Roll Call 125, March 14, 2019, 116th Cong., 1st sess., http://clerk.house.gov/evs/2019/roll125.xml.

References

Abel, Arthur L. 1985. "The Burger Court's Unified Approach to Standing and Its Impact on Congressional Plaintiffs." *Notre Dame Law Review* 60: 1187–1213.

Ackerman, Bruce. 1995. "An Open Letter to Congressman Gingrich." *Yale Law Journal* 104: 1539–1544.

Adler, David Gray. 2000. "The Clinton Theory of the War Power." *Presidential Studies Quarterly* 30 (1): 155–168.

———. 2002. "The Steel Seizure Case and Inherent Presidential Power." *Constitutional Commentary* 19: 155–213.

———. 2007 "Termination of the ABM Treaty and the Political Question Doctrine: Judicial Succor for Presidential Power." In *The Political Question Doctrine and the Supreme Court of the United States*, edited by Nada Mourtada-Sabbah and Bruce E. Cain, 231–242. Lanham, MD: Lexington Books.

Alexander, Larry, and Evan Tsen Lee. 1995. "Is There Such a Thing as Extraconstitutionality? The Puzzling Case of *Dalton v. Specter.*" *Arizona State Law Journal* 27: 845–874.

Alford, Ryan. 2017. *Permanent State of Emergency: Unchecked Executive Power and the Demise of the Rule of Law.* Montreal: McGill-Queen's University Press.

Barber, Sotirios. 1975. *The Constitution and the Delegation of Congressional Power.* Chicago: University of Chicago Press.

Barkow, Rachel E. 2007. "The Rise and Fall of the Political Question Doctrine." In *The Political Question Doctrine and the Supreme Court of the United States*, edited by Nada Mourtada-Sabbah and Bruce E. Cain. Lanham, MD: Lexington Books, 23–45.

Baum, Lawrence. 2003. "The Supreme Court in American Politics." *Annual Review of Political Science* 6: 161–180.

Bessette, Joseph M., and Gary J. Schmitt. 2009. "Executive Orders." In *The Constitutional Presidency*, edited by Joseph M. Bessette and Jeffrey K. Tulis. Baltimore: Johns Hopkins University Press, 28–53.

Beth, Richard S. 2001. *Disapproval of Regulations by Congress: Procedure under Congressional Review Act*, Congressional Research Service Report RL33160, October 10.

Bickel, Alexander M. 1962. *The Least Dangerous Branch: The Supreme Court at the Bar of Politics.* New Haven, CT: Yale University Press.

———. 1971. "Congress, the President, and the Power to Wage War." *Chicago-Kent Law Review* 48: 131–147.

———. 1986. *The Least Dangerous Branch: The Supreme Court at the Bar of Politics.* 2nd ed. New Haven, CT: Yale University Press.

Binder, Sarah A., and Steven S. Smith. 1997. *Politics or Principle? Filibustering in the United States Senate.* Washington, DC: Brookings Institution Press.

Blank, Adam L. 1998. "Raines v. Byrd: A Death Knell for the Congressional Suit." *Mercer Law Review* 49: 609–624.

Brownell, Roy E. II. 2000. "The Coexistence of *United States v. Curtiss-Wright Export Corp.* and *Youngstown Sheet & Tube v. Sawyer* in National Security Jurisprudence." *Journal of Law & Policy* 16: 1–111.

———. 2008. "Foreign Affairs and Separation of Powers in the Twenty-First Century." *Journal of National Security Law & Policy* 2: 367–415. (Book review of John Yoo, *The*

Powers of War and Peace: The Constitution of Foreign Affairs after 9/11, Chicago: University of Chicago Press, 2005.)

Burgess, Susan R. 1992. *Contest for Constitutional Authority: The Abortion and War Powers Debates*. Lawrence: University Press of Kansas.

Campbell, Tom. 2004. *Separation of Powers in Practice*. Stanford, CA: Stanford University Press.

Choper, Jesse H. 1980. *Judicial Review and the National Political Process: A Functional Reconsideration of the Role of the Supreme Court*. Chicago: University of Chicago Press.

——. 2005. "The Political Question Doctrine: Suggested Criteria." *Duke Law Journal* 54: 1457–1523.

Christenson, Dino P., and Douglas L. Kriner. 2017. "Constitutional Qualms or Politics as Usual? The Factors Shaping Public Support for Unilateral Action." *American Journal of Political Science* 61 (2): 335–349.

Ciarrocchi, Robert J. 1987. "U.S., Soviet, and Western European Naval Forces in the Persian Gulf Region," Congressional Research Service Report 87-956F, December 8.

Clark, Robert D., Andrew M. Egeland Jr., and David B. Sanford. 1985. *The War Powers Resolution: Balance of War Powers in the Eighties*. Washington, DC: National Defense University Press.

Coenen, Dan T. 2012. "The Originalist Case against Congressional Supermajority Voting Rules." *Northwestern University Law Review* 106 (3): 1091–1152.

Cole, Jared P. 2014. *The Political Question Doctrine: Justiciability and Separation of Powers*. Congressional Research Service Report R43834, December 23.

Cushman, Barry. 2008. "The Great Depression and the New Deal." In *The Cambridge History of Law in America*, vol. 3, edited by Michael Grossberg and Christopher Tomlins. New York: Cambridge University Press, 268–318.

Dahl, Robert. 1957. "Decision-Making in a Democracy: the Supreme Court as National Policy Maker." *Journal of Public Law* 6: 279–295.

D'Arcy, Rebecca. A. 2003. "The Legacy of *Dames & Moore v. Regan*: The Twilight Zone of Concurrent Authority between the Executive and Congress and a Proposal for a Judicially Manageable Nondelegation Doctrine." *Notre Dame Law Review* 79 (1): 292–326.

Dessem, R. Lawrence. 1986. "Congressional Standing to Sue: Whose Vote Is This Anyway?" *Notre Dame Law Review* 62: 1–31.

Devins, Neal, and Louis Fisher. 2004. *The Democratic Constitution*. New York: Oxford University Press.

——. 2015. *The Democratic Constitution*, 2nd ed. New York: Oxford University Press.

Dolan, Alissa M. 2016. House of Representatives v. Burwell *and Congressional Standing to Sue*, Congressional Research Service Report R44450, September 12.

Dueholm, James A. "Lincoln's Suspension of the Writ of Habeas Corpus: An Historical and Constitutional Analysis," *Journal of the Abraham Lincoln Association* 29, no. 2 (2008): 47–66.

Edelson, Chris. 2013a. *Emergency Presidential Power: From the Drafting of the Constitution to the War on Terror*. Madison: University of Wisconsin Press.

——. 2013b. "In Service to Power: Legal Scholars as Executive Branch Lawyers in the Obama Administration." *Presidential Studies Quarterly* 43 (3): 618–640.

Ellis, Richard J. 2009. *Judging Executive Power: Sixteen Supreme Court Cases That Have Shaped the American Presidency*. Lanham, MD: Rowman and Littlefield.

Elsea, Jennifer K. 2015. Zivotofsky v. Kerry: *The Jerusalem Passport Case and Its Potential Implications for Congress's Foreign Affairs Power*. Congressional Research Service Report R43773, September 28.

Ely, John Hart. 1993. *War and Responsibility: Constitutional Lessons of Vietnam and Its Aftermath*. Princeton, NJ: Princeton University Press.

Entin, Jonathan L. 2015. "The Curious Case of the Pompous Postmaster." *Case Western Law Review* 65 (4): 1059–1081.

Epstein, David, and Sharyn O'Halloran. 1999. *Delegating Powers: A Transaction Cost Politics Approach to Policy Making under Separate Powers*. New York: Cambridge University Press.

Epstein, Lee, and Eric A. Posner. 2016. "Supreme Court Justices' Loyalty to the President," *Journal of Legal Studies* 45: 401–436.

Farrier, Jasmine. 2004. *Passing the Buck: Congress, the Budget, and Deficits*. Lexington: University Press of Kentucky.

———. 2009. "Presidential Budget Power, Constitutional Conflicts and the National Interest." In *Constitutional Presidency*, edited by Joseph M. Bessette and Jeffrey K. Tulis. Baltimore: Johns Hopkins University Press, 173–202.

———. 2010. *Congressional Ambivalence: The Political Burdens of Constitutional Authority*. Lexington: University Press of Kentucky.

———. 2011. "Barack Obama and Budget Deficits: Signs of a Neo-Whig Presidency?" *Presidential Studies Quarterly* 41 (3): 618–634.

———. 2016. "Judicial Restraint and the New War Powers." *Presidential Studies Quarterly* 46 (2): 387–410.

Finkelstein, Maurice. 1924. "Judicial Self-Limitation." *Harvard Law Review* 37: 338–364.

Fisher, Louis. 1987. "The Administrative World of *Chadha* and *Bowsher*." *Public Administration Review* 47 (3): 213–219.

———. 2000a. *Congressional Abdication on War and Budgets*. College Station: Texas A&M University Press.

———. 2000b. "Litigating the War Power with 'Campbell v. Clinton.'" *Presidential Studies Quarterly* 30 (3): 564–557.

———. 2001. *The Pocket Veto: Its Current Status*. Congressional Research Service Report RL 30909, March 30.

———. 2005. "Judicial Review of War." *Presidential Studies Quarterly* 35 (3): 466–495.

———. 2007. "Presidential Inherent Power: The 'Sole Organ' Doctrine." *Presidential Studies Quarterly* 37 (1): 139–152.

———. 2011. *Defending Congress and the Constitution*. Lawrence: University Press of Kansas.

———. 2013. *Presidential War Power*. 3rd rev. ed. Lawrence: University Press of Kansas.

———. 2014. *The Law of the Executive Branch: Presidential Power*. New York: Oxford University Press.

———. 2016. "The Staying Power of Erroneous Dicta: From *Curtiss-Wright* to *Zivotofsky*." *Constitutional Commentary* 31: 149–219.

———. 2017a. "A Challenge to Presidential Wars: Smith v. Obama." *Congress & the Presidency* 44 (2): 259–282.

———. 2017b. *Supreme Court Expansion of Presidential Power: Unconstitutional Leanings*. Lawrence: University Press of Kansas.

Frisch, Morton J., ed. 2007. *The Pacificus-Helvidius Debates of 1793–1794: Toward the Completion of the American Founding*. Indianapolis: Liberty Fund.

Glennon, Michael J. 1990. *Constitutional Diplomacy*. Princeton, NJ: Princeton University Press.

Henkin, Louis. 1976. "Is There a 'Political Question' Doctrine?" *Yale Law Journal* 85 (5): 597–625.

———. 1996. *Foreign Affairs and the United States Constitution*. 2nd ed. New York: Oxford University Press.

Garcia, Michael John. 2012. *War Powers Litigation Initiated by Members of Congress since Enactment of the War Powers Resolution.* Congressional Research Service Report RL30352, February 17.

Genovese, Michael A., and Robert J. Spitzer. 2005. *The Presidency and the Constitution: Cases and Controversies.* New York: Palgrave Macmillan.

Ginsburg, Ruth Bader (The Honorable). 1981. "Inviting Judicial Activism: A 'Liberal' or 'Conservative' Technique?" *Georgia Law Review* 15: 539–558.

Goodman, Sophia C. 1990. "Equitable Discretion to Dismiss Congressional-Plaintiff Suits: A Reassessment." *Case Western University Law Review* 40: 1078–1108.

Gunther, Gerald. 1964. "The Subtle Vices of the 'Passive Virtues': A Comment on Principle and Expediency in Judicial Review." *Columbia Law Review* 64: 1–25.

Halchin, L. Elaine, and Harold C. Relyea. 2019. *National Emergency Powers.* Congressional Research Service Report 98-505. February 27.

Harris, Kevin, and Mario Espinosa. 1981. "Issues and Policy: Reform, Repression, and Revolution in El Salvador." *Fletcher Forum* 5 (2): 295–318.

Henkin, Louis. 1976. "Is There a Political Question Doctrine?" *Yale Law Review* 85 (5): 597–625.

Horowitz, Donald L. 1977. *The Courts and Social Policy.* Washington, DC: Brookings Institution.

Howell, William G. 2003. *Power without Persuasion: The Politics of Direct Presidential Action.* Princeton, NJ: Princeton University Press.

Howell, William G., and Jon C. Pevehouse. 2007. *While Dangers Gather: Congressional Checks on Presidential War Powers.* Princeton, NJ: Princeton University Press.

Kagan, Elena. 2001. "Presidential Administration." *Harvard Law Review* 114 (8): 2245–2383.

Kassop, Nancy. 2003. "The War Powers and Its Limits." *Presidential Studies Quarterly* 33 (3): 509–529.

Kelman, Maurice. 1971. "Introduction: Courts and the Constitutionality of the Vietnam War." *Wayne Law Review* 17: 71–78.

Keynes, Edward. 1982. *Undeclared War: Twilight Zone of Constitutional Power.* University Park: Penn State University Press.

Kiewiet, D. Roderick, and Mathew D. McCubbins. 1991. *The Logic of Delegation: Congressional Parties and the Appropriations Process.* Chicago: University of Chicago Press.

Kleinerman, Benjamin A. 2009. *The Discretionary President: Promise and Peril of Executive Power.* Lawrence: University Press of Kansas.

Koger, Gregory. 2010. *Filibustering: A Political History of Obstruction in the House and Senate.* Chicago: University of Chicago Press.

Koh, Harold Hongju. 1990. *The National Security Constitution: Sharing Power after the Iran-Contra Affair.* New Haven, CT: Yale University Press.

Korn, Jessica. 1996. *The Power of Separation: American Constitutionalism and the Myth of the Legislative Veto.* Princeton, NJ: Princeton University Press.

Kriner, Douglas L. 2010. *After the Rubicon: Congress, the President, and the Politics of Waging War.* Chicago: University of Chicago Press.

LeoGrande, William M. 1981. "A Splendid Little War: Drawing the Line in El Salvador." *International Security* 6 (1): 27–52.

Mangum, David G. 1982. "Standing versus Justiciability: Recent Developments in Participatory Suits Brought by Congressional Plaintiffs." *Brigham Young University Law Review*: 371–387.

Mann, Thomas E., and Norman J. Ornstein. 2012. *It's Even Worse Than It Looks: How the American Constitutional System Collided with the New Politics of Extremism.* New York: Basic Books.

Mansfield, Harvey C., Jr. 1993. *Taming the Prince: The Ambivalence of Modern Executive Power*. Baltimore: Johns Hopkins University Press.

Marks, Lee R., and John C. Grabow. 1982. "President's Foreign Economic Powers after *Dames & Moore v. Regan*: Legislation through Acquiescence." *Cornell University Law Review* 68 (1): 68–103.

Marshall, William P. 2008. "Eleven Reasons Why Presidential Power Inevitably Expands and Why It Matters." *Boston University Law Review* 88: 505–522.

Maskell, Jack. 2013. *Independent Counsels, Special Prosecutors, Special Counsels, and the Role of Congress*, Congressional Research Service Report R43112, June 20.

Mayer, Kenneth R. 2001. *With the Stroke of a Pen: Executive Orders and Presidential Power*. Princeton, NJ: Princeton University Press.

———. 2009. "Executive Orders." In *The Constitutional Presidency*, edited by Joseph M. Bessette and Jeffrey K. Tulis. Baltimore: Johns Hopkins University Press, 149–172.

McGinnis, John O., and Michael B. Rappaport. 1995. "The Constitutionality of Legislative Supermajority Requirements: A Defense." *Yale Law Journal* 105 (1995): 483–511.

McGowan, Carl (the Honorable). 1981. "Congressmen in Court: The New Plaintiffs." *Georgia Law Review* 15 (2): 241–267.

Michaels, Peter S. 1987. "Lawless Intervention: United States Foreign Policy in El Salvador and Nicaragua." *Boston College Third World Law Journal* 7 (2): 223–262.

Mikva, Abner J., and Gerald L. Neuman. 1982. "The Hostage Crisis and the 'Hostage Act.'" *University of Chicago Law Review* 49 (2): 292–354.

Moe, Ronald C. 2002. *Reorganizing the Executive Branch in the 20th Century: Landmark Commissions*. Congressional Research Service Report RL 31446, June 10.

Moe, Terry M., and William G. Howell. 1999. "The Presidential Power of Unilateral Action." *Journal of Law, Economics, and Organization* 15 (1): 132–179.

Mosely, Layna, ed. 2013. *Interview Research in Political Science*. Ithaca, NY: Cornell University Press.

Mulhern, J. Peter. 1988. "In Defense of the Political Question Doctrine." *University of Pennsylvania Law Review* 137: 97–176.

Neustadt, Richard E. 1991. *Presidential Power and the Modern Presidents: The Politics of Leadership from Roosevelt to Reagan*. Rev. ed. New York: Free Press.

Nichol, Gene R., Jr. 1986. "Injury and the Disintegration of Article III." *California Law Review* 74: 1915–1950.

Orren, Karen, and Christopher Walker. 2013. "Cold Case File: Indictable Acts and Officer Accountability in *Marbury v. Madison*." *American Political Science Review* 107 (2): 241–258.

Perry, H. W., Jr. 1991. *Deciding to Decide: Agenda Setting in the United States Supreme Court*. Cambridge, MA: Harvard University Press.

Pfiffner, James P. 2008. *Power Play: The Bush Presidency and the Constitution*. Washington, DC: Brookings Institution Press.

Pickerill, J. Mitchell. 2004. *Constitutional Deliberation in Congress: The Impact of Judicial Review in a Separated System*. Durham, NC: Duke University Press.

Pious, Richard M. 1979. *The American Presidency*. New York: Basic Books.

———. 2009. "Military Tribunals, Prerogative Power, and the War on Terrorism." In *The Constitutional Presidency*, edited by Joseph M. Bessette and Jeffrey K. Tulis. Baltimore: Johns Hopkins University Press, 132–148.

Posner, Eric A., and Adrian Vermeule. 2011. *The Executive Unbound: After the Madisonian Republic*. New York: Oxford University Press.

Prakash, Saikrishna, and Michael D. Ramsey. 2001. "The Executive Power over Foreign Affairs." *Yale Law Journal* 111: 231–356.

Pyle, Christopher H., and Richard M. Pious. 1984. *The President, Congress, and the Constitution: Power and Legitimacy in American Politics.* New York: Free Press.

Redish, Martin H. 1985. "Judicial Review and the 'Political Question.'" *Northwestern University Law Review* 79: 1031–1061.

———. 1995. *The Constitution as Political Structure.* New York: Oxford University Press.

Rosenberg, Gerald N. 2008. *The Hollow Hope: Can Courts Bring about Social Change?* 2nd ed. Chicago: University of Chicago Press.

Rubenfeld, Jed. 1996. "Rights of Passage: Majority Rule in Congress." *Duke Law Review* 46: 73–90.

Rubin, Herbert J., and Irene S. Rubin. 2012. *Qualitative Interviewing: The Art of Hearing Data.* 3rd ed. Los Angeles: Sage.

Rubner, Michael. 1985. "The Reagan Administration, the War Powers Resolution, and the Invasion of Grenada." *Political Science Quarterly* 100 (4): 627–647.

Rudalevige, Andrew. 2006. *The New Imperial Presidency: Renewing Presidential Power after Watergate.* Ann Arbor: University of Michigan Press.

Ryan, Allan A. 2015. *The 9/11 Terror Cases: Constitutional Challenges in the War against Al Qaeda.* Lawrence: University Press of Kansas.

Saturno, James V., and Megan S. Lynch. 2019. *Changes to House Rules Affecting the Congressional Budget Process Included in H.Res. 6 (116 th Congress).* Congressional Research Service Report R45552, March 4.

Savage, Charlie. 2015. *Power Wars: Inside Obama's Post-9/11 Presidency.* Boston: Little, Brown.

Scharpf, Fritz W. 1966. "Judicial Review and the Political Question: A Functional Analysis." *Yale Law Journal* 75 (4): 517–597.

Scheppele, Kim Lane. 2012. "The New Judicial Deference." *Boston University Law Review* 92: 89–170.

Schmitt, Gary J. 2009. "President Washington's Proclamation of Neutrality." In *The Constitutional Presidency,* edited by Joseph M. Bessette and Jeffrey K. Tulis. Baltimore: Johns Hopkins University Press, 54–75.

Seidman, Jeffrey. 2013. *Interviewing as Qualitative Research: A Guide for Researchers in Education and the Social Sciences.* New York: Teachers College Press.

Shampansky, Jay R. 2001. *Congressional Standing to Sue: An Overview.* Congressional Research Service Report R42454, June 19.

Shesol, Jeff. 2010. *Supreme Power: Franklin Roosevelt v. Supreme Court.* New York: W. W. Norton, 2010.

Silverstein, Gordon. 1997. *Imbalance of Power: Constitutional Interpretation and the Making of American Foreign Policy.* New York: Oxford University Press.

———. 2009. *Law's Allure: How Law Shapes, Constrains, Saves and Kills Politics.* New York: Cambridge University Press.

Sparrow, Bartholomew H. 2006. *The Insular Cases and the Emergence of American Empire.* Lawrence: University Press of Kansas.

Spitzer, Robert J. 2001. "The 'Protective Return' Pocket Veto: Presidential Aggrandizement of Constitutional Power." *Presidential Studies Quarterly* 31 (4): 720–732.

Sugarman, R. P. 1974. "Judicial Decisions concerning the Constitutionality of United States Military Activity in Indo-China: A Bibliography of Court Decisions." *Columbia Journal of Transnational Law* 13: 470.

Sunstein, Cass R. 1999. "Nondelegation Canons." John M. Olin Law and Economics Working Paper No. 82 (2nd ser.). Chicago: University of Chicago Law School.

Sweet, Barry. 1996. "Legal Challenges to Presidential Policies on the Use of Military Force." *Policy Studies Journal* 24: 27–41.

Synar, Mike, Vincent LoVoi, and Donald R. C. Pongrace. 1987. "Congressional Perspective on the Balanced Budget and Emergency Deficit Control Act of 1985." *Pace Law Review* 7 (3): 675–694.

Thayer, James B. 1893. "The Origin and Scope of the American Doctrine of Constitutional Law." *Harvard Law Review* 7 (3): 129–156.

Tigar, Michael E. 1970. "Judicial Power, the 'Political Question Doctrine,' and Foreign Relations," *UCLA Law Review* 17: 1135–1179.

Tulis, Jeffrey K. 2017. *The Rhetorical Presidency.* 2nd ed. Princeton, NJ: Princeton University Press.

Turner, Michael J. 2009. "Fade to Black: The Formalization of Jackson's Youngstown Taxonomy by *Hamdan* and *Medellin.*" *American University Law Review* 58 (3): 665–698.

Turner, Robert F. 1996. "Truman, Korea, and the Constitution: Debunking the 'Imperial President' Myth." *Harvard Journal of Law & Public Policy* 19 (Winter): 533–535.

Tushnet, Mark. 1999. *Taking the Constitution Away from the Courts.* Princeton, NJ: Princeton University Press.

———. 2007. "Law and Prudence in the Law of Justiciability: The Transformation and Disappearance of the Political Question Doctrine." In *The Political Question Doctrine and the Supreme Court of the United States,* edited by Nada Mourtada-Sabbah and Bruce E. Cain. Lanham, MD: Lexington Books, 47–74.

Wagner, Jonathan. 1982. "The Justiciability of Congressional Plaintiff Suits." *Columbia Law Review* 82: 526–552.

Warmuth, Francis D., and Edwin B. Firmage. 1989. *To Chain the Dog of War: the War Power of Congress in History and Law,* 2nd edition. Champaign: University of Illinois Press.

Wawro, Gregory, and Eric Schickler. 2006. *Filibuster.* Princeton, NJ: Princeton University Press.

Wechsler, Herbert. 1959. "Toward Neutral Principles of Constitutional Law." *Harvard Law Review* 73 (1): 1–35.

Weed, Matthew C. 2017. *The War Powers Resolution: Concepts and Practice.* Congressional Research Service Report R42699, March 28.

Westerfield, Donald L. 1996. *War Power: The President, the Congress, and the Question of War.* Westport, CT: Praeger.

Whittington, Keith E. 2007. *Political Foundations of Judicial Supremacy: The Presidency, the Supreme Court, and Constitutional Leadership in U.S. History.* Princeton, NJ: Princeton University Press.

Wildavsky, Aaron. 1966. "The Two Presidencies." *Trans-Action* 4 (2): 162–173.

Yoo, John. 2003. "Judicial Review and the War on Terror." *George Washington Law Review* 72: 427–476.

———. 2010. *Crisis and Command: A History of Executive Power from George Washington to George W. Bush.* New York: Kaplan Books.

Zeisberg, Mariah. 2013. *War Powers: The Politics of Constitutional Authority.* Princeton: Princeton University Press.

Zinn, Jeffrey A., and Betsy Cody. 1998. "American Heritage Rivers," Congressional Research Service Report 98-111, August 3.

Index

Adams, John, 17, 22, 100
Adler, David Gray, 169n77
Administrative Procedure Act (APA; 1977), 81, 82, 160n27
Affordable Care Act (ACA). *See* Patient Protection and Affordable Care Act
Afghanistan War, 51, 52
Alexander, Lamar, 143
Algerian Declaration release agreement, 107
Alito, Samuel, 82, 114
American Civil Liberties Union (ACLU), 144
American Heritage Rivers Initiative (AHRI), 129–32
Antiballistic Missile (ABM) Treaty with Russia, unilateral abrogation of, 132–36, 156n47
Anti-Deficiency Act (1982), 131
Arab Spring, 49
armed forces, desegregation of, 141
Arms Export Control Act (1976), 67
Authorizations for the Use of Military Force (AUMF), 46, 47, 48, 51–52, 110–11

Baker v. Carr (1962), 5–6, 20, 41, 42, 81, 87, 128, 153n86, 157n3
Balanced Budget and Emergency Deficit Control Reaffirmation Act (1987), 76, 77, 79
Bas v. Tingy (1800), 22–23
Base Realignment and Closure Commission (BRAC) decisions, overriding, 75, 79–83, 86
Bates, John D., 134–35
Bazelon, Judge, 121
Beacon Products Corp. v. Reagan (1986), 169n75
Berk v. Laird (1971), 153n77
Bickel, Alexander, 5, 20–21
Biden, Joe, 91
Bipartisan Legal Advisory Group, 161n48
Bishop, Maurice, 42–43
Black, Hugo, 104, 106
Blackmun, Harry, 65, 68, 70–71, 79, 82, 127–28
Boehner, John, 50, 154n93
Boland, Edward P., and Boland Amendment, 41–42
border wall with Mexico, 115–16, 139, 143, 145
Bork, Robert H., 43

Boumediene, Lakhdar, 112
Boumediene v. Rumsfeld (2008), 112
Bowsher v. Synar (1986), 64, 75, 76–79, 80, 82, 89, 91
Brandeis, Louis, 101
Brennan, William, 65, 68, 70, 78, 128–29
Breyer, Stephen, 87–88, 89, 111–12
Brownell, Roy E., II, 128
Buckwalter, Ronald, 81–82
Burger, Warren, 65–66, 72–73, 78, 127, 128
Burton, Harold, 104, 163–64n32
Burwell, Sylvia Matthews, 136
Bush, George H. W., 10, 34, 39, 44–46, 74, 80–81
Bush, George W.: legislative processes under, 89; unilateral executive actions by, 109–13, 132–36, 141, 165n77; war powers under, 7, 10, 34, 35, 39, 48, 49, 51, 156n47
Byrd, Harry, 125, 126–27
Byrd, Robert C., 46, 86

Cambodia, invasion/bombing of, 1, 8, 9, 28, 30, 32–35, 131, 152n60, 152n65
Campbell, Tom, 47
Campbell v. Clinton (1999), 46–48, 91, 132, 135
Cardozo, Benjamin, 60–61
Carle, Robin, 84
Carter, Jimmy, 40, 107, 122, 124–29, 164n47
Carter v. Carter Coal Company (1936), 157n9
Chadha, Lagdish, 64–65
Chadha case (*INS v. Chadha*; 1983), 11, 62–67, 71, 72–73, 78–79, 87, 88, 91, 143
Chase, Salmon, 22–23
Cheney, Richard, 80–81
Chenoweth, Helen, 130, 131
Chenoweth v. Clinton (1999), 129–32
Chicago Democratic National Convention (1968), 27
China, foreign relations with, 124–29
Choper, Jesse, 6, 21
Civil War, 24–25, 99
Clark, Tom, 104, 164n32
Cleveland, Grover, 100

CPSIA information can be obtained
at www.ICGtesting.com
Printed in the USA
LVHW011753160120
643876LV00004B/386